SOCIETY FOR NEW TESTAMENT STUDIES
MONOGRAPH SERIES
General Editor: G. N. Stanton
Associate Editor: M.E. Thrall

52

THE APOCALYPSE AND SEMITIC SYNTAX

The Apocalypse and Semitic Syntax

STEVEN THOMPSON

Senior Lecturer in New Testament
Newbold College, Bracknell

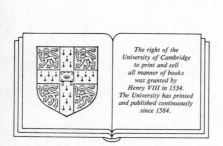

The right of the
University of Cambridge
to print and sell
all manner of books
was granted by
Henry VIII in 1534.
The University has printed
and published continuously
since 1584.

CAMBRIDGE UNIVERSITY PRESS

CAMBRIDGE
LONDON   NEW YORK   NEW ROCHELLE
MELBOURNE   SYDNEY

Published by the Press Syndicate of the University of Cambridge
The Pitt Building, Trumpington Street, Cambridge CB2 1RP
32 East 57th Street, New York, NY 10022, USA
296 Beaconsfield Parade, Middle Park, Melbourne 3206, Australia

First published 1985

Printed in Great Britain at the University Press, Cambridge

Library of Congress catalogue card number: 84–12081

British Library cataloguing in publication data
Thompson, Steven
The Apocalypse and Semitic syntax. – (Society
for New Testament Studies monographs series; 52)
1. Bible. N.T. Revelation – Language, style
2. Grammar, Comparative and general – Syntax
I. Title   II. Series
228'.066   BS2825.5

ISBN 0 521 26031 0

BB

CONTENTS

Contents

PREFACE

At a time when the student of the New Testament is confronted by its urgent social and theological issues, he may be tempted to question whether the writing of a monograph on its grammar can be justified. During the dozen years of continuous pressure from pastorate and lecture room since beginning this research, I have often faced this question. My affirmative answer to it stems from a conviction that a thorough understanding of the language of the New Testament is the key to its message. I am especially indebted for this conviction to my first teacher of Greek, Dr Philip Scoyle, and to Matthew Black who, as professor of biblical criticism in the University of St Andrews, suggested the topic and supervised the dissertation from which this book has grown. He inspired me by the suggestion that it could someday appear in print. I am grateful to Drs A.J.M. Wedderburn and Nigel Turner for reading the dissertation and offering valuable suggestions. Sympathetic scrutiny of my work by Professor R.McL. Wilson, Dr Margaret Thrall, and Professor G.N. Stanton of the Society for New Testament Studies accompanied its acceptance for publication in the Monograph Series. Their suggestions, along with those of the sub-editor appointed by the Cambridge University Press, have led to remarkable improvements which I appreciate. Thanks are due to the Seventh-day Adventist Church of the British Isles for making adjustments to my pastoral duties in order to accommodate my research. I pay tribute to my typists Wendy Brown and Elaine Ginbey, and to the administration of Newbold College for funding the preparation of the typescript. My tenderest tribute is reserved for Ellen Kristin, who during those years of intensive research remained, in the words of Apocalypse 1:9, my 'companion in tribulation . . . and patient endurance'.

April 1984   S.T.

ABBREVIATIONS

Apc.	The Apocalypse
BAG	W. Bauer, W.F. Arndt and F.W. Gingrich, *A Greek–English Lexicon of the New Testament*
BDB	F. Brown, S.R. Driver, C. Briggs, *A Hebrew and English Lexicon*
BGU	Aegyptische Urkunden aus den königlichen Museen zu Berlin
Bl-D	F. Blass and A. Debrunner, *A Greek Grammar of The New Testament* (trans. by R. Funk)
Charles I (II)	R.H. Charles, *A Critical and Exegetical Commentary on the Revelation of St. John*, 2 vols.
GK	Gesenius–Kautzsch (Cowley), *Hebrew Grammar*, 2nd edn
JBL	*Journal of Biblical Literature*
JTS	*Journal of Theological Studies*
LS-J	Liddell and Scott-Jones, *Greek–English Lexicon*, 9th edn (with a Supplement)
LXX	The Septuagint
MT	Masoretic Text
NTS	*New Testament Studies*
PSI	Publicazioni della Società Italiana: Papiri Greci e Latini, I–XI, 1912–35
Symm.	Symmachus
Theod.	Theodotion
TDNT	*Theological Dictionary of the New Testament*
ZAW	*Zeitschrift für die alttestamentliche Wissenschaft*
ZNW	*Zeitschrift für die neutestamentliche Wissenschaft*

Among the standard text-critical abbreviations employed are the following:

al	others (alia)
*	reading of original hand of a manuscript
boh	Bohairic

copt	Coptic
ethio	Ethiopic
gig	Gigas (Old Latin manuscript)
latt	combined Latin versions
mg	textual evidence contained in manuscript margins
minusc.	minuscule
sah	Sahidic
syr	Syriac
vg	Vulgate

Please note that the convention of omitting breathing and accent marks on variant readings cited in brackets is followed in this work.

INTRODUCTION

The justification for this study is found in the fact that it puts forward a number of explanations for the peculiar language associated with the verb and with clauses in the Apc. which have for centuries been a source of perplexity and misunderstanding to students and especially to translators of the book.

At least since the time of Dionysius, bishop of Alexandria (died A.D. 265), questions have been expressed about the un-Greek nature of the language of the Apc. Dionysius drew attention to the fact (see Eusebius, *Ecclesiastical History*, 7, 25, 7ff) that the Greek of the Apc. contained a number of unusual constructions which cannot be explained in terms of Greek grammar and syntax. This peculiar disregard has perplexed modern scholars as well. In the words of R.H. Charles, who studied the book for many years while preparing his commentary, the Apc. possesses a distinctive character of its own which makes it 'absolutely unique' linguistically.[1] More recently Matthew Black observed that 'there is one New Testament book, Revelation, whose crude Greek is particularly stained by "Semitisms" '.[2]

While one could not pretend at this stage to be able to explain all linguistic oddities in the book, yet this introductory survey demonstrates that the major part of the peculiarity attached to the un-Greek use of the verb in the Apc. can be ascribed to the influence of Semitic syntax, primarily biblical Hebrew (and Aramaic). Nigel Turner supports this view: 'some of the sources [of Revelation] may have been Aramaic originally. However, the Semitic influence in Revelation is mainly Hebrew.'[3]

In addition, this study cites evidence strongly supporting the argument that *biblical* Hebrew and Aramaic, not a later variety, is reflected in the Greek of the Apc. The presence of Hebrew infinitives absolute in Greek dress[4] indicates biblical Hebrew was the model for the Seer, since the construction was absent from later Hebrew.[5] G. Mussies, who argues that the language of the Apc. is patterned after later Hebrew and Aramaic, concedes that this is one of the points of difference between biblical and Mishnaic

Hebrew visible in translation.[6] Other telling features of *biblical* Hebrew syntax influencing the Greek of the Apc. are the Hebrew *Waw*-consecutive;[7] the resolving of a participle into a finite verb;[8] and possibly the occurrence of the absolute object.[9] Needless to say, any theory of the nature and purpose of the Apc. and of its relation to the OT cannot afford to ignore these direct links with the syntax of OT Hebrew.

Historical survey of linguistic observations

With the turn of the century as the starting point for a survey, we begin with the sixth edition of Meyer's *Kritisch-exegetischer Kommentar über die Offenbarung Johannis* (1906), by Wilhelm Bousset. Under section 7 of the introduction he begins a discussion, entitled 'Gebrauch des Verbums',[10] by stating that verbs in the Apc. are characterised by haphazard shifts between present and future tense. Especially in chapter 11 is this evident. He also notes that the use of the imperfect is not frequent in the Apc., but in those places where it has been employed, it has been done deliberately. It is preferred, for instance, in descriptive, explanatory relative clauses such as those in 1:12, 2:14 and 6:9. Outside such special categories the imperfect is not in general use in the Apc.

Noteworthy also is the nearly exclusive use of aorist infinitives, with seemingly little sense for the distinction between aorist and present infinitive.

While he points to Hebrew parallels to the language of the Apc., Bousset does not go so far as to see behind the use of the verb traces of direct Semitic influence, although at certain places in the book he recognises the possibility of direct translation from Hebrew sources.

Another study touching on the use of the verb in the Apc. is that of T.C. Laughlin, *The Solecisms of the Apocalypse.*[11] The book (a published Ph.D. thesis) surveys briefly various peculiarities in the language of the Apc. traceable to Hebrew influence. Concerning the verb two points are noteworthy: first, the absolute use of the participle λέγων,[12] as found for example in Apc. 11:1. This is LXX usage, he says, based on Hebrew *lē'mōr*; the second point concerns the tenses: the mixing of present and future tense verbs in the same clause or sentence when, according to Greek usage, we should expect only future verbs.[13] The observations of Laughlin, though brief, are valuable for the LXX parallels which are cited to illustrate the Hebraic nature of the usage he discusses.

A comprehensive survey of the grammar of the Apc. was provided by R.H. Charles in his commentary.[14] His observations about the Semitic influence on the verb will be surveyed briefly.[15] He notes the frequent wavering of the text of the Apc. between present and future tenses, but notes that in most cases the changes are not arbitrary.[16] A careful study of context will show that, while in some places the future is rightly employed, there are other places where the present occurs when we would expect the future or participle. This may be due to the influence of Hebrew tense usage, since a Hebrew imperfect (and perfect) may be rendered as past, present, or future, according to context. Cases of confusion of this nature can be amply illustrated from the LXX. The possibility of a confusion of future tenses for pasts on the basis of Semitic idiom is suggested by Charles at Apc. 4:9–10.[17] The past imperfect or historical present is frequently replaced in the Apc. by a participle. Note the following: 1:16 ἐκπορευομένη, 4:2 καθήμενος. He notes this use of the participle for a finite verb is frequent in late Hebrew, and the same use is even more frequent in both Aramaic and Syriac; thus its displacement of the past imperfect in our author is probably due largely to Hebraic influence.[18] Regarding the use of the infinitives, Charles notes that they are at times used in the sense of finite verbs in conditional clauses, as well as in principal sentences, while the infinitive plus the article serves as a finite verb.

Charles maintains that the criteria of grammar and syntax in the Apc., including syntax of the verb, can be employed in separating portions of the book which originated with the Seer from sections which were based on sources.[19] Concerning the nature of the language of the Apc., he expressed the opinion that while its author wrote in Greek, he remained in the thought world of the Hebrew Bible.[20] Furthermore, while related closely to Greek as found in the LXX and other Greek OT versions, and the apocrypha and pseudepigrapha, the Apc. nevertheless possesses a distinct character of its own.[21]

The next significant work on the language of the Apc., drawing heavily on that of Charles, was by R.B.Y. Scott who, in 1928, published his Ph.D. thesis, *The Original Language of the Apocalypse.*[22] Scott stated his premise at the outset: 'the Apocalypse as a whole is a translation from Hebrew or Aramaic'.[23] Though basing his conclusion ultimately on alleged mistranslations of the Semitic original, Scott also examined certain Hebrew idioms frequently encountered in the book. Regarding the verb, he follows Charles in referring to participles used as finite verbs. He also pointed to a number of cases in which the Greek of the Apc. employs the participial forms of ἔχω to represent possessive *lamedh* in Hebrew. The occurrence of a peculiar Hebrew construction is also noted: a finite verb is used with a noun that has the particle of comparison, where in Greek a participle would be used.[24]

Since the majority of Hebrew verbs have causative stems, while in

Greek separate verbs must be added to express causation, and since in Hebrew causative expressions are comparatively more frequent than in Greek, Scott finds it natural to expect that in the Apc. clumsy phrases with ποιέω or δίδωμι would be found to express the causative idea.[25] Cf. Apc. 13:13: πῦρ ποιῇ ... καταβαίνειν. Scott also notes a number of cases where confusion of tense has occurred. He makes two observations on the matter: first, that the difficulty often arises from the various meanings of the Hebrew imperfect (i.e. time past, present and future) and, where that does not operate, a misunderstanding of a *Waw*-consecutive for simple *Waw* or *vice versa* may have occurred when the Seer rendered an unpointed Hebrew text into Greek. Scott also feels that present participles are found where aorist or perfect participles are expected in several places.

In his conclusion, Scott reaffirms his premise that the Apc. originated in Hebrew and was translated into Greek by an early Christian. By this he does not deny the possibility that the book is composite in origin, nor does he ignore the fact that distinctions in style and diction are apparent in the book. These differences he sees, though, in the Hebrew original, not in Greek.

In his commentary on the Apc., E.-B. Allo of the University of Fribourg notes that certain participles must be given the sense of finite verbs.[26] This he also ascribed to Hebrew influence, and especially to Aramaic. He noted the appearance of the impersonal plural verb, and asked if it could be due to Aramaic influence.

In his final work, published posthumously, C.C. Torrey sets forth his reasons for believing the Apc. was written originally in Aramaic and later translated into Greek.[27] His arguments touching the use of the verb include the use of the indefinite third person plural in place of the passive voice, in line with Aramaic usage. Torrey sees evidence in the Apc. of very frequent use of the Aramaic participle, which prompted the translator to employ a Greek corresponding participle where a finite verb would have sufficed. Similarly, where the Greek present tense occurs, Torrey felt an Aramaic participle could be taken for granted. This is cause for a number of places where the Greek has a present tense verb where one expects a future tense. Finally, he mentions the confusion of tenses which arises over the similarity between Aramaic peal participles and perfect tense verbs in unpointed texts.

Torrey has no time, however, to consider influence of the Hebrew tense system on the verbs of the Apc. - 'In short there is in Revelation no trace of Hebrew usage in the tenses employed. Whatever evidence there is of falsely or too literally rendered verbs points to Aramaic rather than to Hebrew.'[28]

The first monograph devoted to a study of the verb in the Apc. is Angelo Lancellotti's *Sintassi Ebraica nel Greco Dell'Apocalisse*, I, 'Uso delle forme verbali'.[29] He attempts to show how the verb in the Apc. is employed along Semitic, and more specifically, Hebraic, lines by analysing certain verbs in the Apc. in the light of Hebrew grammar. His first chapter discusses the distinction between the Hebrew and Greek concept of verbal tenses; following chapters present descriptions of verbs in the Apc. which conform to the Hebrew qatal, yiqtol; the participle in its differing Hebrew and Greek roles, especially employed nominally and verbally; the infinitive in its nominal and independent employment is discussed last, followed by a final chapter of *recapitolazione* and a conclusion.

Regarding tense, Lancellotti notes that the aorist for the most part is employed along normal Greek lines, but in a few cases a Hebraic sense is displayed when the Greek aorists in the Apc. express the sense of Hebrew perfects. The perfect tense in the Apc. has little connection with Hebrew syntax, although a possible connection with Hebrew perfect is suggested. The present tense more than the others is used abnormally. Omitting the cases in which the present is found in indirect discourse, dependent on a past tense verb, Lancellotti asserts that the so-called 'quasi atemporal' use of the present in the Apc. is due to Semitic influence. Finally, the futuristic present is attached by him to the Hebrew imperfect referring to future events (but wrongly, as we shall see below). While the future in the Apc. is generally used along Greek lines, its substitution for the aorist subjunctive is unusual, and its use with the value of an imperfect[30] is based on Hebrew imperfect tense usage. Also, its modal use with the value of a Hebrew jussive and as cohortative is Hebraic.

Lancellotti discusses Semitic influence on attributive and circumstantial participles, bringing out several specific points at which, he says, Semitic influence is at work. The participial clause also is included in his discussion. Finally, he presents the case for Hebrew influence on the infinitive.

The study is wide-ranging and suggests many possibilities for further research. While specific criticisms of his findings are included at the appropriate places in this study, we could note here two general weaknesses of his monograph: (1) inadequate documentation; and (2) inadequate illustration from Hebrew and the LXX of the existence of the many syntactical equations which he suggests.

The significant study of the morphology of the Apc. by G. Mussies requires mention here since its concluding chapter is titled 'The Use of the Verb in the Apocalypse'.[31] It gives a detailed discussion, plus statistics, of use of the voice (pp. 330ff), moods (pp. 321ff), participles (pp.

324ff), and the durative, aoristic, futural and perfective categories (pp. 330ff). Again, specific criticisms of his chapter are to be found in the main portion of this work.

In a later expansion and update entitled 'The Greek of the Book of Revelation',[32] Mussies surveys the language of the Apc., finding what he terms 'absence Semitisms', which are Greek constructions having no Hebrew/Aramaic counterpart. The genitive absolute is the most striking of these, being absent from the Apc., and from Hebrew/Aramaic. Another is the Greek accusative plus infinitive. When taking the opposite approach, looking for Hebrew/Aramaic constructions with no exact counterpart in Greek, he notes the occurrence in the Apc. of the infinitive absolute. The conjunctive form of the adverbial participle is singled out for special discussion,[33] but its peculiar usage by the Seer in the Apc. is attributed by Mussies to stylistic preference rather than to specific Hebrew influence.

At this point attention should be drawn to three recent monographs in the field of Hellenistic Greek syntax which are valuable to the student of the NT for the light they throw on the language of the NT. From Sweden comes L. Rydbeck, *Fachprosa, Vermeintliche Volkssprache und Neues Testament*, Studia Graeca Upsaliensia 5 (Uppsala, 1967); from Greece comes B. Mandilaras, *The Verb in the Greek Non-literary Papyri* (Athens, 1973), and from the Netherlands comes W.F. Bakker's *Pronomen Abundans and Pronomen Coniunctum* (Amsterdam and London, 1974). Discussions in relevant parts of this study have been enriched by the findings of these authors, and appreciation is expressed for the attention given by each to the influence of his research on the Greek of the NT as seen in its Hellenistic matrix.

The publication of the fourth volume on 'Style' (1976) by Nigel Turner in the Moulton-Howard-Turner *Grammar of New Testament Greek* makes available to grateful students of the language of the Apc. an entire chapter devoted to a discussion of its special linguistic features. Turner's wide-ranging contributions to the elucidation of the Semitic element in NT Greek are already well-known to users of his previous volume in the series, on 'Syntax'. No discussion of Semitisms in the Apc. can afford to overlook this his latest statement on the topic.

This introductory survey could not be concluded without reference to two classic studies devoted to the Semitic element in the language of the New Testament. First, a work which is so widely established and recognised that it hardly requires mention is Matthew Black's *An Aramaic Approach to the Gospels and Acts*.[34] It serves as the standard presentation of the Aramaic element in the Greek of the Gospels and Acts. The usefulness of this store of information has a wider application than that

implied by the title, and although its author excluded from his study
Semitisms due exclusively to Hebrew (cf. p. 34), yet anyone acquainted
with *An Aramaic Approach* will observe how this present study has, with
certain modifications to allow for a difference in subject matter, patterned
itself after Black's work.

In a more recent monograph Klaus Beyer has made his important contribution to the understanding of NT Greek. His *Semitische Syntax im
Neuen Testament*,[35] of which Part I only has appeared, brings to bear a
great deal of Semitic evidence which illuminates un-Greek usage of the
clause. His study, rich in Hebrew and Aramaic examples, has been drawn
upon in several places where it discussed constructions found in the Apc.

1

TEXTUAL CONSIDERATIONS

The preparation of this present work has been greatly facilitated by the excellent textual studies of the Apc. published during this century, making it the most thoroughly studied NT book, from the viewpoint of text.

1. Survey of twentieth-century developments

The commentaries of Bousset and Allo are rich in textual references; both however were superseded by the commentary of R.H. Charles, who in vol. II included the Greek text of the Apc. with extensive critical apparatus. Latin sources, meanwhile, were carefully presented by H.J. Vogels.[1] These works, in their turn were superseded by the masterly apparatus prepared by H.C. Hoskier representing thirty years of labour collating and recording *in toto* the variants found in every Greek manuscript of the Apc. known in his day, plus a comprehensive treatment of the ancient versions.[2] While today some doubt is expressed about the accuracy of his citations of some versions, his careful work on the Greek text is definitive and irreplaceable.

The Greek material presented in Hoskier's apparatus has been studied and carefully analysed by J. Schmid of Munich, who has aimed at determining manuscript families and the allegiance of the Fathers. In his major work his task is sixfold:[3] (1) accurately to define the two medieval forms of the text of the Apc. (*Koine*, and the text used for the Commentary of Andreas); (2) to note the relationship of these two forms to one another; (3) to demonstrate the twofold nature of the earlier tradition made possible by the discovery of Chester Beatty Papyrus p^{47}; (4) to consider the possibility of a 'neutral' text; (5) to note the relation of the *Koine* and Andreas texts to this earlier tradition; (6) to test the manuscript tradition by the criteria of the language and usage of the Apc.[4] In addition to these main objectives Schmid notes that so far no trace of a Western text of the Apc. has been found.[5]

Since the publication of Hoskier's apparatus the early text of the Apc. has been further illuminated by discovery of p^{47}, a late third-century

manuscript containing chapters 9:10–17:2.[6] Several manuscript discoveries
of minor significance are described by J. Schmid.[7] He concludes, after
describing some thirty-one previously unknown or unnoticed manuscripts
of the Apc., that these are not of any help in illuminating the early character of the text (they date mostly from the tenth to the seventeenth centuries).[8]

2. Current status of studies on the text of the Apocalypse

'In the Book of Revelation the Textual scene and its history differ greatly
from the rest of the New Testament.' This statement, from the introduction to the twenty-sixth edition of Nestle–Aland,[9] continues: 'In brief, in
the Apocalypse much (if not all) is different from elsewhere.' The most
significant of these differences, ably summarised by J. Delobel,[10] are the
following: (a) the relative paucity of early Greek witnesses; (b) the absence
of the Apc. in codex B, and its inferior representation in *Aleph* considerably
weakens testimony for the existence of a 'Neutral' text, thus accounting
for Hort's hesitation to distinguish, in the Apc., text types, and to recon-
struct its history; (c) the inferior authority of the few existing papyri containing portions of the Apc.; (d) the exceptional position of the *Textus
Receptus*, which for the Apc. merits much greater attention than it deserves
elsewhere in the NT; (e) the doubt about the existence of a Western text
for the Apc.

3. Use of linguistic criteria and textual eclecticism

Major advances in the task of the recovery of a more primitive NT text
have been made in recent decades by the application of internal linguistic
criteria, and of the eclectic textual method. General questions regarding
the application of both of these to the text of the Apc. have been surveyed
recently by Delobel,[11] who considered the views both of proponents and
opponents. Regarding the textual theory adopted for this present study,
the following statement should be sufficient: in the light of the major
advances made in the study of the text of the Apc. during this century,
it need not be stressed that in the work of analysing the nature of Semitic
influence on syntax, the approach which is based on a single manuscript
or printed NT text is inadequate, and can lead only to unsatisfactory
results. Matthew Black demonstrated the weakness of a similar approach,[12]
relying only on the Westcott and Hort text, for studying the Semitic element in the Gospels and Acts. His practice of granting a hearing to the
more Semitised reading, regardless of its textual pedigree, should be

applied to the Apc. No single manuscript or textual family preserves all the more Semitised and therefore more original readings in those portions of the NT with a Semitic background.

It is all the more surprising, then, to notice that the two most recent studies on the verb in the Apc., i.e. those of Lancellotti and Mussies, ignore in large measure the wealth of textual information readily available, limiting their studies to a single printed text of Merk in the case of Lancellotti, and a single uncial manuscript, Alexandrinus, in that of Mussies. In his monograph Mussies gives the reason for his choice of codex Alexandrinus as the basis for his study of the Apc.: 'Instead of describing the use of language of a text edition which is inevitably eclectic the linguist will have to choose the best ms. available and describe in the first place the idiom of that one alone.'[13] This approach is justified *if* one were aiming to describe the use of language as influenced by the textual tradition responsible for producing the selected manuscript. In the case of the Apc. we have, in fact, the book at a stage of textual transmission which it reached in the hands of fifth-century Alexandrian textual scholars, represented by uncial A, along with is supporting minuscules.

To penetrate behind this stage of the text it is necessary to draw upon a wide range of witnesses for the evidence they contain of the earlier, less polished constructions, especially Semitisms, which were almost certainly removed by certain later copyists. By limiting his work to the basis provided by uncial A, Mussies imposes undue limitations on his findings, especially those in his final chapter on the verb.

The alternative to the single text method pursued by Lancellotti and Mussies is to employ a judicious eclecticism. This means, according to G.D. Kilpatrick,[14] that 'No readings can be condemned categorically because they are characteristic of manuscripts or groups of manuscripts. We have to pursue a consistent eclecticism. Readings must be considered severally on their intrinsic character.' Elsewhere he notes that in principle any variant which occurs in a manuscript that is not a copy of another manuscript may prove to be original.[15] It should not be dismissed because it does not occur in this or that textual type, nor because it has inadequate attestation.[16]

The other factor related to eclecticism in solving textual differences in the Apc. is of course an awareness of Semitic idiom in Greek dress. Metzger observes that 'a knowledge of Hebrew and especially Aramaic will occasionally throw light upon a variant reading in the Gospels'.[17] The same point is made by Kilpatrick regarding the Apc. when he notes that here perhaps the most important consideration is language.[18] Among the writers of the NT the Greek of the Apc. stands out, and would 'invite correction'.

J. Schmid emphasises the importance of understanding the language of the Apc.[19]

This consideration of textual matters concludes with a mention of the criterion of atticism and its implications for the text of the Apc. Atticism became a dominant trend in Greek literary circles during the first and second centuries A.D.; it induced scribes to insert into the NT text classical Greek forms of language in place of original Hellenistic forms. Kilpatrick, in discussing this trend, notes that the most evident stylistic consideration at work on the NT text was this smoothing over or removal of Semitic idioms.[20] He rightly suspects that sometimes the attempt to improve the language of the NT was successful to the point that the more atticised Greek expression appears in our text while the original un-Greek one is relegated to the footnotes. This is evident, for example, in the use of the tenses of verbs, and where an un-Greek tense occurs, there is almost invariably textual evidence of considerable uncertainty among ancient copyists, with many attempts at smoothing. Our findings, presented below, lend additional support to the idea of textual smoothing, showing its extensive nature.

Except in places where the readings of specific NT manuscripts are cited, the Greek text used in this study is that of the United Bible Societies, edited by K. Aland, M. Black, C. Martini, B. Metzger and A. Wikgren (3rd edn, 1975). It was not chosen arbitrarily, but because examination shows that in it, more than in previous printed texts of the Greek NT, an effort was made by the editors to include in the text of the Apc. the more Semitised readings, whenever textual support allowed.[21] For citations of the Hebrew OT the new *Biblia Hebraica Stuttgartensia*, edited by K. Elliger and W. Rudolph was employed. For the LXX the three-volume hand edition by H.B. Swete was relied upon, since its critical apparatus is more extensive than that of Rahlfs.

2

GREEK VERBS WITH HEBREW MEANINGS[1]

In Apc. 17:6 we read that the Seer 'marvelled' at the vision of the great harlot, ἐθαύμασα ἰδὼν αὐτὴν θαῦμα μέγα. Here the traditional meaning of θαυμάζειν, 'marvel', 'wonder', 'be astonished',[2] hardly bears the force required by the passage; better, 'he was appalled' – a sense that is, however, unattested in secular Greek. In an almost identical expression in Dan. 4:16 (MT) we find that Aramaic šĕmam means 'appalled, dumbfounded' – 'Daniel was dumbfounded for a moment.' The reason is given in the following phrase, 'Do not let the dream and its interpretation dismay you.' Note that the LXX of Dan. here uses the verb employed by the Seer: μεγάλως δὲ ἐθαύμασεν ὁ Δανιηλ (4:19). Note the use of corresponding Hebrew qal šāmēm,[3] with identical meaning in Lev. 26:32, which in the LXX is θαυμάσονται ἐπ᾽ αὐτῇ οἱ ἐχθροι, 'the enemies who occupy it shall be appalled' (NEB). Elsewhere in Dan. we find the expression in 8:27 'I was appalled by the vision', καὶ ἐθαύμαζον τὴν ὅρασιν.

On the basis of these occurrences it is suggested that when θαυμάζω is employed, and the meaning 'marvel', 'be astonished', seems too weak, one should understand 'appalled' after the meaning of the Hebrew equivalent. So in the case of Apc. 17:7 Διὰ τί ἐθαύμασας; could be translated why are you appalled?'

The two remaining occurrences of θαυμάζω require separate consideration, based on the fact already noted that the underlying Hebrew word can mean not only 'appalled' but also 'be desolated'. In Apc. 13:3, ἐθαυμάσθη ὅλη ἡ γῆ ὀπίσω τοῦ θηρίου, the traditional rendering is represented by the NEB 'The whole world went after the beast in wondering admiration'; cf. 'followed the beast with wonder' (RSV). Both renderings attempt to deal with the incongruous aorist passive.[4] The traditional explanation, that here we have a passive or deponent form with active meaning is not convincing, because in his two uses of the verb noted above the Seer chose the active voice. A different explanation is called for, and the conjecture to follow is based on the fact already established, that θαυμάζω in the Apc. has the meaning of šāmēm. In 13:3 ἐθαυμάσθη means 'be desolated'

12

in the sense expressed by the Hebrew equivalent; e.g. Ezek. 35:15 *'ăšer-šāmēmâ*, 'which was desolate'. It should be noted in support that while in Greek an increasing sense of 'honour', 'admire', became attached to the verb,[5] Hebrew has no such connotation. Therefore in order to appreciate what effect the sense of Hebrew 'desolate', 'devastate', would give, we must read Apc. 13:3-4 without any trace of the idea of worship – i.e. 'The whole world was devastated in the wake of (ὀπίσω perhaps for *'aḥărê* with the sense 'behind') the beast. So they threw themselves down before[6] the dragon because it gave authority to the beast; then they threw themselves down before the beast, declaring "Who is like the beast? Who can make war against him?"' The final phrase supports the conjecture: the beast is free to devastate and tyrannise the earth because there is no force to oppose it. Finally, verse 7 reveals that the same beast has conquered the saints in battle; furthermore, he exercises ἐξουσία over every tribe, people, language group, and nation. In verse 8 all on earth (except those inscribed in the Lamb's book) again prostrate themselves before the tyrant. The fate of any who refuse to capitulate is stated indirectly 'for those who have ears' in verse 10 – exile and death by the sword, in words taken from Jeremiah's captivity passages, 15:2 and 43:11. The Seer closes this dramatic section with the words 'here is the patience and faith of the saints'.

Seen from this angle, one comes to doubt whether any sense of 'worship', 'marvel', 'admiration' finds its way into the passage. To the contrary, the mood is created by a powerful irresistible tyrant beast who extracts submission from his subjects.

The other passive, θαυμασθήσονται, in Apc. 17:8 should be translated 'those who inhabit the earth shall be devastated'.

Διδόναι, found frequently in the Apc., can be translated in a variety of ways, some of which are un-Greek and betray the influence of Hebrew *nātan*. In the classifications which follow, the six types of 'Hebrew' influence on διδόναι are set forth, along with supporting evidence, where it exists.

(a) Meaning 'set', 'place':[7] Apc. 3:8, δέδωκα ἐνώπιόν σου θύραν, is unusual Greek, but as Helbing in his observations on the cases in the LXX notes,[8] is Hebraic and means 'set', 'place', as does *nātan* in 2 Ki. 4:43, where the LXX renders τί δῶ τοῦτο ἐνώπιον ἑκατὸν ἀνδρῶν; 'How am I to set this before a hundred men?' Cf. also Apc. 13:16 '*place* a mark'; 17:17 '*put* it in their heads'.

(b) Meaning 'requite': N. Turner notes that in Apc. 2:23 διδόναι means 'requite', just as *nātan* does in Ps. 28 (27):4 'requite them according to their work'.[9]

(c) Meaning 'make': The causative sense of διδόναι is clear in Apc. 3:9

διδῶ ἐκ τῆς συναγωγῆς τοῦ Σατανᾶ, 'I will make (those) of Satan's synagogue', where the verb is parallel to ποιήσω in the second part of the verse. This is certainly not Greek but is the literal translation of a Hebrew construction, rendered in 3 Km. 9:22 by ἐκ τῶν υἱῶν Ισραηλ οὐκ ἔδωκεν Σαλωμων εἰς πρᾶγμα, 'Solomon did not make the men of Israel'; cf. Ex. 7:1, 23:27.

(d) Meaning 'to allow, permit': As Black noted,[10] a special feature of the Apc. is its frequent use of ἐδόθη with an impersonal singular, to reflect the sense of *nātan*, meaning 'to allow, to permit', translated in the LXX ἐδόθη: see Lev. 19:20, 4 Km. 25:30, Job 15:19. Occurrences in the Apc. include 6:8, 7:2, 9:5, 16:8, 19:8. This is Hebraic, and not accounted for by the secular use of δίδοναι meaning 'allow', which is found mostly in prayers.[11]

(e) Meaning 'prompt': literally 'put into [the] heart', when linked to καρδία by εἰς: Apc. 17:17 Θεὸς ἔδωκεν εἰς τὰς καρδίας αὐτῶν ποιῆσαι, 'God prompted them to do'. This is a Hebrew idiom found several times in the OT;[12] a close parallel to our verse is Neh. 2:12 *'ēlōhî nōtēn 'el-libbî la 'ăśôt*; LXX (2 Esdras 12:12) Θεὸς δίδωσιν εἰς καρδίαν μου τοῦ ποιῆσαι, 'God prompted me to do'.

(f) Meaning 'appoint': N. Turner maintains that *nātan*, meaning 'to appoint', has influenced Apc. 9:5, ἐδόθη αὐτοῖς ἵνα μὴ ἀποκτείνωσιν αὐτούς, which he translates 'orders were given'.[13] This is questionable, and the passage seems to belong under heading (d) above, meaning 'allow, permit'.

The δώσει ταῖς προσευχαῖς τῶν ἁγίων in Apc. 8:3 is puzzling. Charles suggests one should understand θυμιάματα after δώσει, 'that he might cense the prayers, and so make them acceptable before God'.[14] While not feeling satisfied with his emendation, I have no suitable alternative explanation for the use of δίδοναι here.

Κληρονομεῖν in LXX Deut. 2:24 expresses the idea of taking by force: 'begin to *take possession*, and contend with him in battle' (RSV). This strong sense attached to the verb is not native to the Greek language but derives from the underlying Hebrew *yāraš* 'take possession of', 'displace'; and in a secondary sense 'to inherit'.[15] It is employed elsewhere in the LXX with similar force; Lev. 20:24 'you shall *take over* their land [the land of the nation which Yahweh was to cast out before Israel, verse 23], for I will give it to you to possess' (again, Hebrew *yāraš*).

Such usage can only be described as a Semitism, since nothing like it is to be found in Greek. Many times in the LXX this verb is used in a milder though still Semitic sense of 'acquire', 'possess', without implied force. Isa. 61:7 'in your land you shall possess a double portion' – here again κληρονομεῖν = *yāraš*. Cf. 4 Km. 17:24 '(The king of Assyria brought people . . . and placed them in the cities . . .) so they *took possession* of Samaria.' In the majority of OT passages where κληρονομεῖν translates *yāraš*, the idea of possessing land, cities, fields etc., which were in the hands of others, is expressed. Only in comparatively few places does the term actually denote its Greek sense 'to inherit'.

Since Polybius (second century B.C.) uses κληρονομεῖν twice in the sense 'to acquire', 'obtain', τὴν . . . δόξαν in *History* 15, 22, 3, φήμην in 18, 55, 8,[16] it is not a pure Hebraism. Apart from these two passages, its only attestation meaning 'acquire', 'possess' comes from second century A.D. authors such as Lucian and Phrynichus. Never does it take this meaning in classical Greek.[17]

In line with OT usage and opposed to Hellenistic Greek, the verb meaning 'inherit' is rare in the NT; according to Bauer it occurs only once,[18] at Gal. 4:30: οὐ γὰρ μὴ κληρονομήσει ὁ υἱός, 'this son (of a slave) shall by no means inherit', which cites LXX Gen. 21:10, where κληρονομεῖν = *yāraš*. Other NT occurrences (about seventeen) conform to Hebraic usage, e.g. Matt. 5:5 αὐτοὶ κληρονομήσουσιν τὴν γῆν, 'they shall possess the land' (a citation of LXX Ps. 36:11); no idea of inheritance in the legal sense is implied; this refers to the taking possession of a territory in the OT sense, although allowance may be made for a metaphorical, not literal 'territory'; cf. Matt. 19:29 'whoever has left houses . . . or lands for my sake . . . shall gain possession of (κληρονομήσει) eternal life'.

In Apc. 21:7, immediately following his vision of a new heaven and a new earth (land), the Seer reports the promise of the one on the throne: ὁ νικῶν κληρονομήσει ταῦτα, 'the one who is victorious shall take possession of all this'. Here is the final canonical echo of the promise of a land and heritage first made to Abram, according to Gen. 15:7. In neither passage does the verb κληρονομεῖν/*yāraš* denote 'inherit', so it must be understood in its Hebraic sense. The idea of heirship is expressed in both passages, however, and it is certainly not coincidental. In Gen. 15:1–4 Abram's chief concern is his lack of a male heir; he was childless, so the possession of the promised land meant little, if it could not be passed on to a legitimate heir.

The Seer dealt with a similar concept, which included, in common with the Gen. passage, a 'new land', a city (cf. Heb. 11:10: Abraham looked forward to a city), and the issue of legal heir: Apc. 21:7*b*, ἔσομαι αὐτῷ Θεὸς καὶ αὐτὸς ἔσται μοι υἱός; the matter in the Apc. was resolved by conferral of sonship.

Black, in his article cited above, has dealt with the various Hebrew meanings expressed by ἀδικεῖν when it translates *'āšaq* 'to oppress', or more specifically, 'to defraud', 'to cheat'; e.g. Hos. 12:8(7) 'False scales are in merchants' hands and they love to cheat' (NEB).

Of the ten occurrences of ἀδικεῖν in the Apc., nine (22:11 being excepted) were declared by Charles to mean 'hurt'.[19] Black is not so sure, and in his examination makes some interesting suggestions. The difficult 'hurt not (μὴ ἀδικήσῃς) the oil and the wine' of 6:6 could in fact express the sense 'and do not (fraudulently) withhold the oil and the wine'.[20] This suggestion seems to derive support from its context, which is generally understood to refer to a fixing of the maximum price for the main foodstuffs – a whole day's wage for the average daily consumption of a workman.

In a number of passages in the Apc. which refer to God's judgments 'harming' – i.e. smiting, or destroying the earth, Black agrees that ἀδικεῖν has the sense of hiphil of *nkh* 'to smite': e.g. Isa. 10:20. Generally, the English versions render 'to harm', but a stronger sense of 'to smite' seems justified in Apc. 7:2, 3; 9:4, 10, and possibly 2:11.

Charles suggests that ποιμαίνειν should be given the secondary sense of Hebrew 'to devastate' in Apc. 2:27 and 19:5, based on the LXX mistranslation in Ps. 2:9.[21] Black, however, dissents, pointing out the fact that the LXX mistranslated does not imply that the Seer intended to express the sense of 'devastate': it means 'rule' only. But although he notes that ποιμαίνειν is paralleled with συντρίβεται in Apc. 2:27 and πατάξῃ in 19:15, Black does not explain how the concepts of 'rule' and 'smash' the nations are to be combined. Certainly behind both passages lies the idea of conquest, patterned after the conquest of Canaan by the Hebrews under Yahweh's command, with the goal of 'possessing' the territory promised to the patriarch Abraham.[22] In this sense ποιμαίνειν means 'push aside' or 'shepherd away' the heathen to make way for Yahweh's chosen people.

Black notes that the favoured expression νικᾶν in the Apc. (fifteen occurrences) is used along Greek lines for the most part. Abnormal 'Hebraic' usage was claimed for Apc. 5:5 by Scott,[23] who would translate 'worthy', 'able', on the basis of Aramaic *zĕkâ*. Black is not convinced, however, and is probably right in accepting the NEB rendering 'the lion of the tribe of Judah . . . has conquered, so that he can open the scroll'.

Εὑρίσκειν. In his volume on New Testament Greek Style,[24] N. Turner suggests that under influence of Hebrew niphal of *mṣ'*,[25] εὑρέθη means simply 'to be', not 'to be found'. So in Apc. 12:8 οὐδὲ τόπος εὑρέθη, 'no place was'; likewise in 20:11; cf. 16:20 and 18:21. This is clearly Hebraic, reflecting 1 Sam. 13:22 where *mṣ'* niphal is translated in the LXX (1 Km.

13:22) by οὐχ εὑρέθη ῥομφαία 'sword was not (in the hand of any of the people)'.

Finally, ποιεῖν in Apc. 22:2 used with καρπούς may be a Hebrew idiom, states Turner,[26] since *'āśâ* has the secondary meaning 'to yield'. 2 Ki. 19:30 *wĕ 'āśâ pĕrî* is translated in the LXX (4 Km. 19:30) ποιήσει καρπόν, 'it may yield fruit'. The idiom is found also in Aramaic.[27]

3

SEMITIC INFLUENCE ON VERBAL SYNTAX

1. Voice

a. Third person plural active verbs with indefinite subject

In his *Aramaic Approach* (third edition) Matthew Black draws the follow-ing summary of Aramaic influence on Greek impersonal third-person plural verbs in the Gospels and Acts:[1] 'The passive is less frequently used in Aramaic than in Greek, its place being taken by an impersonal construc-tion, uncommon in Greek apart from λέγουσι, φασί In the appearance of this impersonal construction in the Gospels, Wellhausen detected the influence of Aramaic (*Einl.*[2], p. 18; cf. Wilcox, *Semitisms of Acts*, pp. 127ff.). An examination of the distribution of the construction in the Gospels confirms his view.' R.H. Charles noted the occurrence of this construction a number of times in the Apc., and also pointed to its fre-quent occurrence in biblical Aramaic, citing a number of passages in Daniel.[2] In their NT Grammar, Bl-D recognise that 'the range of ideas expressed by [the impersonal third-person plural] enlarged under the influence of Aramaic (which is not fond of the passive); in classical Greek the construction is used primarily with verbs of saying, etc., as is the case in Modern Greek';[3] Nigel Turner adds several examples illustrating the variety of subjects which can be understood.[4]

In a more recent study on the indefinite third-person plural, Lars Rydbeck has presented new evidence which he believes should bring about a revision of the traditional views of both classical grammarians and NT Greek and Semitic specialists on this construction.[5] In his first chapter, titled 'Subjektlose 3. Person Plural für den Begriff "man" bei Verben ausserhalb der Gruppe der verba dicendi', Rydbeck states as the object of his study a presentation of a hitherto little-known application of the third-person plural, exclusive of verbs of saying, during the various periods of the Greek language.[6] He first notes that grammarians are at fault for always distinguishing between the Greek third-person plural indirect verb and the use of 'one' (German *man*) in modern usage when expressing a general, concrete meaning. While the Greek language has its peculiar sense attached to certain occurrences of the indefinite third-person plural, it is in many cases rendered smoothly and practically by the use of 'one'.[7]

To illustrate this point, several examples of the impersonal third-person plural are drawn from the works of Dioscurides, the Greek medical author of the mid-first century A.D. Rydbeck shows how Dioscurides applied verbs other than those of saying/naming in the third-person plural in a more or less general meaning: examples include δολίζουσιν, χρῶνται, μίσγουσιν, ὑποκαπνίζουσιν, ἀναλαμβάνουσιν, etc. Further, he notes that these and other verbs were employed alternately as passives, as are the verbs of saying. Thus he concludes that these verbs in the impersonal third-person plural always possess a very concrete sense; they lead one to think immediately of the persons who have to do directly with the matter in question. It does not then appear unnatural that a language as concrete as Greek should make use of the third-person plural directly, without an anchorage to a particular subject. While the use of a passive was always open to Dioscurides, yet on occasion he employed the indefinite plural as a necessary variation; one can further formulate that his technical prose needed a linguistic expedient, of itself not meaningful in character, when it came to ascribing to a definite person facts which were of a more general and timeless nature.[8]

Rydbeck continues to develop his view by citing a number of occurrences of the impersonal third-person plural from various periods of Greek literature; from the classical period of Thucydides, Plato, Xenophon, Pseudo-Demosthenes, etc., he finds about fifteen examples, some of which were considered by modern editors to be errors, thus standing altered in the critical apparatus.[9] More classical examples could be found, he asserts, if one took the time to search for them. He further states that in this connection one must concede that when such impersonal passages in the third-person plural form (if they may be called such) occur in classical Greek, it is not improbable that the subject is of a general nature, which appears vaguely to the writer in his actual train of thought, expressed in the third-person, and situated in this verb ending.[10]

In short, by Hellenistic times the impersonal third-person plural was employed as an effective and practical linguistic expedient, whenever general discussion or reference was desired, to 'what one did'.[11]

At this point Rydbeck asks, why have the grammarians not hitherto noted this construction's more general existence by the time of Hellenistic Greek? The reason given is that in nearly every case their conclusions

are based on linguistic material only down to Aristotle, thus giving phenomena such as the impersonal third-person plural the designation of 'exception'. The line of continuing development shown by Greek prose is thus
not recognised, and the artificial demarcation (between various periods of
the language) is created, upon which rests our estimation of the manner
of expression, thus aggravating our prospects of understanding such an
elementary type of expression in Greek.[12]

While having reservations about his concluding assertion, we nonethe-
less recognise that Rydbeck has made a valuable contribution in assembling
examples which demonstrate the existence of the impersonal third-person
plural from earliest Hellenistic times right through to the beginning of the
third century A.D.; his book should be consulted for the twenty or so
examples cited.

Turning his attention to NT Greek, Rydbeck makes a special examination of this phenomenon in Luke, and confesses that he is unqualified to
handle the Aramaic and Hebrew antecedents which might lie behind this
construction in biblical Greek; nor does he discuss whether the phenomenon can be found in the LXX. He then cites NT grammarians, and notes
the case made by Dalman for Semitic influence in the form of the third-
person plural as an indirect reference to God; he then cites seventeen
Lukan passages which contain the construction and makes the following
observations: while Luke's impersonal third-person plural verbs usually
occur in the future and narrative tenses, the non-biblical examples, with a
few exceptions, were always in the present tense. He concludes that the
impersonal and general meaning of the construction is easier to understand intuitively when the verb is present tense. Also, Dalman's suggestion
that reference to God stands behind several at least of the Lukan occurrences Rydbeck cannot criticise. He does note, however, that even in
those cases where Semitic influence must be reckoned with, they are not
of such a nature that they would not have been subject to the more powerful influence of Hellenistic Greek usage, since the inherent Greek characteristics were evolving along similar lines to those of the Semitic languages.
Also of significance to Rydbeck was his final point, that some occurrences
of the construction in Luke (i.e. 6:44, 12:11, 14:35) are so similar to
those shown from secular prose that they are indistinguishable.[13]

From the foregoing summary of Rydbeck's first chapter two firm conclusions can be drawn: first, the occurrence of impersonal third-person
plural verbs (excluding those of saying) in classical Greek is more widespread than was previously recognised; secondly, it becomes increasingly
evident that this construction underwent development during the history

of the Greek language, with an apparently increasing frequency of use in later periods. In short, Rydbeck has succeeded in legitimising the construction in literary secular Greek, and has shown its acceptable use in various periods of the language. What he admittedly failed to do, however, was to explain how an acceptable, albeit infrequent, point of grammar such as the third-person plural came to be used with significantly greater frequency just in those Greek documents which have a direct or indirect link with an Aramaic source, i.e. Theodotion's Greek version of Daniel, the Gospels, and quite possibly, some portions of the Apc. Nor has he satisfactorily shown that in Greek there was the same distinction between the indefinite plural subject ('one') which is commonly found in colloquial speech in many languages, and the truly Aramaic (and, to a much lesser degree, Hebraic) indefinite subject which admits of *no* particular human agent and is thus equivalent to a passive.[14] His discoveries thus have not done away with the need for seeking an explanation for many NT occurrences of impersonal third-person plural verbs on lines other than those of Greek usage.

A survey of the biblical occurrences of this construction reveals that it is found in the OT very frequently to express the ordinary indefinite plural subject 'they', 'one', when reference is made to people generally. This, then, would correspond to the category of the Greek construction demonstrated by Rydbeck. There are, however, a few occurrences of the third-person plural to express an indefinite subject, where the context would not admit of a human agent, or at least not of several.[15] In this case the third-person plural comes to have the meaning of a true passive, as in Aramaic. Of the ten examples of this latter category cited by GK, which have their parallel in the LXX,[16] only one was rendered by a Greek impersonal third-person plural, *viz.* Gen. 34:27 ἐμίαναν, 'they polluted Dinah'.

This paucity of occurrences contrasts sharply with the concentrated cluster found in the Aramaic portions of the OT, and their corresponding rendering in Greek, especially in Theodotion's Dan. Charles cited eight from Dan.:[17] 4:13, 22, 23, 29; 5:20, 21; 7:12, 26; also Ezra 6:6. Five of these are rendered by the Greek third-person plural.

The construction appears in the Apc. in the following passages: 2:24 ὡς λέγουσιν, 'what they call' (i.e. 'what is called'); 8:2 καὶ εἶδον τοὺς ἑπτὰ ἀγγέλους . . . καὶ ἔδωκαν αὐτοῖς (copt), 'and I saw the seven angels . . . who were given' (literally 'and they gave to them').

In his book *Words of Jesus*, Gustaf Dalman drew attention to the tendency of Aramaic, noted by Rydbeck, of preferring the passive voice of the verb in order to avoid naming God as subject.[18] Often the Aramaic passive was in fact expressed by an active third-person plural. This Dalman illustrates with passages from Dan. It is significant to note that the following passages from the Apc. fall into the same category, where reference to God is made: 10:11 καὶ λέγουσίν (א A p⁴⁷: corrected to λεγει by many minusc. plus the versions) μοι Δεῖ σε πάλιν προφητεῦσαι, 'and they said to me, you must prophesy again' (literally 'and God said to me'); 12:6 ἵνα ἐκεῖ τρέφωσιν (τρεφει 2026) αὐτήν, 'that there they (God?) might feed her'; 16:15 καὶ βλέπωσιν (βλεπει 1852, βλεπη 2071) τὴν ἀσχημοσύνην αὐτοῦ, '[blessed is he . . . who keeps his garments, that he go not naked] and they (i.e. God) see his indecency'. It is evident that uncertainties arose over the construction in each case, but nowhere was a correction made to a passive form.

b. Intransitive active verbs expressing causative sense[19]

In the LXX

Conybeare and Stock note that in the LXX an intransitive active verb may express a causative sense, most certainly due to Hebrew influence. For example, βασιλεύειν in Greek means 'to be king', but it is often found in the LXX with the sense 'to make king'. In their discussion of this phenomenon, Bl-D recognise this and other verbs in the LXX as causative, although they are less certain of its Hebraic nature than is, for example, W. Schmid,[20] who in a review of R. Helbing's volume on *Kasussyntax* in the LXX lists (along with βασιλεύειν), ζῆν, 'to animate', as an example of numerous verbs which in secular Greek are intransitive, but which take on a causal meaning in the LXX under influence of the Hebrew piel and hiphil stem verbs, which are then usually followed by direct objects in the accusative case. Such constructions made no significant appearance in classical Greek, or in the language of the papyri, but are abundant in the LXX; note Gen. 3:18 ἀκάνθας καὶ τριβόλους ἀνατελεῖ σοι, 'thorns and thistles it shall cause to come forth to you', which translates a Hebrew hiphil imperfect *taṣmîaḥ*. Note also the objects in the accusative case. P. Katz remarked that some LXX translators, such as those responsible for Lamentations, go far in the use of these intransitive active verbs in a causative sense.[21]

In the NT

In the NT μαθητεύειν often occurs with a causative sense, as do other verbs.[22] In the Apc. two occurrences of the verb εὐαγγελίζεσθαι are suggested as intransitives with causative sense; cf. also Acts 16:17D*; Apc.

10:7 ὡς εὐηγγέλισεν (-σατο minusc.) τοὺς ἑαυτοῦ δούλους τοὺς προφήτας. Charles notes that only here is εὐαγγελίζεσθαι plus accusative as an active found in the NT. Cf. 14:6 ἔχοντα εὐαγγέλιον αἰώνιον εὐαγγελίσαι (-γγελίζασθαι p⁴⁷) ἐπὶ τοὺς καθημένους. The causative sense of both is, however, disputed by Bl-D, who prefer the wider Hellenistic sense of 'to announce the good news' for these occurrences.

R.B.Y. Scott, in his published thesis *The Original Language of the Apocalypse*,[23] drew attention to what he described as 'periphrasis' for Hebrew verbs in the causative stem. In Greek, the causative sense must be expressed by use of a second verb, auxiliary to the main one. Such constructions are much less common in Greek than in Semitic languages, which expressed causatives by a simple modification of the verbal stem. A helpful study of these two distinctive methods of rendering the Semitic causative into an Indo-European language has recently been published by Keder-Kopfstein of Israel in an article titled 'Die Wiedergabe des hebräischen Kausative in der Vulgata'.[24] His observations, though directed primarily toward the translation methods found in the Vulgate, apply quite well to Greek also, especially in regard to the different modes of translating Hebrew causatives. The first, which was pointed out earlier by Conybeare and Stock, as mentioned above, in which a single Greek verb is given the causative sense, is termed *synthetic*, while the mode which employs an auxiliary verb (referred to by Scott) is called *analytic*. Thus for example, the Hebrew verb wĕhiṣmîhaḥ, 'making it to bring forth', in Isa. 55:10 is translated in the LXX synthetically, καὶ ἐκβλαστήσῃ, but by Symmachus analytically, καὶ βλαστῆσαι αὐτὴν ποιήσει. Keder-Kopfstein gives the following examples of analytic translations in the LXX, for illustration: Isa. 29:21 οἱ ποιοῦντες ἁμαρτεῖν for ('dm) mḥṭy'y; Isa. 42:16 πατῆσαι ποιήσω αὐτούς for 'drykm.[25] He also observes that, while in the LXX the analytic form occurs here and there, it is the synthetic which as a rule predominates. In the later translation of Symmachus however, the analytical form is somewhat more frequent.[26] This is clearly the case in the Apc. as well, for while only two somewhat uncertain cases of the synthetic type of causative εὐαγγελίζειν occur, there are numerous cases of the analytic type, employing a form of ποιεῖν plus main verb (usually in the infinitive). Scott cites as an obvious example Apc. 13:13 πῦρ ποιῇ ... καταβαίνειν.[27] The manuscripts evince a widespread uncertainty about this construction, with a strong tendency to omit the very un-Greek ποιῇ, while changing infinitive καταβαίνειν into a finite form. Scott cites also the following: 3:9 ἰδοὺ ποιήσω αὐτοὺς ἵνα ἥξουσιν καὶ προσκυνήσουσιν;[28] 13:12 καὶ ποιεῖ ... ἵνα προσκυνήσουσιν (verse 15) καὶ ἐδόθη αὐτῷ δοῦναι ... καὶ ποιήσῃ ἵνα ... προσκυνήσωσιν;[29] (verse 16) καὶ ποιεῖ ... ἵνα δῶσιν.

Thus we see here a demonstration of how the modes of translating Semitic hiphil causatives into Greek, plainly documented in the Greek versions of the OT, have made their way into the language of the Apc., especially in the analytic form, by which a Semitic causative stem verb is rendered by use of the verb ποιεῖν plus main verb, which is often (not always) intransitive, and which occurs as an infinitive or aorist subjunctive/ future indicative.

Along similar lines we note that the auxiliary use of the verb as discussed by Black, *Aramaic Approach*, pp. 125f, which is based again on Semitic usage, occurs also in the Apc.: 16:1 Ὑπάγετε καί ἐκχέετε τὰς ἐπτὰ φιάλας, 'go and empty the seven bowls'; cf. verse 2 καὶ ἀπῆλθεν ὁ πρῶτος καὶ ἐξέχεεν τὴν φιάλην. J. Jeremias in his *Die Abendmahlsworte Jesu*, second edition, pp. 88ff (cited by Black, *loc. cit.*) also mentions Apc. 8:5 καὶ εἴληφεν ὁ ἄγγελος τὸν λιβανωτὸν καὶ ἐγέμισεν αὐτόν, 'The angel took and filled the censer.'[30]

Passive of Θαυμάζειν

Several commentators have called attention to the strange use of passive forms ἐθαυμάσθη (-μασεν, PQ) in Apc. 13:3 and θαυμασθήσονται (AP 1611 syr[ph]: θαυμασονται, *Koine*) in 17:8.[31] Grimm-Thayer's NT Greek *Lexicon* would make these occurrences in the Apc. middle; the construction is 'neither Greek nor Hebrew', remarked H. Gunkel! That the Seer himself knew the proper use of the active form of the verb is evident from verses 6 and 7 of chapter 17, where the active form occurs twice. One must therefore seek some external influence which led the Seer, deliberately or otherwise, to employ passive forms just in these two passages.

According to H. St J. Thackeray, a tendency of the Greek language during Hellenistic times was for many deponent verbs, particularly those expressing emotion, to adopt the aorist passive suffix -θην in place of the aorist middle. A further stage of this development included the substitution of the passive for the old middle futures.[32] On the analogy of this trend, he would account for the deponent use of the aorist passive and future passive forms in Apc. 13:3 and 17:8, respectively.

Turning to the biblical literature, we find that θαυμάζειν occurs a number of times in the LXX, where it translates a variety of Hebrew verbs. Thackeray observed that 'ἐθαυμάσθην, θαυμασθήσομαι in LXX are used passively (in class. sense), not as deponents, as in the Apocalypse'.[33] An examination of the other occurrences of θαυμάζειν in the LXX suggests a possible exception: Isa. 61:6 ἐν τῷ πλούτῳ αὐτῶν θαυμασθήσεσθε, 'you shall glory in their riches' (MT *ûbikbôdam tityammārû*). The significance of this passage lies in the fact that the passive ϑαυμασϑήσεσϑε renders an underlying hithpael verb.[34]

The explanation for the passive forms, which are true passives, is to be found in the conjecture developed earlier,[35] that the verbs are to be understood as meaning 'be desolated', a sense expressed by the underlying Hebrew *šāmēm*.[36] Thus I would translate Apc. 13:3 'the whole world was devastated by ('in the wake of'?) the beast', and 17:8 'those who inhabit the earth shall be devastated'.

Passive use of Μνησϑῆναι[37]

Charles draws attention to the passive use of μνησϑῆναι in Apc. 16:19 καὶ βαβυλὼν ἡ μεγάλη ἐμνήσϑη ἐνώπιον τοῦ ϑεοῦ δοῦναι αὐτῇ, 'and Babylon the great was remembered before God to give to her' (as opposed to the idiomatic RSV rendering 'and God remembered').[38] This verb obviously fits into the class, termed 'theological passives' by M. Zerwick,[39] which are employed in order to avoid directly naming God as agent. That this construction is used widely throughout the NT, with a variety of verbs, he demonstrates from the beatitudes: Matt. 5:5ff 'they shall be comforted', etc. Jeremias considered this construction in the gospels as an Aramaism which is found frequently in the discourses, thus perhaps serving to indicate the *ipsissima verba* of Jesus.[40] The same verb which occurs in Apc. 16:19 is also found, with identical meaning, in Acts 10:31, where Peter declared to Cornelius εἰσηκούσϑη σου προσευχὴ καὶ αἱ ἐλεημοσύναι σου ἐμνήσϑησαν ἐνώπιον τοῦ ϑεοῦ, 'your prayer was heard and your charities remembered before God'. It could be argued that this particular use of the passive voice as an indirect reference to God has no special Semitic flavour were it not for obvious OT antecedents employing an identical construction, as noted by Charles: Ezek. 3:20 οὐ μὴ μνησϑῶσιν αἱ δικαιοσύναι αὐτοῦ, 'his righteous deeds will not be remembered'; cf. 18:24. In both places the Greek passive translates a Hebrew third-person plural niphal *tizākarnâ*. This is no doubt a case of Hebrew influence on the voice of the verb, since such usage is neither classical, nor is it found in the papyri.[41]

Summary of chapter 3, section 1

In drawing this section to a close we summarise our findings, noting first that while the pioneering work of Rydbeck shows the impersonal third-person plural construction in Hellenistic Greek to be more widespread than previously assumed, still it cannot account for the greatly expanded use of it in Greek documents under direct Aramaic influence. Thus the occurrence of the third-person plural, to avoid naming God, also is found in the Apc. We argued also that the two occurrences of intransitive εὐαγγελίζεσθαι in the Apc. express a causative sense, based on the Hebrew piel and hiphil stem verbs. The Semitic custom of employing an auxiliary verb has probably left its mark on the Apc. in those places where we read such constructions as 'go and pour out', 'take and pour out'. Regarding the long-standing puzzle of passive forms of θαυμάζειν with active sense in the Apc. we have cited new evidence showing them not to be merely deponent preferring the aorist passive endings, but rather to express the Hebrew sense 'devastate'. Finally, the passive μνησθῆναι was presented as a member of that group of 'theological passives' used to avoid naming God. This is due to the influence of Hebrew niphal.

2. Mood

a. Deliberative use of the present indicative[42]

The deliberative question is one expressing doubt or perplexity, in which a person asks what is to be done, rather than simply what will happen. Such questions may be real, asking for information, or simply rhetorical, taking the place of a direct assertion. Classical examples include ποῖ πορευθῶ; 'whither shall I go?', εἴπω ταῦτα; 'shall I say this?', τί πάθω; 'what shall I undergo?' In common Greek usage, the deliberation is expressed by the verb in the subjunctive mood, chiefly in the first person.[43] Occasionally also in classical Greek the deliberative is expressed by the indicative mood, but then always in the future tense.[44] In the NT the deliberative is most often expressed by the subjunctive, but with several occurrences of the future indicative.[45] In addition to the first-person, the second- and third-person forms of the deliberative are found in the NT. Conybeare and Stock note that, in biblical Greek,[46] questions of deliberation are sometimes expressed in the non-classical present indicative ('very rarely' Bl-D) instead of the accepted Greek subjunctive or future indicative. The corresponding Latin present indicative is pointed out: *quid ago?*; any case for Latin influence on biblical Greek at this point is weakened, however, by occurrences of the same type in the LXX. Examples in the NT of the present indicative are found only in John 11:47 τί ποιοῦμεν; possibly 1 John 3:17 πῶς ἡ ἀγάπη τοῦ θεοῦ μένει (-εῖ preferred by Bl-D, §366 (4)) ἐν αὐτῷ. In the Apc. there is also one case, 6:10 ἕως πότε . . . οὐ κρίνεις (altered to future κρινεῖς in 1854 2046 598) καὶ ἐκδικεῖς (εκδικησεις 2321). This strange usage is found by Conybeare and Stock in

Gen. 37:30 ἐγὼ δὲ ποῦ πορεύομαι ἔτι; 'but I, where shall I go?' Note also the following: Gen. 44:16 τί ἀντεροῦμεν τῷ κυρίῳ; 'what shall we say to the Lord?'; Judg. 18:18 τί ὑμεῖς ποιεῖτε; 'what are you going to do?'[47]

A plausible explanation for this un-Greek use of the present indicative is that in the Hebrew underlying two of the passages cited the participle is used;[48] Gen. 37:30 πορεύομαι = bā'; Judg. 18:18 ποιεῖτε = 'ōśîm. Thus it would appear that the tendency to render Hebrew participles into Greek present indicative verbs was sufficiently strong to lead translators to introduce a new form of the Greek deliberative into their Greek translations, on the analogy of the Semitic participle. The occurrence from the Apc. cited above follows the pattern noted here in the LXX.[49]

It is of interest at this point to note that in several places where the deliberative verb in the LXX is stated with the future indicative, the underlying Hebrew verb is in the imperfect tense; e.g. Ps. 12(13):2f ἀποστρέψεις (Bא) = tastîr; θήσομαι = 'āšît; ὑψωθήσεται = yārūm. In Ps. 61:4 ἐπιτίθεσθε = tĕhôtĕtû.[50] Thus there emerges a basic pattern for translating Semitic tenses into Greek. When rendering Hebrew imperfects expressing deliberation, the Greek future indicative was used. For a deliberative Hebrew participle, the Greek present served.[51] There are, of course, exceptions to the general pattern traced here, which prevent the formation of an absolute rule. Yet this basic pattern played a vital role in the phenomenon of biblical Greek.[52]

Other deliberative questions in the Apc. are expressed by δύνασθαι in the second- and third-persons, followed by an infinitive: 6:17 and 13:4 (cf. Matt. 12:34).[53] This use of the infinitive has a partial parallel in the papyri, however, where in one case an indirect question of deliberation is expressed by τί ποιῆσθαι; (PSI IV, 368, 26).[54]

b. Aorist subjunctive replaced by future indicative following ἵνα[55]

It is a well-known fact that in NT Greek there is apparent confusion between the aorist subjunctive and the future indicative, especially following ἵνα. Most of these confusions are in the Apc., and perhaps the best-known example is 22:14 μακάριοι οἱ πλύνοντες τὰς στολὰς αὐτῶν ἵνα ἔσται ἡ ἐξουσία.[56] Bl-D list examples from other parts of the NT (§369), plus extensive literature on the matter. The reason usually put forward for this phenomenon is the Hellenistic tendency to blur the distinction between the future indicative and aorist subjunctive suffixes. It is thus widely assumed that in the NT as well as in Hellenistic Greek at large the future indicative has been introduced in those very places where it would not have been tolerated in classical times.

Since the LXX contains some of the earliest examples of ἵνα plus future indicative,[57] it is worthwhile to investigate the possibility of Semitic influence behind this strange preference for the future indicative. Examination of the Hebrew text underlying twelve occurrences of ἵνα plus future indicative revealed that in each case the Hebrew *imperfect* was being translated mechanically by Greek future indicative.[58]

It seems most satisfactory, on the evidence presented from the LXX, to conjecture that where in the Apc. the future indicative follows ἵνα it reflects a Hebrew imperfect tense verb.[59] Alongside this, of course, we allow for the fact that in some places the Hellenistic blurring of subjunctive and indicative forms influenced certain copyists. Unfortunately there is no reliable method for distinguishing one from the other.

c. Modal use of the future indicative for Hebrew jussive

Mussies notes that the Semitic verb system lacked not only a special subjunctive category, but a third-person imperative as well.[60] Therefore the Semitic imperfect tense has a jussive aspect which can be equated with the Greek third-person imperative. He expects that certain future indicative verbs in the Apc. betray an incidental jussive or imperatival colour,[61] and cites the following instances: 4:9f;[62] 9:4; 19:7; 22:18, 19. His point seems to be weakened, however, by the fact that all the above except 19:7 (which, he notes, is in the first-person) are best understood as indirect, therefore taking the form of requests rather than commands. This would seem not to reflect any influence of the Semitic jussive use of the verb. While in the LXX and in the NT the hortatory is usually expressed by the subjunctive, cases can be cited for the use of the future indicative on the model of the Hebrew cohortative imperfect: Gen. 18:21 καταβὰς οὖν ὄψομαι (wĕ'er'eh); cf. Ps. 58(59):10 τὸ κράτος μου πρὸς σὲ φυλάξω ('uzzô 'ēlēkā 'ešemōrâ). Perhaps this best explains the future indicative δώσομεν in Apc. 19:7 [χαίρωμεν (-ομεν 2019 2022 180 2053 *al*) καὶ ἀγαλλιῶμεν (-μεθα 2048 808 Syr^ph)] καὶ δώσομεν (א^a A 2042 2067 2055 *al*) ['Let us rejoice and exult] and give Him glory', which stands in place of the Greek hortatory subjunctive.[63] This is probably Semitic influence, because it corresponds to the Hebrew lengthened imperfect expressing the sense of the cohortative.[64]

Summary of chapter 3, section 2

In this section we noted how the deliberative question is cast in the present indicative, instead of the customary subjunctive mood, under influence from the Hebrew participle, which is used often for deliberative questions in the OT, since the Greek present indicative served as a formal translation equivalent for Semitic participles. Where in biblical Greek the deliberative question is stated by a future indicative verb, this can be traced to an underlying Hebrew imperfect tense.

Concerning the substitution of future indicative for aorist subjunctive, we noted how in the Apc. and elsewhere this can be explained as due to the tendency to translate Hebrew imperfect by Greek future indicative. The related use of future indicative for the Semitic jussive, while well-attested elsewhere in the NT, does not seem to enjoy much use in the Apc. The cohortative, however, does appear.

3. Tenses of the finite verb

The task of determining the nature of Semitic influence upon Greek verb tenses seems at first to yield results less convincing than in other areas. C.F.D. Moule, who takes a generally cautious view about alleged Semitisms in NT Greek, is sceptical; 'most possible Semitisms of tense seem to me to be too uncertain to be profitably discussed'.[65] Semitic scholars, on the other hand, have been more confident. They realise perhaps more fully than others how striking is the difference between Semitic and Greek languages in the matter of tenses.[66]

a. Futuristic use of the Greek present indicative

A point of biblical Greek grammar not yet adequately explained by grammarians is the strange yet obvious future sense expressed by certain present indicative Greek verbs. Speaking of the classical period, Eduard Schwyzer remarks that the futurist use of the present indicative is 'infrequent, and bound to specific conditions',[67] while Turner notes that the present indicative sometimes occurs in the NT referring to an obviously future event; he quotes Moulton (*Grammar of New Testament Greek*, I, 120), suggesting that these presents differed from the future tense 'mainly in the tone of assurance which is imparted'.[68] They express a note of confidence in the approaching event. Turner himself noted the (rare) futuristic present in classical Greek, used in a prophetic sense which corresponds to the frequent NT references to the Coming One with the verb ἔρχομαι. Blass–Debrunner give limited recognition to the presence of futuristic present indicative verbs in the NT,[69] especially in prophecies (again, with ἔρχομαι), and also verbs of coming/going. This latter category is the only one widely-employed in classical Greek, and takes its sense from the fact that ἐλεύσομαι is ordinarily not used in Attic prose, its sense being expressed by εἶμι as the future of ἔρχομαι.[70]

In Greek literature of the Hellenistic period, L. Radermacher cites as futuristic the verbs βαπτίζω, φέρω, ὑπόκειμαι, πείθω, and ἔρχομαι.[71] Jannaris observes that the present indicative in animated speech is often used for the future, especially in post-classical and NT Greek.[72] He cites numerous examples, mostly from NT and other Christian literature; however, in his Appendix IV, which treats the future indicative since Attic times, several secular examples are cited.

The state of the futuristic present indicative in the Greek non-literary papyri was described by Mayser in his *Grammatik*; with a measure of caution he cites the possible (but not always certain) occurrences from a few of the papyri.[73] For expanded treatment of this category we now have the newly-published work of B. Mandilaras,[74] who cites a total of twenty-eight examples from the papyri examined by him, grouped in the following categories: (a) those giving temporal indication of future time; (b) those with verbs of coming/going; (c) the present as apodosis in conditional sentences; (d) in prophecies, and particularly in questions to oracles. Aside from a remarkable passage illustrating this last category, from Oxyrhynchus papyrus 1477, dating from *c.* A.D. 300, and containing a mixture of present and future tense verbs, with mostly future sense, the futuristic present indicative in the papyri seems to occur with no greater frequency than in the classical period. Certainly there is no expanded use of the tense in the period which produced the bulk of the papyri.

These occurrences, plus those cited earlier, clearly illustrate two facts: first, that the futuristic use of the present was current during the Hellenistic era, and second, that the widely-scattered examples of it in secular literature do not compare at all in frequency with the multitude of examples to be found in biblical and other Jewish translation Greek.

For the sake of illustration, a few examples are cited here to demonstrate the widened use of the Greek present with future sense: Gen. 41:25 καὶ εἶπεν Ἰωσηφ τῷ Φαραω Τὸ ἐνύπνιον Φαραω ἕν ἐστιν ὅσα ὁ θεὸς ποιεῖ ἔδειξεν, 'Joseph said to Pharaoh, "The dream of Pharaoh is one; God has shown . . . what he will do".' The case often cited by grammarians is Mark 9:31 παραδίδοται (periphrastic future in Matt. parallel) followed by the future ἀποκτενοῦσιν. From Theodotion's version of Daniel comes an example, influenced by the Hebrew portion of the underlying MT: 10:11 σύνες ἐν τοῖς λόγοις οἷς ἐγὼ λαλῶ σε, 'attend to the words I *shall speak* to you'. Examples could be multiplied, testifying to the relative frequency of the futuristic present indicative in biblical and Jewish translation Greek, in contrast to occasional appearances of it in secular literature of the period.

This preponderance of the construction leads one to examine the Semitic antecedents of such Greek to determine a cause for this over-worked usage. In Hebrew and Aramaic the expression of future events certain to occur ('prophetic' futures) was often made by use of the participle which represents the event as already beginning; the name of *futurum instans* is applied to this use of the participle when it asserts future events, especially divine acts.[75] In this role the participle usually stands as the predicate of a noun clause; it frequently expresses deliberative questions, as well as future actions.[76]

A selection of these participles from the OT has been compared with the rendering of each in the LXX (including Dan. Theod.),[77] revealing the following facts: of a total of fifty-four examples, thirty-eight were rendered by Greek present indicative while the future indicative was employed in only thirteen cases, giving the following percentages:

Greek present indicative: 70% of cases
Greek future indicative: 24% of cases.

Of course the translators did not limit the futuristic present to the category represented by the Semitic prophetic participle, and exceptions can be found. But in spite of these, the over-working of an acceptable Greek usage permits us to look to Semitic influence on the Greek composers and translators as the explanation for this construction. Further LXX examples include the following: Gen. 6:17 ἐγὼ δὲ ἰδοὺ ἐπάγω, 'and I, behold, I will bring'; 19:13 ὅτι ἀπόλλυμεν ἡμεῖς, 'about to destroy'; 1 Sam. 3:11 ποιῶ, 'shall do'; 1 Ki. 13:2f τίκτεται, 'shall be born'; cf. 2 Ki. 22:20; Isa. 13:17, 26:21; Mic. 1:3; Zech. 3:8.

These are but a sampling of the many occurrences which could be cited. It is noteworthy that all are more or less of the category of oracular, or prophetic present tenses; thus some would insist that they can be accounted for along the lines of Greek usage and that the Semitic tense of *futurum instans* plays no role here, but that the frequent usage of this construction in biblical Greek is due merely to an over-working of the Greek construction. If this were the case, we could expect to see a corresponding tendency toward over-use in the secular Hellenistic Greek documents. Mayser,[78] however, cites but few examples from the papyri, and points out that even some of them are disputable, due to the close connection of the adverbs εὐθύς or ταχύ(ς), giving an immediate rather than truly future sense to the verbs in question. The use of this special futuristic sense of the present indicative, then, in biblical Greek has developed quite independently of

Hellenistic literature. In addition to the 'prophetic' occurrences cited above, there are others of a patently non-prophetic nature, e.g. Deut. 1:20 δίδωσιν ὑμῖν, 'shall give to you'; Dan. 8:19 (Theod.) καὶ εἶπεν Ἰδοὺ ἐγὼ γνωρίζω σοι 'and he said, "I shall make known to you"'.

C.F. Burney was among the first to apply the Semitic participle of *futurum instans* in explaining futuristic present verbs in the NT. He explains the futuristic ἔρχομαι found often in the fourth Gospel as due to Aramaic influence of this nature, and notes that in a majority of cases where the futuristic ἔρχομαι occurs, the Peshitta represents it by a participle.[79] Burney appended a list of examples of the futuristic present in the Apc. also, but the passages listed were limited to those containing the verb ἔρχομαι. Thus, while being the first to point to the Semitic construction behind these verbs, he did not make his case sufficiently strong since, as noted above, the verb ἔρχομαι with futuristic sense can be explained solely on Greek grounds. In order to demonstrate the case made for Semitic influence on the Apc. at this point. it is necessary to find verbs other than ἔρχομαι with futuristic sense.

Black recognised the existence in the Gospels of futuristic present indicative verbs, apart from ἔρχομαι, which show the influence of the Aramaic participle.[80]

In the Apc. these present verbs fall into two categories: those in which the verb is preceded by ἰδού, and those without it. Examples of the former include Apc. 2:22 ἰδοὺ βάλλω (βαλω ℵ[a] 046 P 325 *al*) αὐτὴν εἰς κλίνην, 'behold, I *shall cast* her into a bed'.[81] Charles notes that βάλλω 'represents a participle in the Hebrew which can refer to the future, the present, or the past, according to context. Since it is parallel here with ἀποκτενῶ in verse 23*a* it refers, of course, to the future'.[82] Also noteworthy here is the fact mentioned above that the introductory ἰδού precedes the Greek rendering of a Semitic participle of *futurum instans*; on this point S.R. Driver observed, 'when applied to the future, the Hebrew participle is very frequently strengthened by an introductory *hinnê*'.[83] Hebrew examples are too frequent to require illustration, and their Greek equivalent, ἰδού plus present tense verb, appears a number of times in the Apc. in addition to the clear case cited. Further occurrences are: Apc. 3:9 ἰδοὺ διδῶ (future in boh ethio latt); 2:16 ἴδε (88) εἰ δὲ μή, ἔρχομαι . . . καὶ πολεμήσω; 3:11 Ἰδοὺ (·Ιδου CAP minsuc.) ἔρχομαι ταχύ; 9:12 ἰδοὺ ἔρχεται;[84] 16:15 ἰδοὺ ἔρχομαι; 21:5 ἰδοὺ καινὰ ποιῶ (ποιησω 522 copt). In this passage we see a literal rendering of a Hebrew expression from Isa. 43:19, *hinnî ʿōśeh ḥădāšâ*, for which the LXX gives Ἰδοὺ ἐγὼ ποιῶ καινά; cf. Isa. 65:17 *kî hinnî bôrē'*. In both places the Hebrew participle occurs with future sense.

Thus, while recognising that the present ἔρχομαι alone has no special

Semitic flavour, even when its sense is future, we have demonstrated that when preceded by ἰδού the resulting biblical Greek construction can represent the literal rendering of Hebrew *hinnê* plus participle.[85]

The second category of futuristic present verbs in Apc. includes those not preceded by ἰδού, and those not expressing coming/going, which are thus less explicable from Greek precedents. Examples follow: Apc. 1:11 ὃ βλέπεις (βλεψεις 2200) γράψον εἰς βιβλίον, 'write what you shall see in a book'. The future sense of this verb led the copyists of a single extant minuscule to alter the tense to future, there is Coptic evidence, however, which shows the temptation to read a future here was more widespread; 'shall hear' (for 'see') (boh); 'which you see and shall see' (sah). Further examples include 2:27; 3:7, 9; 5:10 (A 046); 7:15, 17 (82 91); 9:6;[86] 11:5, 9 (ℵ CA), 10,[87] 15 (325); 13:10;[88] 14:9, 10, 11; 17:11, 12; 19:3, 11;[89] 22:5.[90]

Charles was one of the first to consider seriously the future sense of certain present verbs in the Apc. as due to Semitic influence; in fact, he devoted a section of his *Short Grammar of the Apocalypse* to discussing the phenomenon, but he ascribed it to the Hebrew imperfect tense rather than to the participle of *futurum instans.*[91] Strangely, Charles also recognised the future sense of certain present tense verbs under influence of the Semitic participle, but mentioned it only in a brief note (cf. Charles I, 71) and did not develop it in his Grammar.

A. Lancellotti, in his monograph on Hebraic influence on verbs in the Apc., follows Charles in attributing the futuristic present to Hebrew imperfect, taken with future sense, and adds the following examples:[92] Apc. 22:5; 14:11; 11:5, 9; 9:6; 17:12, 13, 16. Unlike Charles, Lancellotti gives no consideration at this point to the influence of the Hebrew participle on the verbs in the Apc. outside the group preceded by ἰδού. Nor does he support his position by illustrations from the LXX; in fact, the single passage of biblical Greek outside the Apc. which he cites is Isa. 24:10 LXX,[93] which renders Hebrew imperfect by a future, not present, tense. Thus nothing is demonstrated; yet he can still argue thus:[94] 'Now, since the yiqtol, having itself the "durative" value of the present and the past, corresponds in Greek to the present stem, the author of the Apocalypse, influenced by Hebraic syntactical categories, displays not infrequently the tendency to employ the present for the future.'

G. Mussies, in the final chapter of his recent work on the morphology of the Apc. ventures into a discussion of 'The Use of the Verb in the Apocalypse'. Earlier in the book he proposed that the Semitic substrate of the language of the Apc. was limited to the form of Hebrew and Aramaic current in Palestine during the first Christian century; namely, Mishnaic

Hebrew and the Aramaic dialect represented by the Palestinian Pentateuch Targum.[95] Although Mussies admits that biblical Hebrew also had its influence on the author of the Apc., he makes little allowance for it. A more balanced view would certainly consider the influence of spoken Semitic vernacular, but, of necessity, it would not overlook the influence of Hebrew/Aramaic of the OT and Pseudepigrapha, since it was *primarily* to this literature, more than to later material, that the Seer made reference. In its repeated allusions to OT passages and in its general idiom, the Apc. shares in the full, flowing style found in classical Hebrew prophets, while on the other hand it displays none of the terse, highly-compressed and sometimes abbreviated style so characteristic of Mishnaic language.

Mussies counts thirty-nine occurrences of the future present indicative, including five where he would expect future subjunctive (11:5; 14:4, 9 twice; 14:11 - all from codex A), as compared with my own total of thirty-three. He neglects to list the references, however, so the two lists cannot be compared.

Since neither Mussies nor his predecessors gave convincing demonstrations from the LXX or other translation Greek to establish that there was a pattern for translating futuristic Semitic imperfects by Greek present indicative, we prefer to accept instead the explanation demonstrated here that the Semitic participle of *futurum instans* was the prime influence behind futuristic present verbs in the Apc.

b. Present tense passing into future tense

T.C. Laughlin, in his thesis *The Solecisms of the Apocalypse*,[96] followed a suggestion made earlier by G. Ewald,[97] that Hebrew influence is responsible for the passages in the Apc. where present and future tenses occur co-ordinately in the same clause or sentence where we should expect the future of all verbs. The following examples are cited: Apc. 1:7 ἰδοὺ ἔρχεται μετὰ τῶν νεφελῶν καὶ ὄψεται αὐτὸν πᾶς ὀφθαλμός, 'Behold, He shall come with the clouds, and every eye shall see Him'; 2:5 εἰ δὲ μὴ ἔρχομαι σοι καὶ κινήσω τὴν λυχνίαν σου ἐκ τοῦ τόπου αὐτῆς, 'I shall come . . . I shall move'; 2:22f ἰδοὺ βάλλω (βαλω ℵ[a] BP minusc.) αὐτὴν εἰς κλίνην . . . καὶ τὰ τέκνα αὐτῆς ἀποκτενῶ ἐν θανάτῳ, 'Behold I shall cast her . . . shall kill'; 3:9 ἰδοὺ διδῶ . . . ἰδοὺ ποιήσω; 17:12-14 λαμβάνουσιν . . . διδόασιν . . . πολεμήσουσιν . . . νικήσει (all have future sense).

This passing from present to future tense is found also in the LXX: Zech. 2:13 ἰδοὺ ἐγὼ ἐπιφέρω τὴν χεῖρά μου ἐπ' αὐτοὺς καὶ ἔσονται σκῦλα, 'Behold, I will shake my hand over them, and they shall become plunder';

cf. verse 14 διότι ἰδοὺ ἐγὼ ἔρχομαι καὶ κατασκηνώσω, 'for behold, I will dwell'.

The explanation for this is closely connected with that of the previous section on futuristic Greek present indicative, i.e. the Greek renders a Hebrew participle of *futurum instans*. In Zech. 2:13 *menîp* = ἐπιφέρω; in 2:14 *bā'* = ἔρχομαι.[98] The following Hebrew verb in each case was a perfect tense, plus *Waw*-consecutive, rendered in the LXX by a Greek future tense. Thus added support is given for our hypothesis that in the Apc. most present indicative verbs with future sense are influenced by the Semitic participle of *futurum instans*.

c. Present tense verbs with past or imperfect sense[99]

Under this heading come two divisions under which several passages from the Apc. will be considered.

Historic present with verbs of saying

First to be considered is the widely-discussed historic present, since it occurs several times in the Apc. In his thesis C.G. Ozanne referred to several occurrences of the verbs ᾄδουσιν, κράζουσιν as historic (aoristic) presents which reflect 'an essentially Semitic influence'.[100] Most grammarians think otherwise, however, agreeing that the historic present, especially with verbs of saying and proclaiming, was acceptable Greek idiom during the classical period, the time of the papyri, the LXX, literary *Koine*, and in Modern Greek, especially in vivid narrative.[101] Thus, 'apart from its over-use [in Mark and John], there is nothing specially Semitic about the tense', concludes Black.[102]

Other present verbs with past sense

When verbs in this category are excluded, however, we are left with numerous present tense verbs, not of the category of saying, which have a past sense. While some would prefer to explain them merely as historic presents along Greek lines, it is well to recall the tendency, noted previously, for Semitic authors to employ, when writing Greek, the present tense along the lines of Semitic participles, which can refer to future, present, or *past* actions. This past sense of a present indicative is not unknown in the LXX: Judg. 14:4 ὅτι ἐκδίκησιν αὐτὸς ζητεῖ (εκζητει A) ἐκ τῶν ἀλλοφύλων, 'for he was seeking vengeance against the Philistines' (literally 'foreigners'; Hebrew participle *mĕbaqēš*). Further examples could be found, but this demonstrates the existence of a present indicative verb with past sense or, more specifically, an imperfect sense, with emphasis sometimes on the duration of the action or state. The Hebrew participle with past durative sense[103] is obviously responsible for the LXX translation with a present tense verb at this point.

The identical phenomenon occurs in the Apc. The sequence of imperfect and present tenses in 9:9–11 for example, has caught the attention of recent scholars: καὶ εἶχον . . . καὶ ἔχουσιν (ειχον 2020 2067 vg gig) . . . ἔχουσιν (2067: εχοντες 2080). Lancellotti, pp. 59f, observes that Semitic nominal constructions expressing possession are often translated by a form of ἔχω (cf. below, pp. 83–8, the section on Noun clauses). So in this passage the present ἔχουσιν, found in a sequence of other tenses of the same verb, seems to express the atemporal sense of the Semitic nominal phrase.

Other present tense verbs with past sense include Apc. 9:17 ἐκ τῶν στομάτων αὐτῶν ἐκπορεύεται (εξεπορευετο 2020 2080 *al*), 'from their mouths was issuing fire'; 9:19 καὶ ἐν αὐταῖς ἀδικοῦσιν (ηδικουσιν 2020 2080 *al*), 'and by their tails they were stinging'; 13:11–17 Καὶ εἶδον ἄλλο θηρίον ἀναβαῖνον ἐκ τῆς γῆς καὶ εἶχεν κέρατα δύο ὅμοια ἀρνίῳ καὶ ἐλάλει (present gig) ὡς δράκων . . . ποίει (εποιει 2080 *al*) . . . καὶ ποίει (BE *al*) . . . καὶ ποίει (εποιει E 2016) . . . καὶ ποίει (εποιει 1611), 'Then I beheld another beast arising from the earth, and it had two horns like a lamb, and was speaking like a dragon . . . he made . . . and he made' etc. Here we find a mixture of tenses, mostly present but with seemingly little logic employed in their use. Charles notes that the vision begins in the past tense, so he gives a past sense to the following cluster of present tense verbs. The only reasonable explanation is that they here represent a Semitic participle with past sense. Note also Apc. 14:3 καὶ ἄδουσιν ὡς ᾠδὴν καινὴν . . . καὶ οὐδεὶς δύναται (2038) μαθεῖν τὴν ᾠδήν, 'and they sang a new song . . . and no one was able to learn the song'; 16:21 καὶ χάλαζα μεγάλη ὡς ταλαντιαία καταβαίνει (κατεβαινεν 1611) ἐκ τοῦ οὐρανοῦ, 'and hail stones large like talents fell from heaven'; 19:15 καὶ ἐκ τοῦ στόματος αὐτοῦ ἐκπορεύεται (εκπορευετε 792) ῥομφαία ὀξεῖα (preceded in the previous verse by imperfect ἠκολούθει), 'and from his mouth issued a sharp sword'.

Several explanations have been put forward by commentators for this anomalous use of the present tense for past, mostly on stylistic grounds. None have explained it as we have here, by demonstrating its dependence upon the Semitic participle used as a finite verb and expressing past or imperfect action. It cannot be denied that the Greek historic present could be used to express similar sense in *Koine* Greek, although it was never used on a large scale. But in such a text as the Apc., which is noted for its Semitic constructions, this use of the present tense can be described as yet another point of contact with Semitic verbal syntax.

d. Greek aorist indicative for Semitic perfect verbs[104]

In the LXX

One finds in the LXX a number of aorist verbs which cannot be made to bear the Greek punctiliar sense; they seem to have the continuing sense of a state, though not that of the gnomic aorist,[105] which in classical Greek expresses timeless maxims. Most of the LXX aorists so employed appear to be simple statements of fact, with emphasis on the present. Examination of these occurrences shows that there was a tendency for the LXX translators to render Hebrew perfects by the Greek aorist. From lists of the Hebrew perfect (with either present or future sense) given by Driver, in *Hebrew Tenses*, and GK, I examined a selection of ninety-five occurrences, and studied the Greek rendering of each in context to ascertain that the sense was identical with the Hebrew passage from which it derived. The following list presents relative frequencies by which these Hebrew perfects were rendered into the various Greek tenses:

	Greek	aorist	45
		present	21
		future	16
		imperfect	2
		perfect	7
		participles	3
		subjunctive	1
			──
	Total		95

A surprising 47% were translated by the Greek aorist, while the combined total of the present and future Greek tenses, which would logically express the meaning of a Hebrew stative or prophetic perfect, reaches only 39%.

Among the more frequent Hebrew stative perfects represented by Greek aorists are ἐμεγαλύνθη, 'I am great': Ps. 91:6; 103:1, 24; ἤλπισα, 'I hope': Ps. 7:2; 31:2, 7; 130:6; ἐμίσησας, 'you hate': Ps. 5:6, 30:7. Also note:

'I know not', οὐκ ἔγνων	Gen. 21:26
'we remember', ἐμνήσθημεν	Nu. 11:5

'is like', ὡμοιώθη	Ps. 143:4
'is full', ἐπληρώθη	Ps. 103:24
'rejoices', ἐστερεώθη	1 Km. 2:1
'requireth', ἐξεζήτησεν	Isa. 1:12
'wait', ὑπέμεινεν	Ps. 129:5
'delight', ἐβουλήθην	Ps. 39:9
'abhor', ἐβδελύξαντο	Job 30:10
'stand aloof', ἐφείσαντο	Job 30:10
'abides', παρασυνεβλήθη	Ps. 48:13, 21
'am weary', ἐκοπίασα	Ps. 6:7
'delighteth', εὐδόκησεν (Theod., Symm.)	Isa. 42:1

The following Hebrew perfect verbs, which occur in direct discourse to express actions in process of accomplishment, are rendered by Greek aorist: ὤμοσα, 'I swear': Jer. 22:5; συνεβούλευσα, 'I counsel': 2 Km. 17:11; εἶπον, 'I decide': 2 Km. 19:29; εἶπον, 'I declare': Job. 9:22.

The Hebrew prophetic perfect (and related *perfectum confidentiae*), which has as its primary function the expression of a future event certain to occur, is also frequently rendered in the LXX by a Greek aorist. Driver quotes the Greek Grammar of Jelf, §403, to show that the Greek aorist is similarly used, at least in the apodosis, to 'express future events which must certainly happen';[106] several passages from Plato are cited. Though it appears in classical Greek, yet there is little doubt that the greater frequency of this usage in the LXX is due more to the adoption of the Greek aorist as the equivalent of the Hebrew perfect tense than to any tendency in Greek usage. The biblical Greek grammarians mention no occurrences of the classical 'futuristic' aorist in Hellenistic literature, so appeal cannot be made on this point to a developing tendency in Greek. Yet numerous examples of 'prophetic' aorists are found in the LXX; especially striking is Jer. 5:6 ἔπαισεν αὐτοὺς λέων ἐκ τοῦ δρυμοῦ, 'a lion from the forest *shall slay* them' (note also following verbs 'shall destroy', 'is watching', also rendered by Greek aorist); others include:

'shall be full', ἐνεπλήσθη	Isa. 11:9
'will destroy', ἔθραυσεν	2 Chr. 20:37
'shall be [exiled]', ἐγενήθη	Isa. 5:13
'shall fall', ἔπεσεν	Amos 5:2
'is laid waste', ἀπώλετο	Isa. 23:1 (cf. verse 14)
'shall speak', εἶπεν	Isa. 23:4
'shall be exiled', ἠχμαλωτεύθησαν	Mic. 1:16 (cf. verses 9, 12)

Especially striking are the examples of this Semitic usage of the aorist in Dan. (Theod.), where extensive passages of discourse and prophetic description call for numerous instances of the Semitic perfect verb forms.[107] Note the following: Dan. (Theod.) 2:45 ὁ θεὸς ὁ μέγας ἐγνώρισεν τῷ βασιλεῖ, 'The great God is making known to the king' (Aramaic perfect *hôdaʿ*); 5:16 ἤκουσα περὶ σοῦ, 'I hear concerning you' (repeated in verse 14*a*) (Aramaic perfect *šimʿēt*); 5:14*b* καὶ σοφία περισσὴ εὑρέθη ἐν σοί, 'and great wisdom is found in you' (Aramaic *hištĕkahat*); 10:17 νῦν οὐ στήσεται ἐν ἐμοὶ ἰσχύς καὶ πνοὴ οὐκ ὑπελείφθη ἐν ἐμοί, 'Now no strength remains in me, and no breath is left in me' (Hebrew *niš'ārâ*); along with these should be listed the following, still with present sense: 6:8 συνεβουλεύσαντο πάντες, 'all the presidents of the kingdom . . . are agreed' (Aramaic *'ityā'aṭw*); cf. 4:36, 9:24, 10:11.

The following aorist verbs are employed to render the Semitic prophetic perfect or *perfectum confidentiae*: Dan. (Theod.) 4:31 ἡ βασιλεία παρῆλθεν ἀπὸ σοῦ, 'the kingdom shall be taken from you' (Aramaic *'ădāt*); 5:28 διῄρηται ἡ βασιλεία σου καὶ ἐδόθη, 'your kingdom is taken . . . and shall be given' (Aramaic *wîhîbat*).

The Greek aorist verbs listed, which do not express the sense of punctiliar past time, represent a Semitic perfect verb with stative or future sense.

In the New Testament

The existence of this futuristic sense of the aorist in the NT is noted by Bl-D,[108] who draw scattered parallels from Homer and Modern Greek to demonstrate that an aorist after a future condition can have a future sense. They note that since 'the Hebrew perfect serves not only as a narrative tense, but also to denote a timeless act, the Greek aorist also appears for this second kind of perfect in lyrical passages in the LXX, and hence also in the Magnificat, Luke 1:46ff'. Zerwick also senses the Hebraic flavour of certain aorists in the Magnificat,[109] while Moule recognises Semitic antecedents for the aorists employed in John 15:6, noting that they 'may be explained as representing the Hebrew perfect, which is not used "gnomically" as is sometimes claimed, but to emphasise immediacy'.[110]

We now realise that these writers greatly underestimated the extent to which the Greek aorist in the NT was influenced by Semitic perfect verbs. A much more accurate summary of this phenomenon in the Gospels and Acts is provided by Black, who notes that the Greek aorist renders not only the Hebrew prophetic perfect, but also the stative perfect; reference to his work can be made for examples he cites to support these points.[111]

Only one of the occurrences of this tense in the Gospels is cited here:

John 15:25 cites a LXX expression attested primarily in the Psalms, 'they hate', ἐμίσησαν, which speaks of present or stative sense, as is clearly illustrated by Ps. 5:6 and 31:7.

In the Apc.

Turning to the Apc., we find a number of passages in which the aorist tense must be rendered with the sense of the Semitic perfect.[112] For the sake of convenience, these are divided into three categories: those which express present sense, those with future sense, and those which are described by Charles as 'timeless'. The three appear to correspond to the Semitic stative perfect, prophetic perfect, and the perfect expressing general truths (which is similar to the gnomic aorist).[113] These categories must be understood as merely suggestive; they are not rigid and distinctively separate, since some of the following verbs can be placed in two or even all three with equal plausibility.

(i) Aorist with present sense: Apc. 1:2 ἐμαρτύρησεν – translated as present by Allo,[114] who considered it an epistolary aorist; 2:21 καὶ ἔδωκα αὐτῇ χρόνον ἵνα μετανοήσῃ, 'and I gave her time that she might repent' (note following present tense verbs οὐ θέλει . . . ἰδοὺ βάλλω);[115] 2:24 οἵτινες οὐκ ἔγνωσαν τὰ βαθέα τοῦ Σατανᾶ ὡς λέγουσιν, 'who know not the deep things of Satan, as some are speaking'; 3:4 ἃ οὐκ ἐμόλυναν τὰ ἱμάτια αὐτῶν, 'who stain not their garments'; 3:8 καὶ ἐτήρησάς μου τὸν λόγον καὶ οὐκ ἠρνήσω τὸ ὄνομά μου, 'yet you are keeping my word, and not denying my name'; 3:9c ἐγὼ ἠγάπησά σε (cf. Isa. 43:4 LXX ἐγὼ σε ἠγάπησα), 'I love you'; 3:10 ὅτι ἐτήρησας τὸν λόγον, 'because you are keeping the word'; 11:17d ἐβασίλευσας καὶ τὰ ἔθνη ὠργίσθησαν, 'you are reigning; and the nations rage' (cf. Ps. 98:1 κύριος ἐβασίλευσεν ὀργιζέσθωσαν λαοί); 13:14 τὰ σημεῖα ἃ ἐδόθη αὐτῷ ποιῆσαι, 'the signs which it is allowed to perform' (cf. also verse 13 ἐθεραπεύθη; verse 15 ἐδόθη); 14:4f οὗτοι ἠγοράσθησαν ἀπὸ τῶν ἀνθρώπων . . . καὶ ἐν τῷ στόματι αὐτῶν οὐκ εὑρέθη ψεῦδος, 'These are redeemed from among men . . . and in their mouth no falsehood is found' (cf. Zeph. 3:13 LXX, where the same verb appears in the subjunctive mood); 22:16 Ἐγὼ Ἰησοῦς ἔπεμψα τὸν ἄγγελόν μου, 'I, Jesus, am sending my angel'.

(ii) Aorist with future sense: Apc. 10:7 ἀλλ᾽ ἐν ταῖς ἡμέραις . . . καὶ ἐτελέσθη (τελεσθησεται 2026 2038[mg]) τὸ μυστήριον, 'but in those days . . . the mystery shall be finished';[116] 11:2 ὅτι ἐδόθη τοῖς ἔθνεσιν, 'for it shall be given to the gentiles'; 11:10–13 οὗτοι οἱ δύο προφῆται ἐβασάνισαν . . . εἰσῆλθεν . . . καὶ ἔστησαν . . . ἐπέπεσεν. The extensive series of aorists in these verses have long puzzled Bible translators, as the recent English versions indicate. That some of the verbs are futuristic is clear, but others are best classified as 'timeless' or even as stative. So, for example, 12:8 οὐκ ἴσχυσεν - this is an idiom, corresponding to Hebrew *lō'-yākōl* (perfect tense), according to Charles, who cites on this point Dan. (Theod.) 7:21 (cf. Apc. 20:11); Apc. 14:8 ἔπεσεν ἔπεσεν βαβυλὼν ἡ μεγάλη, 'Babylon the Great is falling, is falling';[117] 18:17, 19 μιᾷ ὥρᾳ ἠρημώθη ὁ τοσοῦτος πλοῦτος, 'in one hour so much wealth is laid waste';[118] 21:23 ἡ γὰρ δόξα τοῦ θεοῦ ἐφώτισεν αὐτήν, 'for the glory of God shall illuminate (or 'illuminates') it'.

(iii) Timeless aorists: a third category of the Greek aorist in the Apc. is mentioned because of the important role it plays in certain visions of the Apc. Verbs in this category have close affinity with the Hebrew perfect used to express a general truth, and are best rendered by the English present. This category of the Semitic perfect tense is evident from the OT, as shown by the following examples from Dan. (Theod.): 7:14 καὶ αὐτῷ ἐδόθη ἡ ἀρχὴ καὶ ἡ τιμὴ καὶ ἡ βασιλεία καὶ πάντες οἱ λαοί, φυλαί, γλῶσσαι δουλεύουσιν αὐτῷ, 'and to him is given dominion and glory and kingdom, and all peoples, nations, and languages shall serve him'; 7:27 καὶ ἡ βασιλεία . . . ἐδόθη ἁγίοις ὑψίστου, 'and the kingdom . . . is given to the saints of the most High'; 11:21 καὶ οὐκ ἔδωκαν ἐπ' αὐτὸν δόξαν βασιλείας, 'and the glory of a kingdom is not granted him'.

While some would argue that the examples cited here are merely Greek gnomic aorists, it is noteworthy that again the verbs in the underlying Hebrew/Aramaic text are in the perfect tense.

In the Apc. I cite the following examples of the timeless aorist: 5:9 καὶ ἠγόρασας τῷ θεῷ ἐν τῷ αἵματί σου, 'and are ransoming men for God by your blood'; 5:10 καὶ ἐποίησας αὐτοὺς τῷ θεῷ ἡμῶν βασιλείαν, 'and are making them a kingdom to our God'; 14:4 οὗτοι ἠγοράσθησαν ἀπὸ τῶν ἀνθρώπων . . . καὶ ἐν τῷ στόματι αὐτῶν οὐκ εὑρέθησαν ψεῦδος, 'these are redeemed from among men . . . and in their mouth no falsehood is found'; 16:20 οὐκ εὑρέθη, 'is not found'; cf. 20:11 ἔφυγεν ἡ γῆ . . . καὶ τόπος οὐκ εὑρέθη. Charles (II, 53) noted this is a Hebrew idiom: *wĕlō'-nimṣā'* (niphal perfect); cf. Ps. 37:36. Apc. 17:17 ὁ γὰρ θεὸς ἔδωκεν εἰς τὰς καρδίας αὐτῶν ποιῆσαι τὴν γνώμην, 'For God puts it into their hearts to carry out his purpose'. Both Charles and Allo note the Hebraic flavour of ἔδωκεν, in that it reflects the verb *nātan*, both in tense and in causative meaning. Apc. 19:2 ὅτι ἔκρινεν τὴν πόρνην . . . καὶ ἐξεδίκησεν τὸ αἷμα;[119] 19:6 ὅτι ἐβασίλευσεν;[120] 20:12 καὶ βιβλία ἠνοίχθησαν, 'and books were open'; this is an echo of Dan. 7:10, where a passive perfect verb is employed.

In determining the date or time of the aorist verbs cited in this section, one must always rely upon the context of the passage in question, just as is necessary in determining the time of perfect tense verbs in Semitic texts.

e. Greek perfect for Semitic derived conjugation verbs[121]

In this chapter allowance has been made so far for the rendering into Greek of the Semitic primary conjugation verbs, i.e. Hebrew qal and Aramaic peal, in their perfect, imperfect and participial forms. Anyone translating from one of these Semitic languages into Greek, however, would be obliged to deal not only with the primary conjugation, but would also have to translate verbs of the derived conjugations such as Hebrew niphal, piel, pual, hiphil, and their Aramaic counterparts.

The Greek OT provides evidence to indicate that in many places its translators attempted to indicate that a derived conjugation verb occurred in the Hebrew text by making an alteration in the tense or mood of the corresponding Greek verb.

A striking illustration of this is seen in the use of the Greek perfect indicative in a context where the sense of the perfect seems not to fit at all, the only justification for its presence being to indicate an underlying Semitic verb of a derived conjugation. For example, Ezek. 3:10 πάντας τοὺς λόγους οὓς λελάληκα μετὰ σοῦ, 'all the words which I *shall declare* to you'. The only justification for the perfect here is the underlying Hebrew piel *ădabēr*. Ezek. 5:13 καὶ ἐπιγνώσῃ διότι ἐγὼ Κύριος λελάληκα ἐν ζήλῳ is best rendered 'and they shall know that I, Yahweh, declare in my jealousy' – the context of the passage is future, the Hebrew verb is piel (the same construction is repeated in verse 17). In Dan. (Theod.) 9:18 τῆς πόλεώς σου ἐφ᾽ ἧς ἐπικέκληται, 'the city which is called [by thy] name', the perfect verb represents a niphal *niqrā'*. Likewise Ex. 2:14 ἐμφανὲς γέγονεν τὸ ῥῆμα τοῦτο, 'the thing is known', is not the most natural construction; it represents an attempt by the translator to signal the presence of a niphal verb in the underlying Hebrew, *nôda' haddābār*.

The hiphil could also be represented by a Greek perfect, as in Ezek. 8:12 Ἑώρακας ... ἃ οἱ πρεσβύτεροι τοῦ οἴκου Ἰσραὴλ ποιοῦσιν, 'do you see ... what the elders of the House of Israel are doing?' (*hărā'îtā*).

Especially striking in this respect is Ex. 32:1 ἰδὼν ὁ λαὸς ὅτι κεχρόνικε Μωϋσῆς, 'The people noticed that Moses delayed'. Moulton noted the problematic perfect tense in this verse,[122] but his attempt to explain it as merely *oratio obliqua* is not convincing. One should look at the under- lying Hebrew text where the rare *bōšēš* occurs, a polel form of *bôš*. Once

again the translator attempted, by employing a Greek perfect, to signal
the presence of a derived conjugation Hebrew verb. Elsewhere the LXX
translator of Ezek. employed the Greek perfect in its proper sense,
demonstrating that he suffered no misunderstanding of the proper use of
the tense, but in the occasions just cited he sacrificed idiomatic meaning
for slavish literalness, using the perfect tense in a way wholly against its
natural use.

In the NT

The application of this previously unnoticed characteristic of translation
Greek to relevant passages in the NT should bring about a re-evaluation of
those perfects which have long been known to stand in opposition to the
rules of Greek syntax.

There are perfects in the NT which have no more than simple aorist
meaning, and in fact have been described thus by grammarians.[123]
Burton,[124] for example, notes that while NT writers had an adequate concept of the distinction between perfect and aorist, he has to admit some
perfect tenses had the force of aorists. A good example is Matt. 13:46
πέπρακεν πάντα ὅσα εἶχεν καὶ ἠγόρασεν αὐτόν, or Mark 11:2 κεκάθικεν
(א BC *al*). Note also the sudden change of tense in John 3:32: ὃ ἑώρακεν
καὶ ἤκουσεν τοῦτο μαρτυρεῖ. This latter passage may not represent direct
Semitic influence since the perfect ἑώρακα is a favourite form in the
fourth Gospel, occurring more than twenty times. More difficult to
account for on Greek grounds is Acts 21:28 Ἕλληνας εἰσήγαγεν εἰς τὸ
ἱερὸν καὶ κεκοίνωκεν τὸν ἅγιον τόπον. According to Bl-D,[125] the perfect
here denotes 'a continuing effect on the object'. This seems too subtle –
I maintain that Semitic influence is at work here, the Greek perfect representing an Aramaic pael verb, perhaps *hallêl* (from *hǎlal*), 'to profane'.
The simple peal of this verb is nearly an antonym, meaning 'to purify' –
thus is was important to distinguish between peal and pael, even in Greek
translation. It is of interest at this point to compare the Hebrew piel
hillēl, 'to profane', in Dan. 11:31. The piel *wattĕhallehā* in Ex. 20:25, 'if
you use a tool on [the altar], you *profane*', is translated by a perfect
tense (μεμίανται) in the LXX, although Greek grammar would not tolerate
a perfect verb in the apodosis of such a conditional sentence.

Matthew Black cites other NT perfects which might belong here,[126]
including Matt. 22:4 ἡτοίμακα, which was apparently altered to ἡτοίμασα
(Θ, *Koine*), a case of assimilation to other aorists in the context. Interest-
ingly, in biblical Hebrew the equivalent of this verb is chiefly hiphil of
kûn; the niphal and other conjugations mean 'be established', 'certain',

'ready'.[127] As a more certain instance, Black cites Mark 10:28 where ℵΘ *al* read ἠκολουθήσαμεν against BCD *al* ἠκολουθήκαμεν and argues that the aorist is a mistaken assimilation to the preceding aorist ἀφήκαμεν, which probably belongs to aorist class ('we have (just) left', etc.). An aorist is expected here, not a perfect.

In the Apc.

Josef Schmid,[128] in his discussion of the text of the Apc., is puzzled when he observes that the perfect repeatedly stands in place of the aorist, or in parallel with it, as if there were no distinction of meaning between the two tenses. He cites Apc. 2:3 ὑπομονὴν ἔχεις καὶ ἐβάστασας ... καὶ οὐ κεκοπίακες (AC: ουκ εκοπιασας ℵ); 16:6 ἐξέχεαν καὶ ... δέδωκας (AC 1611: ἔδωκας p[47] ℵ *al*). Cf. 18:3 πέπτωκαν (πεπτωκασιν ℵ 046 1611 *al*: ἐποτισε(ν) 2071 2072 2074 *al*) πάντα τὰ ἔθνη.

G.D. Kilpatrick accounts for this odd use of the perfect by noting that the classical perfect tense was in decline in Hellenistic Greek, so he assumes that where it exists as a variant for the aorist, the aorist is original while the perfect is an atticising alternative.

The most striking occurrence of this type of perfect is Apc. 7:14 καὶ εἴρηκα αὐτῷ, 'and I said to him', which was altered to εἶπον by 046. It probably represents piel *dibbēr*, which occurs often in the MT, where it is usually (not always) translated by λαλέω. It is worthy of note that in Nu. 12:2 *dibbēr* is translated by λελάληκεν: μὴ Μωϋσῇ μόνῳ λελάληκεν Κύριος; οὐχὶ καὶ ἡμῖν ἐλάλησεν; 'Did Yahweh speak only by Moses? Did He not also speak by us?' Here the copyists of A and F altered the perfect to aorist, to harmonise with the second ἐλάλησεν. Note also Apc. 19:3 καὶ δεύτερον εἴρηκαν Ἀλληλουϊά. Apc. 5:7 ἦλθεν καὶ εἴληφεν has caught the eye of grammarians,[129] as has the similar usage in 8:5 εἴληφεν ὁ ἄγγελος ... καὶ ἐγέμισεν, 'the angel took ... and filled'. In both passages there was probably Semitic influence to account for the perfect tense Greek verb.

Mixing perfect and present tenses

The mixing of perfect and present tenses in Apc. 3:20 is puzzling: ἰδοὺ ἔστηκα ἐπὶ τὴν θύραν καὶ κρούω, 'behold, I stand by the door and knock'.[130] The Seer is fond of the perfect tense of ἵστημι, using it either as a finite verb or participle about twelve times, often in places where another tense would be expected; e.g. 8:2 ἑπτὰ ἀγγέλους ... ἑστήκασιν; 12:4 ὁ δράκων ἔστηκεν. At the same time the Seer correctly employs the aorist and future tenses of the same verb. Could it be that in those places

3. Tenses of the finite verb

where the perfect occurred, it was influenced by Hebrew *nāṣab*, which in the OT occurs in the niphal conjugation meaning 'to stand'? The likelihood of this explanation is greatly increased when it is observed that in the LXX of Ex. 17:9 identical usage is found, where ἔστηκα translates the niphal *niṣṣāb*: καὶ ἰδοὺ ἐγὼ ἔστηκα, 'behold, I will stand'. Finally, the phrase in Apc. 19:13, καὶ κέκληται τὸ ὄνομα αὐτοῦ ὁ λόγος τοῦ θεοῦ, is similar to the LXX of Isa. 43:7 πάντες ὅσοι ἐπικέκληνται τῷ ὀνόματί μου, which translates niphal *hanniqrā'*. Other passages where a Greek perfect is used to translate niphal of *qārā'* include Jer. 7:10, 11, 14, 30; Amos 9:12. Note also Dan. (Theod.) 9:18 and Ex. 2:14, cited above.

It hardly requires saying that if the proposal maintained here is accepted – i.e. that a Greek perfect is used in the NT in a manner not acceptable to Greek syntax where translation from a Semitic source has occurred – the tense can be ignored, since it merely indicates a derived conjugation Semitic verb. The temporal sense of the verb would thus be determined by context. This would remove the need for exegetes to account for the 'perfect' or 'completed' nature of the action of verbs where this was not evident. Thus when Charles noted that in Apc. 7:14 the perfect 'seems to be used as an aorist',[131] he needed only to modify his statement to say that εἴρηκα means the same as piel *dibbēr*, which could have a past, present, or even future sense, depending on context.

f. Greek future indicative for Semitic imperfect verbs[132]

The debate over the past sense of certain future tense verbs in the Apc. is an old one,[133] and will here receive a brief summary. A key passage for discussion has been Apc. 4:9–10 καὶ ὅταν δώσουσιν (δωσωσιν ℵ 046: δωσιν *Koine*) . . . πεσοῦνται . . . καὶ προσκυνήσουσιν . . . καὶ βαλοῦσιν (βαλλουσιν 046). The presence of variants attests to scribal efforts to improve the sense by altering the problematic futures. Ewald,[134] as early as 1828, noted that in this passage the Seer represented the Hebrew imperfect by the Greek future tense, and he implies that as a result the meaning here could be past. Most commentators since have followed either Ewald's position, viewing the future tense verbs as having past meaning, or that of Winer, who sees the verbs as true futures. Simcox,[135] for example, doubts that future time is to be understood here; 'it is always a question in this book [Apc.] whether the use of the tenses be not accommodated to the rules of Hebrew rather than Greek grammar; the sense may, after all, be merely frequentative'. Charles (I, cxxiv) takes δώσουσιν as frequentative, then notes that on the basis of Hebrew idiom the futures in this passage could be rendered by a past. Turner goes further in stating that the

futures in this passage are due entirely to Semitic influence.[136] Zerwick
(§281) and Lancellotti (p. 42), in their notes on Apc. 4:9–10 likewise
see a Hebraic past sense for these future tense verbs, but Mussies (341ff)
makes an extensive and closely argued appeal for understanding them as
true futures, following Winer.

The first step in this study is to determine whether there is any precedent in biblical Greek for employing the future indicative when referring
to the past, since secular Greek literature appears devoid of such usage.
A startling illustration is found in Ps. 103:6 ἐπὶ τῶν ὀρέων στήσονται
ὕδατα, 'waters stood upon the mountains' (MT 104:6 *'al-hārîm ya'amdû-
māyim*). The reference is clearly to the past – the creation in Gen. 1 – yet
the Greek future στήσονται is employed, apparently as a servile rendering
of the Hebrew imperfect tense verb. Turner notes two occurrences in verse
7 ἀπὸ ἐπιτιμήσεώς σου φεύξονται . . . δειλιάσουσιν (MT *yenûsûn . . .
yeḥāpēzûn*), 'they fled from your rebuke . . . they took flight'. Again, the
past sense is unmistakable. Another passage to which Ewald, followed by
Lancellotti, made reference is Nu. 17:25.[137] From these examples it is
evident that the equation of Greek future indicative and Hebrew imperfect, though somewhat rare, does exist in biblical Greek, in spite of the
protests from some modern commentators that such an equation is highly
illogical!

We now turn to examine occurrences in the Apc. with an allegedly past
sense. In addition to 4:9–10 we note the following: 5:10 καὶ ἐποίησας
αὐτοὺς τῷ θεῷ ἡμῶν βασιλείαν καὶ ἱερεῖς καὶ βασιλεύσουσιν (βασι-
λεύουσιν A 046 1006 1611 1859 2020 2065 2081 2138) ἐπὶ τῆς γῆς.
The sense here, though, could be properly future, 'and they shall reign
upon the earth'. Again, 11:15 ἐγένετο ἡ βασιλεία τοῦ κόσμου τοῦ κυρίου
ἡμῶν . . . καὶ βασιλεύσει εἰς τοὺς αἰῶνας τῶν αἰώνων. Perhaps we should
render this 'and he continues reigning forever and ever', which is also a
possibility with the Hebrew imperfect tense. Or there is 18:8 καὶ προσκυνήσουσιν αὐτὸν . . . οἱ κατοικοῦντες ἐπὶ τῆς γῆς, which is preceded by a
series of past tense verbs ἐδόθη . . . ἤνοιξεν . . . ἐδόθη. Mussies, however,
explains this future as due to a shift of viewpoint, not a 'confusion of tenses' to use his term.[138] Charles (I, 353) also proposed future sense, and
suggested the Seer translated an original *Waw*-consecutive as if it were
simple *Waw*. In any case, the future sense is not demanded by the context.
A further example occurs in 17:8 καὶ θαυμασθήσονται (θαυμασον 2031)
οἱ κατοικοῦντες ἐπὶ τῆς γῆς. Lohmeyer called attention to the contrast
between the description of the beast in chapter 17 and that given in chapter 13, which includes the different tenses of the verb θαυμάζειν;[139] cf.
13:3 καὶ ἐθαυμάσθη ὅλη ἡ γῆ. The sense of the Hebrew imperfect could

be taken here, thus reading 'and those dwelling on the earth constantly
marvel'.[140] While we are not obliged by context to render all the passages
cited by past tenses, yet the possibility is open, should the sense be better
suited thereby. Another example is Apc. 21:3 σκηνώσει (gig has a past
tense), noted by Allo.

The documentation of this long-disputed usage by means of examples
from the LXX helps to establish it as a true Semitism, for which non-
biblical Greek has no parallel whatever. We are led to the conclusion that
here we are dealing with translation Greek and, furthermore, Greek which
is intelligible primarily to readers familiar with Semitic languages. An ordinary non-Jew could hardly be expected to understand that the future
tense contains a past reference, along the lines of the LXX instances cited
above.[141]

g. The problem of shifting tenses[142]

On the basis of Semitic influence adduced for irregular use of the present,
aorist and future tenses, we can now consider the related phenomenon of
sudden and seemingly inexplicable shifts among aorist/present/future
tenses of verbs in connected narrative, without a corresponding shift in
the time during which the action being described actually takes place.
While related shifts are found to a limited degree in other parts of the
NT,[143] the phenomenon is more pronounced in the Apc.

Nearly 150 years ago Ewald observed that sometimes one finds in the
Apc. an astonishing mixture of future and past tenses, such as in 20:7-10,
where aorist and future verbs are scrambled in apparently random fashion,
all with future sense.[144] Bousset in his commentary on the Apc. described
this tendency as an irregular fluctuation (*regellose Schwanken*) and considered it a characteristic of the author's style, distributed in the epistles
to the seven churches, and especially in chapter 11.[145] Mussies ascribed the
phenomenon to the fact that the Seer usually began recounting his visions
in the past tense, then quickly shifted to the present because 'he is no
longer telling what he saw in the past, but rather what he is seeing again
before his eyes, and as such these present indicatives give the idea of lively
presentation'.[146]

A further complication in the Apc. is the fact that the visions are supposed to predict future events. Most other commentators who have considered the question of shifting tenses have explained them along similar
lines.

Charles, in his explanation of un-Greek tense usage as due to the influence
of the Semitic tense system,[147] also offered the clue to explain these

remarkable shifting tenses. This point has been taken up by Lancellotti and applied to the question of shifting tenses in continuous narrative passages in the Apc.[148] While this explanation has hypothetical appeal, it has not proved convincing to Mussies (and probably to others) because Lancellotti failed to demonstrate from a Semitic text and its Greek translation that such shifts of tense were actually caused by corresponding shifts in the underlying Semitic original. If the Seer could produce such strange yet acceptable phenomena, then surely there must have been some precedent for it. The explanation, of course, is clear in the light of the Semitic influence on the Greek tenses, especially that of aorist for prophetic perfect. Several examples of shifting Greek tenses, always based on shifts in the underlying Semitic verb tenses, illustrate clearly the identical shifts in the Apc. A good illustration is Daniel (Theod.) 4:31f ἡ βασιλεία παρῆλθεν ἀπὸ σοῦ καὶ ἀπὸ ἀνθρώπων σε ἐκδιώκουσιν (Β) . . . καὶ χόρτον ὡς βοῦν ψωμιοῦσιν σε καὶ ἑπτὰ καιροὶ ἀλλαγήσονται ἐπὶ σέ, 'The kingdom shall be taken from you, and they shall drive you from men . . . and they shall feed you grass as an ox, and seven seasons shall pass over you.' Note how the aorist παρῆλθεν represents a prophetic perfect, 'adāt, while the present ἐκδιώκουσιν renders a participle ṭardîn, and the remaining Greek future verbs, ψωμιοῦσιν and ἀλλαγήσονται, correspond exactly to their Aramaic imperfect counterparts yĕṭa'ămûn and yiḥlĕpûn. Similar shifts are found in Dan. (Theod.) 4:35 καὶ πάντες οἱ κατοικοῦντες τὴν γῆν ὡς οὐδὲν ἐλογίσθησαν καὶ κατὰ τὸ θέλημα αὐτοῦ ποιεῖ ἐν τῇ δυνάμει τοῦ οὐρανοῦ . . . οὐκ ἔστιν ὃς ἀντιποιήσεται τῇ χειρί αὐτοῦ καὶ ἐρεῖ . . . Τί ἐποίησας; 'the inhabitants of earth are counted as nothing, and he does according to his will in the powers of heaven . . . and there is no one who stays his hand and says to him, what are you doing?' Here note that present ποιεῖ = participle 'ābēd, futures ἀντιποιήσεται and καὶ ἐρεῖ = imperfects yĕmaḥē' and wĕyē'mar, and aorist ἐποίησας = perfect 'ābadt. Cf. 7:26f, καὶ τὸ κριτήριον ἐκάθισεν καὶ τὴν ἀρχὴν μεταστήσουσιν . . . καὶ ἡ βασιλεία . . . ἐδόθη ἁγίοις Ὑψίστου, 'And the court shall sit, and they shall take away his dominion . . . and the kingdom . . . shall be given to the saints of the most High.' Aorist ἐκάθισεν = ytb (pointed imperfect in MT; however, it could as well be a perfect yĕtib); future μεταστήσουσιν = hafel imperfect yĕha'dôn and aorist ἐδόθη = perfect yĕhîbat. Now some occurrences from the Hebrew sections of the OT: Hosea 4:10 καὶ φάγονται . . . ἐπόρνευσαν, 'For they shall eat . . . they shall commit whoredom'; future καὶ φάγονται = perfect plus *Waw*-consecutive wĕ'ākĕlû, while aorist ἐπόρνευσαν = hiphil perfect hiznû; cf. 9:3b κατῴκησεν Εφραμ . . . ἀκάθαρτα φάγονται, 'Ephraim shall return . . . he shall eat'. Here aorist κατῴκησεν = perfect wĕšab; future φάγονται imperfect yō'kĕlû. From these examples it is apparent that radical shifts in tense, from future to aorist and *vice versa*, which are inexplicable from a Greek viewpoint, are acceptable in Semitic Greek since they represent a literal rendering of the underlying Semitic tenses, usually influenced by the presence of prophetic perfects.

There are several passages in the Apc. which reflect the same shifts noted above: 20:7-10 καὶ ὅτε ἐτελέσθη (2059 2081 syr^ph) τὰ χίλια ἔτη λυθήσεται ὁ Σατανᾶς . . . καὶ ἐξελεύσεται πλανῆσαι τὰ ἔθνη . . . καὶ ἀνέβησαν ἐπὶ τὸ πλάτος τῆς γῆς καὶ ἐκύκλευσαν . . . καὶ κατέβη πῦρ . . . καὶ κατέφαγεν αὐτοὺς καὶ ὁ διάβολος ὁ πλανῶν αὐτοὺς ἐβλήθη εἰς τὴν λίμνην . . . καὶ βασανισθήσονται ἡμέρας καὶ νυκτός, 'And when the thousand years are ended, Satan shall be loosed . . . and will come forth to deceive the nations . . . and they shall march up over the broad earth and surround . . . but fire shall fall . . . and shall devour them and the Devil who deceives them shall be thrown into the lake [of fire] . . . and they shall be tormented'; 6:15-17 καὶ οἱ βασιλεῖς τῆς γῆς . . . ἔκρυψαν ἑαυτοὺς εἰς τὰ σπήλαια . . . καὶ λέγουσιν τοῖς ὄρεσιν καὶ ταῖς πέτραις . . . ὅτι ἦλθεν ἡ ἡμέρα . . . τῆς ὀργῆς αὐτῶν καὶ τίς δυνήσεται (2053) σταθῆναι; 'And the kings of the earth . . . hid themselves in caves . . . calling to the mountains and rocks . . . because the day of his wrath is come, and who is able to stand?'; 7:16, 17 οὐ πεινάσουσιν ἔτι οὐδὲ διψήσουσιν ἔτι οὐδὲ μὴ πέσῃ . . . ὅτι τὸ ἀρνίον τὸ ἀνὰ μέσον τοῦ θρόνου ποιμαίνει (82 91 314) αὐτοὺς καὶ ὁδηγήσει αὐτοὺς ἐπὶ ζωῆς πηγὰς ὑδάτων καὶ ἐξαλείψει ὁ θεός, 'They shall hunger no more, neither thirst any more; [the sun] shall not strike them . . . because the Lamb in the midst of the throne shall shepherd them, and shall guide them to springs of living water, and God shall wipe away every tear.' This passage seems to be based on phrases taken directly from Isa. 49:10; Ps. 22(23):1, 2; and Isa. 25:8 where a remarkable correspondence with the verb tenses of the MT is apparent:

future πεινάσευσιν	= imperfect *yir'ēbû*
future διψήσουσιν	= imperfect *yismā'û*
present ποιμαίνει	= participle *rō'eh*
future ὁδηγήσει	= imperfect *yĕnahēl*
future καὶ ἐξαλείψει	= perfect + *Waw*-consecutive *ûmāhâ*

14:2*b*-3 καὶ ἡ φωνὴ ἣν ἤκουσα ὡς κιθαρῳδῶν . . . καὶ ᾄδουσιν ὡς ᾠδὴν καινὴν . . . καὶ οὐδεὶς ἐδύνατο μαθεῖν τὴν ᾠδήν, 'and the voice which I heard was like harpers . . . and they sang a new song . . . and no one was able to learn the song'. Allo has noted the irregularity of the tenses in this passage, where the sequence of aorist - present - imperfect occurs in a continuous narrative with past sense.[149] Similar also is Apc. 16:21 where a present tense verb occurs in the midst of a past narrative: καὶ χάλαζα μεγάλη ὡς ταλαντιαία καταβαίνει (corrected κατεβαινεν 1611) 'and hailstones as large as talents fell'.

These demonstrate adequately the presence of shifting tenses in the Apc., indistinguishable in nature from those cited above from the LXX and Dan. Theod.

h. Periphrastic conjugations[150]

The debate over the question of Semitic influence on the periphrastic conjugations in the NT is a long-standing one. Most examples of periphrases are found in the Gospels, so a complete analysis of the matter lies outside the scope of this study. Since a limited number occur in the Apc. however, the occasion will be used first, to criticise previous studies on the subject and afterwards, to re-evaluate the Semitic evidence traditionally cited in discussion of the question.

G. Björck's work, HN ΔΙΔΑΣΚΩΝ *Die Periphrastischen Konstruktionen im Griechischen*,[151] has, together with its French predecessor 'Les Tournines Periphrastiques',[152] set the mood for the current evaluation of the question. Björck (pp. 59–62) seems to seriously discard *any* form of Semitic influence, since scattered occurrences of the construction are to be found in classical authors. Although he discusses briefly the *Semitismusfrage*,[153] yet the validity of his conclusion in this field is seriously undermined by his lack of firsthand acquaintance with Semitic languages, which he openly acknowledges.[154] It becomes immediately apparent that he, and anyone else viewing the phenomenon of periphrasis in the NT only from the Greek side, is working under a serious limitation.

In summary, his thesis of the purely Greek character of periphrasis in the NT is maintained wrongly in the face of three significant facts in the historical evolution of the Greek language: (1) while periphrasis was employed by classical authors in its most common forms (i.e. plus perfect and present participles) yet Hellenistic Greek, even in the papyri, makes only limited use of the construction;[155] (2) even within the Hellenistic period this construction did not receive its most notable development until the post-Christian era, as Björck concedes;[156] (3) at the same time, it is significant that while periphrasis is rare in Hellenistic literature it is found in the LXX with surprising frequency.[157]

On this final point Björck asked an important question: how is the use of periphrasis in the LXX related to the underlying Hebrew? Had he been able to provide the answer, it is likely that his conclusions would have been different.

Periphrasis in biblical Hebrew, employing either the perfect or imperfect of *hāyâ* plus participle, is well-established and widely distributed, if not very frequent.[158] Characteristic of the former, expressing emphasis of a past action, is Gen. 37:2 *yôsēp ... hāyâ rō'eh*, 'Joseph ... was herding', which in the LXX becomes Ἰωσὴφ ... ἦν ποιμαίνων. This is the type of periphrasis most frequently found in the OT. For an example from biblical Aramaic, cf. Dan. 5:19 *hăwô zāyĕ'în*, 'they were trembling' (Theod. ἦσαν τρέμοντες).[159] Not every periphrastic construction in the LXX of course is the result of the underlying Hebrew or Aramaic. Sometimes the translators employed the construction in its own right, to express (usually) a continuing or repeated action, condition, etc. But investigation shows that the construction in the LXX is due primarily to the same construction in the underlying Semitic text. This has recently been shown by W.J. Aerts, in his work *Periphrastica*.[160]

In the NT

The periphrastic tenses in the Gospels are cited and discussed by others.[161]

Occurrences in the Apc. are not so numerous as, for example, in Mark, Luke and the first half of Acts. This is possibly due to the fact that while the latter owe some of their examples to the form of Aramaic current in first-century Palestine, the Apc. reflects the variety of Hebrew/Aramaic found in the OT, which contains proportionately fewer occurrences of periphrasis.

Grammarians customarily include under the heading 'periphrasis' both those with the accompanying auxiliary form of εἶναι and those with the participle alone. Here only examples with the auxiliary verb are discussed such as Apc. 1:18 ζῶν εἰμι, present, and 17:4 ἦν περιβεβλημένη, imperfect. The participle alone, in the sense of a finite verb, receives fuller treatment in section 7*b* of this chapter, 'Participles in the sense of finite verbs', pp. 67–9.

Turner lists as present periphrasis without εἶναι Apc. 3:17,[162] and as imperfect 1:16; 10:2; 21:11, 14, and as perfect (or pluperfect) 7:5, 21:19. In Apc. 1:18 ζῶν εἰμι expresses an obviously continuous sense, as does the periphrastic tense in biblical Hebrew,[163] and in Greek as well. 'I will continue living forever.' It is thereby distinguished from occurrences in the Gospels and Acts in which the sense of continuation has receded into the background, under the influence of later Aramaic usage, where the periphrastic tense tended on occasion to replace the simple tenses.[164] Apc. 17:4 needs special consideration because of textual confusion between ἡ γυνὴ ἡ περιβεβλημένη (*Textus Receptus*) and ἦν περιβεβλημένη (ℵ A 046 *al*). The latter reading is preferred, although it would be difficult to make a case for a continuing sense, since the parallel κεχρυσωμένη has no accompanying ἦν.

The periphrastic tense employing a form of γίνομαι plus participle is well-attested in the LXX, based usually on a form of the underlying Hebrew *hāyâ*, as in Lam. 1:16 *hayû bānay šômēmîm*, 'my children are desolate' (LXX ἐγένοντο οἱ υἱοι μοῦ ἠφανισμένοι).[165] This has been claimed by Mussies and others to represent the construction in Apc. 3:2 γίνου γρηγορῶν.[166] But this is hardly periphrastic in meaning; as noted by Black,[167] it should be rendered 'become watchful'. Likewise Apc. 16:10 καὶ ἐγένετο ἡ βασιλεία αὐτοῦ ἐσκοτωμένη is a doubtful case, since the verb 'to be' usually immediately precedes the participle in the Semitic languages and in genuine NT occurrences of periphrasis.[168] Here the καὶ ἐγένετο is perhaps better understood as introductory, while ἐσκοτωμένη represents a hophal participle meaning 'was caused to become darkened'.[169]

Μέλλειν *plus infinitive*

The use of μέλλειν plus infinitive to express something about to occur is not unknown in classical Greek, so its frequent occurrence in the Apc. cannot be strictly ascribed to Semitic influence. It also appears (infrequently) in the LXX where it usually translates an imperfect Hebrew verb with the sense 'about to occur'. Neither in the Apc. nor in the LXX does μέλλειν plus infinitive seem to be used in the common classical sense to refer to a fixed necessity, something destined to occur, except perhaps Apc. 1:19 'write therefore whatever you see, and whatever is, and whatever is about to come (or, 'must come') after these things', ἃ μέλλει γενέσθαι. It probably means no more than 'things about to come'.

Summary of chapter 3, section 3

This section has developed more clearly than any previous study the formal translation equivalents employed in biblical and Jewish translation Greek. For the sake of clarity the relation between Greek and Semitic tenses is presented in the following table:

Greek (Indicative Mood)	Aramaic/Hebrew

Present Tense
  (Futuristic present)
  (Present with past sense)
	Participles
	  (Participle of *Futurum Instans*)
	  (Participle of past action)

Aorist
  (Futuristic aorist)
  (Aorist with present sense)
  (Timeless aorist)
	Perfect
	  (Prophetic perfect and *perf.*
	    confident.)
	  (Stative perfect)
	  (Perfect expressing general truth)

Future
  (with past sense)
	Imperfect
	  (with past sense)

Perfect (omnitemporal)	Derived Conjugation Verbs

These translation equivalents were, of course, not always adhered to, and exceptions can be found for every category. On the other hand, the very simplicity of this pattern, when seen in the light of the many illustrations cited here, argues for its general validity. In determining the *time* at which the action took place we must deal with biblical Greek tenses with the same technique we would use to render biblical Hebrew/Aramaic – rely on the context of the verb in question.

The related problem of sudden shifts of tense in the Apc., which has puzzled generations of scholars, is likewise solved by appealing to the shift in tense made in an underlying Semitic source.

Regarding the periphrastic conjugations in NT Greek, it can no longer be maintained that they are purely Greek in origin, since they occur also in Hebrew and Aramaic. On the other hand, it must not be assumed that when found in the NT they always show Semitic influence. The true periphrasis, using a participle accompanied by a form of the verb 'to be', is infrequent in the Apc.; when it occurs it seems to stress the continuing nature of the action.

4. Evidence of underlying *Waw*-consecutive constructions

One of the unique characteristics of biblical Hebrew syntax is the use of the *Waw*-consecutive with perfect and imperfect tense verbs. This peculiarity, which is not shared by Aramaic, Syriac, or even the later form of Hebrew found in the Mishnah, is described by GK, §49a, b in the following terms:[170]

The Hebrew *consecution* of tenses is the phenomenon that, in representing a series of past events, only the first verb stands in the perfect, and the narration is continued in the imperfect. Conversely, the representation of a series of future events begins with the imperfect, and is continued in the perfect . . .

This progress in the sequence of time, is regularly indicated by a pregnant *and* (called *waw* consecutive).

This fundamental point of Hebrew syntax requires no illustration here; it is so widely employed in the OT that examples can be found throughout. We will at this point seek to determine the influence exerted by the *Waw*-consecutive on the syntax of the LXX. The results will then be used to evaluate any constructions in the Apc. which are alleged to be the result of Hebrew *Waw*-consecutive influence.

It would be strange indeed if a structure so fundamental as the *Waw*-consecutive left no mark on the LXX, especially in those portions where a more literal method of translation was followed. The examples cited below come from three categories: (a) conditional sentences; (b) causal clauses; and (c) temporal clauses.[171] In each of these a Hebrew *Waw*-consecutive plus perfect tense verb introduces the apodosis. These categories occur frequently in the OT, and when translated into Greek, with καί for *Waw*-consecutive, show an obvious deviation from Greek idiom. Now, some examples from the first category.

a. καί in apodosis of conditional clauses in the LXX

4 Km. 7:4*b* καὶ ἐὰν θανατώσιν ἡμᾶς, καὶ ἀποθανούμεθα, 'and if they kill us, we shall but die', MT *'im-yĕmîtunû wāmātnû*; Nu. 30:16 ἐὰν δὲ περιελὼν περιέλη αὐτῆς . . . καὶ λήμψεται τὴν ἁμαρτίαν αὐτοῦ, 'But if he makes . . . null and void . . . he shall bear his iniquity', MT *wĕnāśā'*; 3 Km. 3:14 καὶ ἐὰν πορευθῇς ἐν τῇ ὁδῷ μοῦ . . . καὶ πληθυνῶ τὰς ἡμέρας σου, 'and if you will walk in my way . . . I will lengthen your days', MT *wĕ'im tēlēk . . . wĕha'araktî*.

In the Apc.

Grammarians have called attention to two passages in the Apc. where the *Waw*-consecutive construction introducing the apodosis in conditional sentences is echoed by redundant καί:[172] 3:20 ἐάν τις ἀκούσῃ τῆς φωνῆς μου καὶ ἀνοίξῃ τὴν θύραν, καὶ (א 046) εἰσελεύσομαι πρὸς αὐτόν, 'if anyone hears my voice and opens the door, I will come in to him'; 14:9f Εἴ τις προσκυνεῖ τὸ θηρίον . . . καὶ λαμβάνει χάραγμα . . . καὶ αὐτὸς πίεται ἐκ τοῦ οἴνου, 'If anyone worships the beast . . . and receives the mark . . . he shall drink the wine'.[173]

b. καί in the apodosis of causal clauses in the LXX

Nu. 14:24 ὅτι ἐγενήθη πνεῦμα ἕτερον ἐν αὐτῷ . . . καὶ (A) εἰσάξω αὐτόν, 'because there was a different spirit in him . . . I will bring him', MT *wahăbî'ōtîw*; Isa. 3:16f Ἀνθ' ὧν ὑψώθησαν αἱ θυγατέρες . . . καὶ πατει-νώσει ὁ θεός, 'because the daughters are haughty . . . God will smite', MT *wĕśippah*; Isa. 37:29 ὁ δὲ θυμός σου . . . καὶ ἡ πικρία σου ἀνέβη πρός με, καὶ ἐμβαλῶ φιμὸν, 'since your anger and your arrogance come to my attention, I will fix my hook', MT *wĕśimtî haḥî*.

In the Apc.

3:10 ὅτι ἐτήρησας τὸν λόγον τῆς ὑπομονῆς μου, κἀγώ σε τηρήσω ἐκ τῆς ὥρας τοῦ πειρασμοῦ, 'Because you kept the word of my patience, I will keep you from the period of temptation'. Note that the conjunction here is separated from the verb, and joined by crasis to ἐγώ. See also 16:6 ὅτι αἷμα ἁγίων καὶ προφητῶν ἐξέχεαν, καὶ αἷμα αὐτοῖς [δ]έδωκας πιεῖν, 'since they shed blood of saints and prophets, you gave them blood to drink'; 18:9 (an inversion, where the apodosis precedes the protasis) καὶ κλαύσον-ται καὶ κόψονται . . . ὅταν βλέπωσιν τὸν καπνὸν τῆς πυρώσεως αὐτῆς, 'they shall weep and wail . . . when they see the smoke of her burning'. That this inversion is Hebraic is shown by the following: Nu. 26:10 καὶ ἀνοίξασα ἡ γῆ τὸ στόμα αὐτῆς . . . ὅτε κατέφαγεν τὸ πῦρ, MT *wattiptaḥ*, 'the earth opened its mouth . . . when the fire devoured'. Possibly also Apc. 3:8f ἐτήρησάς μου τὸν λόγον καὶ οὐκ ἠρνήσω τὸ ὄνομά μου καὶ (syr[ph]) ἰδοὺ διδῶ . . . καὶ (1 181 2023 2037 2038 2067) ποιήσω. The sentence is complex, appearing to have a compound protasis with three verbs, and an apodosis with two verbs, or with one verb, διδῶ, replaced after a paren-thetical digression by ποιήσω. There is limited textual support for καί pre-ceding both verbs of the apodosis; in the first case καὶ ἰδοὺ διδῶ seems not to be a Syriac construction, although attested to only in Syriac. It is good biblical Hebrew, however. The καί with the second verb, likewise weakly-attested, is also hard to account for if not original, unless the sentence is arranged differently, allowing it to be a simple conjunction.

c. καί in the apodosis of temporal clauses in the LXX

1 Km. 2:13 παντὸς τοῦ θύοντος, καὶ ἤρχετο τὸ παιδάριον τοῦ ἱερέως, 'when-ever anyone sacrificed, the priest's servant came', MT *ûbā'*. Gen. 32:18f Ἐάν σοι συναντήσῃ Ησαυ . . . καὶ (A) ἐρεῖς, 'when Esau meets you . . .

you shall say', MT *wĕ'āmartā*. Lev. 19:23 ὅταν δὲ εἰσέλθητε εἰς τὴν γῆν
... καὶ περικαθαριεῖτε, MT *ûnĕṭa'tem*, 'when you enter the land . . . you
shall purge away'.

In the Apc.

Apc. 6:12 ὅτε ἤνοιξεν . . . καὶ σεισμὸς μέγας ἐγένετο, 'when he opened . . .
a great earthquake occurred', note here the verb has become detached
from καί, and separated from it; 10:7 ἀλλ' ἐν ταῖς ἡμέραις . . . ὅταν μέλλῃ
σαλπίζειν, καὶ ἐτελέσθη τὸ μυστήριον, 'but in those days . . . when he is
about to sound, the mystery will be fulfilled'. Here Allo notes that καί
represents the *Waw*-consecutive.[174]

While not every passage from the Apc. cited here is fully convincing,
there are genuine examples in each of the three categories, syntactically
identical to LXX passages where the redundant καί introducing the apodosis is directly traceable to a Hebrew *Waw*-consecutive in the MT. But
before drawing conclusions about the meaning of this phenomenon in the
Greek of the Apc., we will observe another syntactical feature which might
point towards *Waw*-consecutive influence on biblical Greek – the *tense* of
the main verb in the apodosis. A pattern emerges from LXX translators,
who often translated the Hebrew *Waw*-consecutive by καί plus future tense
verb – this is the case in eight of the ten LXX passages cited above. Note
the similar tendency in the eight Apc. passages cited above, where five
employ future tense verbs, reflecting the Semitic imperfect tense.

If these observations are valid, they lead to the conclusion that the
Greek of the Apc. has been, at least in part, modelled on biblical Hebrew,
rather than on a later stage of the language. This could be a very significant point to consider in any theory about the nature of the Greek of the
Apc., and the best method for its translation and elucidation.

The contrasting opinion has recently been expressed by Mussies, who
maintains that 'Mishnaic Hebrew is the best basis for comparison with the
use of Greek in the Apc.; first, because it is contemporary with the book;
second, because it is not classicistic but reveals the development of Hebrew
after the OT period, and third, because the quantity of literature composed in it is sufficient.'[175] He comments in detail about the disappearance
of *Waw*-consecutive tenses in Mishnaic Hebrew,[176] and refers to the tendency of the Qumran Isaiah scroll (1QIs[a]) to avoid the consecutive *Waw*
tenses as if this were simply part of a line of development, traceable from
the early form of the language (i.e. the MT) through Qumran Hebrew to
that preserved in the Mishnah. While we will not at this point examine the
matter in detail, it is important to correct a false impression which Mussies

seems to give, that in 1QIs^a and in other biblical documents from Qumran
the *Waw*-consecutive tenses had all but disappeared. Examination shows
to the contrary that *Waw*-consecutive tenses were still in use; and even in
places where they are avoided,[177] a *Waw*-conjunctive is substituted in
nearly every instance. A sharp contrast is noticed in Mishnaic Hebrew,
where the *Waw*-consecutive is conspicuously absent, except in scattered
OT quotations,[178] and where even the *Waw*-conjunctive coupled with verbs
appears infrequently. While agreeing fully with Mussies that tendencies can
be seen in Qumran Hebrew which point in the direction of Mishnaic Hebrew, we would dispute his supposition that the disappearance of the *Waw*-
consecutive tenses in Mishnaic Hebrew can be seen at an intermediate
stage in 1QIs^a, and suggest instead that, in the use of *Waw* in connection
with verbs, the biblical scrolls of Qumran have far greater affinity to the
MT than to the Mishnah.

Summary of chapter 3, section 4

Here it is shown that the biblical Hebrew *Waw*-consecutive construction
has left its mark on the syntax of the Apc. most clearly where it is used
(translated by καί) to introduce the apodosis of a conditional, causal, or
temporal clause, thus creating a syntactical oddity nearly unknown in
secular Greek. This points to biblical Hebrew, not a later variety, as the
model for the language of the Apc.

5. Imperatives

Mussies notes that since the Greek imperative third-person mood had no
Semitic counterpart,[179] one might expect to find in the Apc. future indicative verbs with the value of an imperative, since Semitic languages
expressed the third-person imperative by the imperfect (or jussive).[180] The
question of Greek future for Hebrew jussive receives discussion elsewhere;[181] here attention will be drawn to alternate constructions which
have a supposed imperative meaning.

a. Infinitive with imperative sense

There are scattered cases in the NT of the infinitive expressing the sense of
an imperative. This is well in line with Greek usage, being attested as early
as Homer[182] and, while less common in Attic literature,[183] was widely employed in the papyri.[184] With such strong attestation in secular Greek it

may appear futile to suggest the possibility of Semitic influence on the infinitive at this point. Moule, for example, notes that 'whether the Hebrew "Infinitive Absolute" has influenced the use of infinitive for imperative at all is hard to judge; but Homeric instances make one cautious about detecting Semitic influence'.[185] While every occurrence of this construction in the NT can be accounted for along Greek lines, yet an instance of it in the Apc. deserves attention because it closely reflects Ezek. 3:1-3. In Apc. 10:9 we read καὶ ἀπῆλθα πρὸς τὸν ἄγγελον λέγων αὐτῷ δοῦναί μοι τὸ βιβλαρίδιον, 'so I went to the angel and said to him, "give me the little book" '. Charles prefers to take the Hebraic sense of λέγων (= 'amar) meaning 'to command', thus translating it 'bidding him to give me the little book'.[186] On the one hand this phrase corresponds with the appearances in the papyri of an imperatival infinitive depending on the verb signifying 'to command', etc., which is either stated in the text or at least understood from context;[187] but at the same time we cannot ignore a similar Hebrew idiom. The use of the Hebrew infinitive absolute to express the imperative idea is 'extraordinarily common',[188] and it seems that, as with the case of Greek, likewise with Hebrew, this infinitive could be used as a kind of fixed word of command.[189] So if δοῦναι in Apc. 10:9 is taken as an imperative, it could perhaps be explained as due to a convergence of Greek and Hebrew influence. An attractive alternative explanation is that suggested by Charles,[190] who takes λέγων to mean 'command', leaving δοῦναι with the true sense of a Greek infinitive. The same can be said of Apc. 13:14 λέγων τοῖς κατοικοῦσιν ἐπὶ τῆς γῆς ποιῆσαι εἰκόνα τῷ θηρίῳ, 'ordering those dwelling on earth to make an image to the beast'. Cf. Acts 21:21 λέγων μὴ περιτέμνειν αὐτούς, 'commanding them not to circumcise'.

Understood either way, this use of the infinitive preceded by λέγων in the Apc. shows the Seer's acquaintance with and awareness of biblical Hebrew idiom.

b. Greek participle for imperative

It is well known that in several places in the NT, especially in Paul and 1 Peter, the participle is employed in place of a finite verb with imperatival sense.[191] The fullest discussion of this phenomenon remains that of David Daube,[192] who disputes Moulton's claim that such usage represented a genuine Hellenistic development. Daube prefers to explain this usage as due to Hebrew or (less probably) Aramaic influence.[193] Mishnaic Hebrew expresses what ought to be done by the use of the participle. In this role the participle comes very close to the sense of the imperative, which Daube illustrates by numerous Hebrew passages from post-biblical material. He thus seeks to explain the imperatival participle in the NT as due to Hebrew, not Hellenistic Greek, influence, and his explanation seems to be sound.[194]

A new evaluation of the evidence from the papyri, cited by Moulton to support his position that the imperatival participle was a Hellenistic development, has been recently made by Mandilaras,[195] who is more reluctant than his predecessor to see a truly Greek imperatival participle: 'Such a use of the participle is indeed rare in the papyri.' He is doubtful of the strong case Moulton made on this point, and reveals that the construction is much less common in the papyri than Moulton believed. Naturally, the case for Semitic influence is enhanced by such findings.

An occurrence of an imperatival participle has not so far been cited from the Apc., but it may be instructive to examine a variant reading in 3:2 γίνου γρηγορῶν, καὶ στηρίζων (336 459 628) τὰ λοιπά, 'awaken, and strengthen what remains'.[196] The participle appears in none of the printed Greek texts, which generally prefer the aorist imperative στήριξον of the *Textus Receptus.* The variant στηρίζων is supported by only one family of rather late minuscules (eleventh to sixteenth century), which were produced by rather careful copyists, probably from an earlier uncial archetype.[197] While the textual pedigree of this variant is admittedly unimpressive, it clearly represents the more difficult reading. It may also be significant that the passage is part of the epistles to the seven churches, and that it consists of admonition. There is no other occurrence of this construction in the Apc.

c. Δεῦτε followed by the imperative

W.H. Simcox, in his comments on the text of the Apc.,[198] seems to imply that the verbal use of δεῦτε immediately preceding an imperative represents a Semitic construction. On this point Ozanne makes even more certain claims for its Hebraic nature,[199] arguing that in Apc. 19:17 δεῦτε, συνάχθητε represents a Hebraism, due to the fact that in the LXX the adverb δεῦτε commonly represents the imperative of *hālak.*[200] The expression is not peculiar to Hebrew however, but is present in many languages in essentially the same form. In Greek the sequence δεῦτε plus imperative has been employed since the time of Homer in poetic passages and appears in later prose works.[201] It seems that this particular use of the imperative has little significance for illustrating Semitic influence on Greek syntax, or for indicating a Hebrew source for the Apc.

Summary of chapter 3, section 5

The infinitive with imperative sense is attested in Hebrew and in Hellenistic Greek, so does not *per se* point to Hebrew influence. The well-established late Hebrew use of the participle for imperative is known from other parts of the NT; in the Apc., however, it has only a single weakly-attested occurrence.

Little significance should be attached to the use of δεῦτε followed by the imperative. The construction occurs in Hebrew, but is well-established in Greek from ancient times onward.

6. Infinitives

Bl-D note that in comparison with classical Greek the use of the infinitive in the NT has shifted greatly, with some categories, such as the infinitive of purpose and certain forms of the substantival infinitive growing more common, while other forms were falling into disuse.[202] This changing syntactical scene, including both the replacement of temporal and causal clauses by the infinitive, and the instrusion of ἵνα and καί constructions into territory formerly held by the infinitive, has motivated a considerable amount of study dealing with the position of the infinitive in Hellenistic Greek.

a. The articular genitive infinitive

Perhaps the most striking point of NT usage of the infinitive is its use preceded by the genitive article τοῦ.[203] In the NT this construction is used 'in a lavish way' (Bl-D, §388) to express a variety of meanings, including purpose, a consecutive sense and a final sense.[204] All these uses can be explained on Greek grounds; indeed, the construction is acceptable Greek. It is found in the language of Plato and Polybius, and was somewhat favoured by Thucydides for expressing purpose,[205] and is used in a wide range of meanings in the papyri.[206]

In addition, Bl-D note (§400 (7, 8)) the Semitic flavour of certain infinitives with prefixed τοῦ, after the pattern of the LXX, which often employed this construction to render the Hebrew infinitive with prefixed *lĕ*. This NT usage falls into two categories: (a) a loose, general tendency to prefix τοῦ onto any sort of infinitive; (b) a use in which Greek consecutive sense all but disappears, where the relation between τοῦ plus infinitive and the remainder of the sentence is very loose.[207]

Under (a) Bl-D list the following examples from the LXX: 3 Km. 1:35 καὶ ἐγὼ ἐνετειλάμην τοῦ εἶναι εἰς ἡγούμενον ἐπὶ Ἰσραηλ καὶ Ἰουδα, 'and I have appointed him to be ruler over Israel and Judah', which translates a Hebrew infinitive construct *lir'ôt*. Ezek. 21:16(11) ἑτοίμη τοῦ δοῦναι αὐτὴν εἰς χεῖρα ἀποκτενοῦντος, 'ready to be placed in the hand of the slayer' (Hebrew *lātēt*). To these we add Ps. 26:13 πιστεύω τοῦ ἰδεῖν τὰ ἀγαθὰ κυρίου ἐν γῇ ζώντων, 'I believe that I shall see the good things of the Lord' (Hebrew *lir'ôt*). The Hebrew construction in each case is the infinitive construct preceded by *lĕ*, which occurs very frequently in the OT with a variety of meanings.[208] It becomes apparent that biblical Greek writers in certain instances employed the τοῦ plus infinitive as the equivalent of Hebrew *lĕ* plus infinitive, thus giving the previously infrequent Greek construction a much wider range of meaning in biblical Greek.

While Charles and others are content to point out the Hebrew antecedent of this genitive articular infinitive, it is worth noting that in Aramaic the same construction occurs with even greater frequency. In biblical Aramaic the infinitive plus *lĕ* stands almost without exception following a governing verb to express command, intention, necessity and coercion.[209] Regarding its frequency Bauer and Leander (§85*b*) made the following observation: 'Die Konstruktion mit *lĕ* ist auch nahezu ständige Regel in den Targumen, weniger häufig im pal. Talmud. So auch immer im Syrischen'.[210] This occurs in biblical Aramaic (always negated with *lā'*) in the following places: Dan. 6:16 *'ĕsār ûqĕyām . . . lā' lĕhišnāyâ*, '[Know, O king, that every] interdict and ordinance . . . cannot be altered'; cf. Theodotion's translation, where τοῦ plus infinitive translates the construction, although the article is widely separated from its infinitive: τοῦ πᾶν ὁρισμὸν καὶ στάσιν ἣν ἂν ὁ βασιλεὺς στήρῃ οὐ δεῖ παραλλάξαι.[211] Cf. 6:9 *kĕtābā' dî lā' lĕhašnāyâ*, 'the decree which must not be altered'. While we recognise that in Hellenistic Greek the genitive articular infinitive was coming into wider use, we cannot account for what Bl-D term the 'lavish use' of this construction by NT writers on the basis of this trend alone. The best explanation of the construction's frequency in biblical Greek, especially in the Apc. is that which recognises the widespread use of the corresponding Semitic construction in Hebrew, Aramaic and Syriac, and which allows the Greek construction to represent this Semitic one by a literal rendering of *lĕ* by τοῦ.

After noting the especially wide use of this construction in Aramaic, it may be instructive to repeat the observation made earlier that outside the Apc. it is found most frequently in Luke–Acts. While the occurrences in the Apc. are probably due to Hebrew influence,[212] it is tempting to conjecture that those in Luke–Acts provide a link, hitherto un-examined, with Aramaic sources.[213]

Previous searches for the genitive articular infinitive in the Apc. have yielded meagre results since they have been based only on the published critical editions of the Greek NT. Bl-D for example find only one certain occurrence (Apc. 12:7), and two that are weakly attested (Apc. 9:10 and 14:15).[214] A construction of this nature would doubtless be smoothed by copyists with an eye towards improving their texts, so it is safe to assume that the Apc. originally contained a greater number of occurrences than do the manuscripts on which printed editions are based. In Hoskier's apparatus attestation is given for several more, four of which seem to reflect the Hebraic *lĕ* loosely attached to an infinitive following a governing verb: Apc. 4:11 ἄξιος εἶ ὁ κύριος καὶ ὁ θεὸς ἡμῶν τοῦ (469) λαβεῖν τὴν δόξαν, 'Thou art worthy, O Lord and our God, to receive glory.'[215] Apc. 5:3 καὶ οὐδεὶς ἐδύνατο . . . τοῦ (2019) ἀνοῖξαι τὸ βιβλίον, 'And no one was able . . . to open the book.' Apc. 9:6 καὶ ἐπιθυμήσουσιν τοῦ (792) ἀποθανεῖν, 'And they shall desire to die.' Here we might add the weakly-attested τοῦ κηρῦξαι in 1:2. Apc. 12:2 καὶ ἐν γαστρὶ ἔχουσα καὶ κράζει ὠδίνουσα καὶ βασανιζομένη τοῦ (468 2017 2040 syr^ph) τεκεῖν, 'And she was with child and she cried out in pangs of birth, and anguished for delivery' (cf. Isa. 26:17 where τεκεῖν renders Hebrew *lāledet* 'about to be delivered', a familiar Hebrew idiom).[216]

Closely related syntactically is a category of the infinitive plus genitive article expressing necessity. While nineteenth-century commentators noticed the Semitic nature of the passage in question (Apc. 12:7), they wrongly ascribed it to the influence of the Hebrew infinitive absolute.[217] R.H. Charles has given the best explanation of the construction, summarised here:

He noted the unconvincing attempts of others to remove the un-Greek construction in this verse either by changing the infinitive into a finite verb, or by removing the subjects, Michael and his angels, or at least by rendering them in the accusative instead of nominative case. 'Some acquaintance with the LXX' has enabled Charles to illustrate convincingly that the infinitive with genitive article, preceded by a subject in the nominative case, represents the literal rendering of a pure Hebraism. As examples from the LXX he cited: Hos. 9:13 Ἐφραιμ τοῦ ἐξαγαγεῖν (*'epraîm lĕhôşî'*), 'Ephraim must bring forth'; also: 1 Chr. 9:25 ἀδελφοί αὐτῶν . . . τοῦ εἰσπορεύεσθαι κατὰ ἐπτὰ ἡμέρας (*'āḥêhem . . . lābô lĕšib'at hayyāmîm*), 'Their brethren had to come in . . . every seven days'; Eccl. 3:15 ὅσα τοῦ γίνεσθαι ἤδη γέγονεν (*'ăšer lihyôt kĕbār hāyâ*), 'What is to be hath already been.'

'Thus in the Hebrew the subject before *lĕ* and the infinitive is in the
nominative, and the Greek translators have literally reproduced this idiom
in the LXX.'[218]

The soundness of Charles' explanation is recognised by Howard;[219] cf.
Turner,[220] who gives a survey of recent opinions on this construction.

In his treatment of Apc. 12:7 Lancellotti recognises this infinitive plus
subject in the nominative case as Hebraic, but argues wrongly for rejection
of the genitive article, primarily because it is attested in manuscripts considered textually inferior; also because, according to his text, the infinitive
generally occurs without the article. He suggests that it perhaps entered
the text as a result of dittography of the final syllable of the preceding
word αὐτοῦ.[221]

Another occurrence of the phenomenon, cited by Charles, is Apc. 13:10
εἴ τις ἐν μαχαίρῃ ἀποκτανθῆναι αὐτὸν ἐν μαχαίρῃ ἀποκτανθῆναι. Here
he would understand αὐτόν as a corruption for αὐτός, and he also notes
that the article τοῦ is not attested in any manuscript. The idiom is still
Hebraic, and should be understood as meaning 'if any man is to be slain
with the sword, he is to be slain with the sword'.[222]

The remaining cases of τοῦ plus infinitive in the Apc. appear to express
either purpose or consequence, and thus can be explained along the lines
of the (infrequent) Greek genitive articular infinitive.[223] If these are indeed
such acceptable Greek as is maintained by Bl-D, one wonders why the
article was subsequently omitted in the major manuscripts containing the
Apc.? Certainly the article represents the more difficult reading in each
case, and the temptation for copyists would be to eliminate it, indicating
perhaps their judgment that the construction was somewhat un-Greek in
character.[224]

Since the widely employed Hebrew infinitive construct plus *lĕ* could
also express purpose and consequence,[225] one could safely postulate that
at least in the Apc. the cases of τοῦ plus infinitive cited above are attributed more to Hebraic than to Greek influence.

b. Infinitive resolved into a finite verb[226]

Charles noted a case in the Apc. where an infinitive is resolved into a finite
verb in the following clause, on the basis of Hebrew practice. He quotes
S.R. Driver: 'it is a common custom with Hebrew writers, after employing
a participle or infinitive, *to change the construction*, and, if they wish to
subjoin other verbs which should logically be in the participle or infinitive
as well, to pass to the use of the finite verb'.[227] This construction is found

also in the so-called 'Zadokite document', as well as in the Aramaic of Ezra (cf. 4:21); it is also attested in the Babylonian Talmud.[228] This change of construction affects infinitives which have prefixed *lĕ* as well as those without it. Examples without the prefix include the following: 1 Ki. 2:37 *bĕyôm ṣe'tĕk wĕ'ābartā ,et-nahal*, 'in the day you go forth (infinitive) and *cross* (finite verb) the brook'; 1 Ki. 8:33 *bĕhinnāgep 'ammĕkā wĕšabû*, 'when your people are smitten (infinitive) and *turn* (finite verb)'. Occurrences of infinitive plus *lĕ* include: Gen. 28:25 *lĕhāmît . . . wĕhāyâ*, 'To slay . . . and *to be*' (which is translated literally in the LXX by τοῦ ἀποκτεῖναι . . . καὶ ἔσται).[229]

In the LXX we find this construction rendered literally in several places: Deut. 4:42 φεύγειν ἐκεῖ . . . καὶ καταφεύξαι . . . καὶ ζήσεται, 'to flee there . . . and to flee . . . and to live'; 3 Km. 8:33 ἐν τῷ πταῖσαι τὸν λαόν σου . . . καὶ ἐπιστρέψουσιν καὶ ἐξομολογήσονται, 'when the people are smitten . . . and turn, and acknowledge' (a hypothetical sentence). Other cases could be cited. These illustrate that the un-Greek resolution of an infinitive into a finite verb preceded by καί is due to the influence of the corresponding characteristic in biblical Hebrew.

This phenomenon appears in the Apc. at 13:15f (cf. Moulton–Turner, IV, 155): καὶ ἐδόθη αὐτῷ δοῦναι . . . καὶ ποιήσει (א *al*),[230] 'And it was given unto him to give . . . and to cause'. Charles tentatively reconstructs the underlying Hebrew which he sees at this point: *wyntn lh ltt . . . wt'š*.[231]

The translation of this verse depends, of course, on whether it is the beast or the image of the beast which is the subject of 'to cause'. I follow Charles in taking the beast to be the subject, since it seems unlikely that if the image of the beast were the subject, it would appear so soon in the same verse as the object of the verb προσκυνήσωσιν. Apc. 12:17f καὶ ἀπῆλθεν ποιῆσαι πόλεμον μετὰ τῶν λοιπῶν . . . καὶ ἐστάθη ἐπὶ τὴν ἄμμον τῆς θαλάσσης, 'And he departed to make war with the remnant . . . and to stand on the sand of the sea.'[232] By understanding the verb ἐστάθη in the sense of an infinitive we would be able to settle the textual dispute over whether the variant ἐστάθην, 'I stood', should be read here as the introduction to what follows in chapter 13. Apc. 13:5f καὶ ἐδόθη αὐτῷ ἐξουσία ποιῆσαι μῆνας τεσσαράκοντα καὶ δύο καὶ ἤνοιξεν τὸ στόμα αὐτοῦ εἰς βλασφημίας πρὸς τὸν θεὸν βλασφημῆσαι τὸ ὄνομα αὐτοῦ, 'And he is allowed to exercise authority forty-two months, and to open his mouth in blasphemies against God, to blaspheme his name.'

In both cases the sentence is relieved of a certain awkwardness when the finite verb following the infinitive is understood as a Semitic second infinitive, resolved in form to a finite verb.

c. Nominal use of the infinitive

Under the heading of the nominal use of the infinitive in his monograph Lancellotti notes the occasional use of an infinitive in a servile manner to supplement the verbs μέλλω, θέλω, δύναμαι, λέγω, etc.[234] While he rightly recognises that such usage is fully acceptable in Greek, he suspects Semitic influence to be at work when the infinitive, in dependence on δίδωμι, is used to express the sense 'concede', 'permit', in Apc. 2:7 and 13:15, and λέγω in the sense of 'demand', 'request' in Apc. 10:9 and 13:14.[235] These definitions are by no means un-Greek,[236] nor is there any irregularity in the fact that they are followed by infinitives. Lancellotti succeeds, however, in drawing attention to the interesting fact that this Greek usage is exactly paralleled by a corresponding Hebrew construction, well-illustrated in the case of λέγω by 1 Chr. 21:17 *hălō 'ănî 'āmartî limnôt bā'ām*, 'Was it not I who commanded to number the people?' (LXX οὐκ ἐγὼ εἶπα τοῦ ἀριθμῆσαι τῷ λαῷ;), and in the case of δίδωμι by Gen. 31:7 *wělō'-nětānô 'ĕlōhîm lěhara' 'immādî*, 'God did not permit him to harm me' (LXX καὶ οὐκ ἔδωκεν αὐτῷ ὁ θεὸς κακοποιῆσαι με); cf. Job 9:18 *lō'-yittnēnî hāšēb rûhî*, 'he will not permit me to draw my breath' (LXX οὐκ ἐᾷ με ἀναπνεῦσαι).

This construction, identical in both Hebrew and Greek, seems not to represent so much a case of Semitic influence on our author's Greek as to be a basic characteristic of many languages, which is used to express a particular idea. This element has found its way into numerous languages in similar form to that shown here in the case of Hebrew and Greek.

Perhaps a similar explanation can be offered to explain the phenomenon, pointed out by Charles,[237] in Apc. 16:19 where we read καὶ βαβυλὼν ἡ μεγάλη ἐμνήσθη ἐνώπιον τοῦ θεοῦ δοῦναι αὐτῇ τὸ ποτήριον. Charles notes that the construction ἐμνήσθη δοῦναι should be compared with Ps. 109:16 and 103:18, where the infinitive 'to give' follows *zākar*. The construction μιμνήσκω followed by an infinitive occurs numerous times in secular Greek,[238] so in itself it shows no direct Semitic influence.[239]

Summary of chapter 3, section 6

In summary, we note that while Charles long ago laid the foundation for explaining the Semitic nature of τοῦ plus infinitive in certain passages of the Apc. as expressing necessity, here for the first time evidence is cited demonstrating that the construction was even better known in Aramaic and Syriac than in biblical Hebrew. By availing ourselves of Hoskier's apparatus we have discovered occurrences in the Apc. not before seen.

In the case of infinitives which are resolved into finite verbs, based upon a well-documented Hebrew practice, further examples have been suggested in addition to those presented by Charles.

Regarding the so-called 'nominal' use of the infinitive ascribed by Lancellotti to Hebrew influence, it was noted here that the construction is found in Greek literature as well, although there is admittedly a Hebraic construction in the OT which is identical.

7. Participles

While Greek participles have many functions in common with their Semitic counterparts, yet they differ from one another on several points. The observations presented in this section deal with those points where a participial usage more or less restricted to Hebrew and/or Aramaic has influenced their use in the Greek of the Apc.

a. Greek participles resolved into finite verbs

The participle in the Apc. is sometimes employed in circumstances where, in the following clause, it is resolved into a finite verb which expresses the sense of a participle. Close attention has been given to this usage by Charles,[240] who explains its Hebraic nature. He cites S.R. Driver:[241] 'it is a common custom with Hebrew writers, after employing a participle or infinitive, *to change the construction*, and if they wish to subjoin other verbs, which logically should be in the participle or infinitive as well, to pass to the use of the finite verb'. Note the following illustrative examples: Gen. 27:33 *ḥaṣṣār ṣayid wayyābe'*, 'who hunted game and *who brought'*. Here the LXX renders idiomatically, using two participles. Ps. 136:13f *lĕgōzēr yam-sûp . . . wĕheʿĕbîr yiśrā'ēl bĕtôkô*, 'to him who divided the Red Sea . . . and *made* Israel *pass* in its midst'. Again the LXX gives an idiomatic rendering: τῷ καταδιελθόντι τὴν ἐρυθρὰν θάλασσαν . . . καὶ διαγαγόντι τὸν 'Ισραηλ; 1 Sam. 2:8 *mēqîm mēʿāpār dāl . . . yārîm 'ebyôn*, 'he raises the poor from the dust . . . *he lifts* the needy'; here the LXX renders ἀνιστᾷ ἀπὸ τῆς γῆς πένητα . . . ἐγείρει πτωχόν. While the construction is primarily Hebraic, Burney notes Dan. 4:22 (MT) as an Aramaic example *wĕlāk ṭārdîn min-'ānāšâ wĕ'iśbā. kĕtôrîn lāk yĕta'ămûn*, 'And they *shall drive* you . . . (literally 'driving you') and with grass like oxen they shall feed you'.[242]

Burney cites two occurrences of the construction from the fourth Gospel: 1:32 Τεθέαμαι τὸ πνεῦμα καταβαῖνον . . . καὶ ἔμεινεν ἐπ' αὐτόν; cf. 5:44 λαμβάνοντες καὶ . . . οὐ ζητεῖτε.[243] Black, in his discussion of parataxis in the Gospels,²⁴⁴ notes that 'in D, καί occasionally introduces a finite verb after a participle'. Among the examples he cites are some similar in function to the cases cited above; e.g. Luke 9:6 ἐξερχόμενοι . . . καὶ ἤρχοντο (D) εὐαγγελιζόμενοι καὶ θεραπεύοντες, literally 'And they departing and going . . . evangelizing and healing'.

C.C. Torrey called attention to this construction in Apc. 1:16 καὶ ἐκ τοῦ στόματος αὐτοῦ ῥομφαία . . . ἐκπορευομένη, καὶ ἡ ὄψις αὐτοῦ ὡς ὁ ἥλιος φαίνει, 'and out of his mouth a sword coming, and his face as the sun *shining*'.²⁴⁵ Burney, in an article devoted to this construction in the Apc., collects from Charles' commentary the following examples of the construction:²⁴⁶ 1:5f τῷ ἀγαπῶντι ἡμᾶς . . . καὶ ἐποίησεν ἡμᾶς, 'Unto him who loves us . . . and *makes* us' (not RV 'and he makes us'); 2:2 τοὺς λέγοντας ἑαυτοὺς ἀποστόλους, καὶ οὐκ εἰσιν, 'Those who call themselves apostles, and *are not*' (not RV 'and they are not'); 2:9 τῶν λεγόντων Ἰουδαίους εἶναι ἑαυτοὺς, καὶ οὐκ εἰσιν, 'Those who claim to be Jews, and *are not*' (Apc. 3:9 identical); 2:20 ἡ λέγουσα ἑαυτὴν προφῆτιν, καὶ διδάσκει, 'Who says . . . and *teaches*' (not RV 'and she teacheth'); 2:23 ἐγὼ εἰμι ὁ ἐραυνῶν . . . καὶ δώσω, 'I am he who searches . . . and who *gives*'; 7:14 οἱ ἐρχόμενοι . . . καὶ ἔπλυναν. Also 14:2, 3; 15:2, 3. Burney adds to Charles' list 13:11 ἄλλο θηρίον ἀναβαῖνον . . . καὶ εἶχεν. He rejects 1:18 and 20:4, which Charles included. Finally I would add 7:2f ἄλλον ἄγγελον ἀναβαίνοντα . . . ἔχοντα . . . καὶ ἔκραξεν.²⁴⁷

b. Participles in the sense of finite verbs

Hjalmar Frisk argues against what he terms the 'wide and growing opinion' that the participle in later Greek was used on occasion as a finite verb.²⁴⁸ He asserts that the participle is always to be understood as a participle. Where it seems to have the sense of a finite verb the explanation can be found in what he describes as 'stylistic peculiarities'.

Frisk, of course, was referring to later (Hellenistic) Greek. In biblical Greek there are occurrences of the participle in place of the finite verb to express finite action. The Hebrew practice of using a participle for a finite verb is responsible for the construction in the LXX. Especially significant are occurrences of sentences or primary clauses in which the participle is the only verb.²⁴⁹ This un-Greek practice owes its explanation to Semitic influence. In Hebrew, the participle is found on occasion in place of a finite verb in a main clause: Gen. 4:10 qôl dĕmê 'āḥîkā sō'ăqîm 'ēlay, 'The voice of your brother's blood *cries* [literally 'crying'] unto me.' Gen. 43:5 wĕ'im - 'ênĕkā mĕšaleaḥ lō' nērēd, 'but if you will not *send* him, we will not go down' (literally 'if you not sending him'); Eccl. 1:4 dôr hōlēk wĕdôr *bā'*, 'One generation *passes* away, another generation *comes*' (literally 'one passing . . . one coming'); Eccl. 1:6 *sōbēb hōlēk hārûaḥ*, 'The wind *turns* about and *goes*' (literally 'turning . . . going the wind'); cf. verse 7: *kol-hannĕhalîm hōlĕkîm 'el-hāyyam*, 'Every stream *runs* to the sea' (literally 'running'). The examples cited so far are rendered in the LXX by present indicative verbs which, as noted earlier in this study, are in the tense frequently preferred for translating Semitic participles. In those which follow, however, the participle was translated literally into Greek: Judg. 13:19 *ûmānôah wĕ'ištô rō'îm*, 'And Manoah and his wife *looked* on' (literally 'looking on'), LXX καὶ Μανῶε καὶ ἡ γυνὴ αὐτοῦ βλέποντες; Judg. 14:4 *ûbā'ēt hahî' pĕlištîm mōšĕlîm bĕyiśrā'ēl*, 'And in that time the Philistines *ruled* in Israel' (literally 'ruling'), LXX καὶ ἐν τῷ καιρῷ ἐκείνῳ οἱ ἀλλόφυλοι κυριεύοντες ἐν Ἰσραηλ.

While this use of the participle is found infrequently in Hebrew, the situation is the reverse in the branches of Aramaic relevant to our subject, where very frequently the participle serves as a finite verb expressing present, past or future sense.[250] In biblical Aramaic, for example, Stevenson notes 'the participle is the ordinary equivalent of a present tense'.[251] Charles and Burney cite biblical Aramaic on this point,[252] noting that in various places in the Aramaic of Dan. participles occur in the sense of ordinary finite verbs. The majority of these participles in Dan. are rendered in LXX and Theod. by the indicative. For example, Dan. 2:8 *min-yaṣṣîb yāda' 'ănah dî 'iddānâ 'antûn zābnîn*, 'Of a certainty *I know* that you are trying to gain time.' Here the participle *yāda'* appears in both LXX and Theod. as οἶδα. This mode of translating is predictable, again because Jewish Greek often uses present indicative to represent Semitic participles. What is worthy of note is that in some places a literal translation of Greek participle for Aramaic participle occurs, apparently unintentionally: Dan. 2:21f *wĕhû' mĕhašĕnē' . . . mĕha'dēh . . . ûmĕhaqêm . . . yāhēb ḥakmĕtā' . . . hû'gālē' . . . yāda'*, 'He changes . . . he removes . . . and sets up . . . he gives wisdom . . . he reveals . . . he knows', LXX καὶ αὐτὸς ἀλλοιοῖ . . . μεθιστῶν . . . καὶ καθιστῶν, διδοὺς . . . ἀνακαλύπτων . . . καὶ γινώσκων. Here the six Aramaic participles with present tense have been translated by one present indicative verb and five participles; Theod. uses four indicative verbs and two participles.

These examples illustrate that while the tendency in the LXX is to translate Hebrew participles using Greek present indicatives, yet on occasion the translators rendered participle for participle in an apparently slavish and unintentional fashion, producing the phenomenon found in NT Greek as well.

From the evidence presented, we can safely conclude that since this use of the participle is standard in Aramaic, while less common in Hebrew, wherever it occurs in the NT it can more probably be ascribed to Aramaic than to Hebrew influence. Wellhausen long ago suggested that in Mark's Gospel certain participles could best be understood as full indicatives.[253] This point has been discussed by Black,[254] and even Moulton, who stressed its existence in the papyri, conceded that the occurrences in Mark, especially in codex D, arise from literal translation from Aramaic.[255] Moule cites a few Pauline passages where the participle has the force of a finite verb,[256] but offers no explanation for the phenomenon.

Torrey,[257] followed by Lancellotti,[258] called attention to this Aramaism in the Apc. when he discussed Apc. 10:8 καὶ ἡ φωνὴ ἥν ἤκουσα ἐκ τοῦ οὐρανοῦ, πάλιν λαλοῦσαν μετ' ἐμοῦ καὶ λέγουσαν, 'then the voice which I heard from heaven again speaks to me and says'. To this I would add Apc. 4:1b καὶ ἡ φωνὴ ἡ πρώτη ἥν ἤκουσα ὡς σάλπιγγος λαλούσης μετ' ἐμοῦ λέγων, 'and the first voice which I heard speaks to me like a trumpet, saying'.[259] Scott adds Apc. 12:2 καὶ βασανιζομένη τεκεῖν and 19:11 καὶ ὁ καθήμενος ἐπ' αὐτὸν πιστὸς καλούμενος καὶ ἀληθινός (א).[260] (The other examples he cites do not properly belong here.) Torrey (p. 43) cites as a passive example Apc. 7:4 ἑκατὸν τεσσαράκοντα τέσσαρες χιλιάδες ἐσφραγισμένοι. (The other passages cited by him do not belong here.)

These passages, which are clumsy Greek, seem to be identical in nature to those noted earlier from the Greek OT, which literally rendered Semitic participles with the sense of finite verbs.

c. Indeclinable λέγων representing *lē'mōr*

In biblical Hebrew the infinitive absolute *lē'mōr* (from *'āmar*) is employed with two meanings. First, it represents in a few places only the simple meaning 'to say' of the finite verb, e.g. 2 Sam. 2:22 'And Abner *said* (*lē'mōr*) again to Asahel',[261] while its other, and best-known, meaning is as an introductory formula meaning 'as he said', 'with these words', and often best rendered simply as 'thus', or even as a pause before direct discourse, the counterpart of Greek ὅτι *recitativum*. In this role *lē'mōr* occurs some 800 times in the OT.[262]

The former usage is not surprising, since elsewhere in Hebrew the infinitive absolute appears as a finite verb,[263] while the latter usage could possibly have arisen from the tendency to follow a verb with an infinitive absolute to intensify the idea of the main verb,[264] although there is admittedly little sign of intensity in most of the verbs followed by *lē'mōr* in the OT.

Ozanne makes a misleading statement in this connection when he describes this construction as 'a pure Hebraism, there being no indigenous equivalent in Aramaic'.[265] He argues that the targumic *lĕmêmar* corresponding to *lē'mōr* is itself a Hebraism. But he should have noted that this 'Hebraism' is found not only in targumic Aramaic, but also in Ezra 5:11, at least three times in the Elephantine papyri,[266] and at least three times in non-Jewish Aramaic sources cited by Vogt in his Aramaic Lexicon.[267] All the examples mentioned are of the same nature as the category of Hebrew cases just described, and are best translated 'thus' or 'as follows'. While the basically Hebraic flavour of this usage is evident, it is only fair to recognise its existence, on a limited scale, in Aramaic.

The redundant *lē'mōr* is translated hundreds of times in the LXX by λέγων/λέγοντες/λέγουσα, which are usually indeclinable. Under the first use of the word ('to say'), *lē'mōr* is rendered by λέγων in the LXX in only a few places, for example 2 Sam. 2:22, Isa. 49:9, Zech. 7:3. All remaining occurrences are of the second category, the redundant λέγων.[268]

Both uses of λέγων are found in NT Greek.[269] The former is found in Matt. 3:2 Ἰωάννης . . . κηρύσσων καὶ λέγων, 'John . . . preaching and *saying*'; cf. Matt. 8:2 καὶ ἰδοὺ λεπρὸς . . . προσεκύνει αὐτῷ λέγων, 'a leper . . . knelt before him *and said*'.[270] The latter use, naturally, is more common so needs no illustration.

Charles and Bousset have commented on this construction, which occurs frequently in the Apc. It is rightly traced by them to Hebrew influence, but neither they nor anyone else, so far as I can determine, has distinguished between the two meanings of λέγων in NT Greek; i.e. 'to say' versus λέγων plus another verb meaning 'thus'. The following examples illustrate. First, those where the term means 'say': Apc. 5:11f καὶ ἤκουσα φωνὴν ἀγγέλων . . . λέγοντες φωνῇ μεγάλῃ, 'I heard the sound of angels . . . *say* in a great voice', 11:1 καὶ ἐδόθη μοι κάλαμος . . . λέγων, 'he gave me a reed . . . and *said*'; cf. also 1:11, 17; 4:8.[271]

The second category, in which λέγων follows another verb of saying, crying, singing, etc. is illustrated by Apc. 5:9: καὶ ἄδουσιν ᾠδὴν καινὴν λέγοντες, 'and they sing a new hymn'; cf. 6:10 καὶ ἔκραξαν φωνῇ μεγάλῃ λέγοντες, 'They cried in a loud voice.' Others include 7:2, 3, 10, 13; 14:18; 15:3; 17:1; 18:2, 15, 16, 18; 19:17; 21:9.

While there is limited evidence for similar use of λέγων in classical Greek (cf. Bl-D, §420), in the case of NT Greek both usages owe their sense to the Semitic influence of *lē'mōr*. This construction alone is not direct evidence of translation Greek though, because an expression of this nature would be quickly stereotyped in Jewish Greek.

d. Perfect passive participles

The perfect passive participle occurs with surprising frequency in the Apc.,[272] always as an attributive. While the construction in itself is acceptable Greek, it was not considered as correct as a relative clause among classical authors.[273] Others have suggested Semitic influence on the use of perfect passive participles in the Apc., and elsewhere in the NT,[274] but a systematic examination of the evidence has been lacking. According to Mussies, the perfect middle (surely he meant middle and/or passive?) participle 'reflects certainly the Semitic gerundive qatul'.[275] There is a well-established convention among LXX translators of employing the perfect passive participle for Hebrew participles, either qal passive or one of the derived conjugations. For example, the qal passive participle *kātûb* occurs 113 times in the MT according to BDB, usually in a fixed formula such as 'written in the book of the law', or similar. At least 90 of these are translated by a Greek perfect passive participle (γεγραμμένον). Many other examples could be given.

The question arises, why the *perfect* tense Greek participle? From the viewpoint of Hebrew grammar, the following comment should precede the answer: while the Hebrew adjective represents 'a fixed and permanent quality (or state)', the participle represents one which 'is in some way connected with an *action* or *activity*'.[276] The passive participle 'indicates the person or thing in a state which has been brought about by external *actions*'.[277] The answer to the question of why a *perfect* tense, is that the period of time indicated by a qal passive participle 'always corresponds to a . . . Greek perfect participle passive'.[278] So I suggest that, due to Hebrew influence, the acceptable but infrequent attributive perfect passive participle came to be used more frequently in biblical Greek. Some examples include 1 Km. 5:4 ἀφῃρημένα for *kĕrutôt* (which is translated by κατειρ-γασμένης in 3 Km. 6:36, and κεκολλαμένης in 7:49). Note the fixed expression for temple adornment and utensils: χρυσίῳ συγκεκλεισμένῳ/κατειλημμένα in 3 Km. 6:20, 2 Chr. 9:20 *et al.* for *zāhāb sāgûr.* In other words, a formal translation equivalent expresses the Hebrew qal passive participle.

For Niphal participle

The LXX, however, contains far more perfect passive participles than there are qal passive verbs in the underlying MT. Often one of the so-called Hebrew 'derived conjugation' verbs seems to be responsible. Note for example οἱ καταλελειμμένοι καὶ οἱ κεκρυμμένοι, 'those left behind and hidden', in Deut. 7:20, the Hebrew niphal participles *hannìš'ārîm wĕhannistārîm*. In Josh. 10:17 κεκρυμμένοι, 'five kings hidden' translates the niphal participle of another Hebrew verb. Identical usage is found in Apc. 2:17 τοῦ μάννα τοῦ κεκρυμμένου. In Isa. 48:1 there is another, seemingly needless, perfect tense passive participle οἱ κεκλημένοι, again for the niphal participle of *qārā'*; cf. the same form of the same verb in Apc. 19:9. Likewise in the LXX Ps. 64:7, περιεζωσμένον corresponds to the niphal participle of *'āzar* – God is 'girded with might' – cf. Apc. 1:13, where one like a Son of Man is 'girded with a golden girdle' – again, employing a perfect tense passive participle. In 3 Km. 7:2 πεπληρωμένος translates a niphal imperfect verb (MT 7:14); note similar usage in the very Hebraic phrase of Apc. 3:2 πεπληρωμένα ἐνώπιον τοῦ θεοῦ.

For pual participle

Περιβεβλημένοι in 1 Chr. 21:16, 'clothed, covered with', translates pual participle of *kāsâ* which in qal/qal passive has a slightly different sense, 'to conceal/be put out of sight'. In Apc. 7:9 the sense of the pual form of the verb is demanded – the great company are *clothed* – περιβεβλημένους. Likewise also Apc. 10:1, 11:3, 17:4, 18:16, 19:13 follow the same pattern.

In Ex. 26:32 κεχρυσωμένων translates pual participle of *ṣāpâ*; note its usage in two of the passages above, Apc. 17:4, 18:16. Elsewhere the LXX uses perfect passive participle to translate pual, as in 3 Km. 7:47, Canticles 5:15, and Ex. 28:20.

For hophal participle

Γῆς ἠρημωμένης in Ezek. 29:12, 'desolated land', is the translation of the hophal participle of *hārēb*, 'laid waste'. The same participle is found in Apc. 17:16. The construction there, ἠρημωμένην ποιήσουσιν, is not Greek, but represents the hophal participle found in Ezek. 29:12, expressing the causative sense of becoming laid waste, with the additional strength of expression provided by the following ποιήσουσιν, giving a very forceful statement of the harlot's grim fate. The weaker sense of the qal stative, 'to be desolate', is inadequate for describing this development. Here again the full force of the passage is felt when the perfect passive participle is understood as a pointer to an underlying hophal verb. This occurs elsewhere in the LXX: Ex. 26:30 τὸ δεδειγμένον; 26:31 νενησμένης; 26:36 κεκλωσμένης (a fixed expression recurring frequently in Ex.).

If the observations here are sound, that Hebrew qal passive participles
and the passive participles of the derived conjugations have influenced
the perfect passive participles in biblical Greek, and especially the Apc.,
what conclusions for syntax and interpretation can be drawn? First, that
one should not insist on finding a precise temporal relationship between
the participle and main verb such as is found in classical Greek. Second
that a close relation between subject and external actions is implied. Without knowing the evidence for Hebraic influence cited in this study, Turner
stated it well: 'It is here . . . that a difference from classical Greek is apparent: there was a distinct tendency in the Hellenistic period to connect
very closely a past action with its present consequences . . . Hence the perfect where classical Greek would have aorist.'[279] It is significant that both
NT examples employed to illustrate his point are *passive* perfect participles – Matt. 5:10 οἱ δεδιωγμένοι and 1 Cor. 1:23 Χριστὸν ἐσταυρωμένον.
Or, in the words from GK cited above, 'a state which has been brought
about by external actions'.[280] Seen in this light, each of the sixty plus
perfect passive participles in the Apc. invites the reader to ask about the
'state' of the subject, and equally important, about the source, nature and
significance of 'external actions' so closely bound up with the subject.
Significant exegetical possibilities could emerge by following this pro-
cedure.

e. Perfect and pluperfect of ἵστημι

It should be noted that the occurrences of the perfect and pluperfect of
ἵστημι in Apc. are probably influenced by Hebrew usage. The Seer employs
the verb at least fifteen times (the pluperfect εἰστήκεισαν in 7:11; the
remainder perfect indicative or perfect participle: ἔστηκεν in 12:4, etc.
and ἑστηκός in 5:6, etc.). The same forms of ἵστημι are found very frequently in the LXX, nearly always for ʿōmēd. For example, pluperfect
(παρ-) εἰστήκει (Gen. 18:8), perfect ἔστηκας (Ex. 3:5), perfect participle
ἑστῶτα (Ex. 33:10).

From this evidence it seems unnecessary to appeal as Mussies has done
to any particular new Greek stem.[281]

f. Participles used as relative clauses[282]

Participles with or without definite articles were widely used in both Greek
and Hebrew for relative clauses. Many were substantival participles, such
as the well-known Johannine ὁ πιστεύων εἰς ἐμέ 'He *who believes* (literally
'the believing one') in me'.[283] As would be expected for a construction

well-rooted in both Hebrew and Greek (but not Aramaic²⁸⁴) there is considerable discussion as to whether the many occurrences in the NT owe
their existence to Semitic or Hellenic influence. Beyer's elaborate discussion of the phenomenon is especially rich in Semitic examples.²⁸⁵ He
analyses NT occurrences of this type of participle according to the following categories, corresponding to their Hebrew equivalents, and draws the
following conclusions: (a) The participle as subject of the main clause.
This is by far the most common in Hebrew and in the NT. The likelihood
of Semitic influence is increased, he feels, when the participle is preceded
by πᾶς (*kōl*), as in Matt. 5:22 πᾶς ὁ ὀργιζόμενος τῷ ἀδελφῷ αὐτοῦ. (b)
The participle as object of the main clause. Here he notes that in Hebrew
the participle is very rarely found when it is not the subject of the main
clause. Thus if there is good reason to suppose an Aramaic origin, this construction could be a primary indication of the Aramaic relative clause.²⁸⁶
(c) The participle which precedes the main clause as *casus pendens*. This
refers to the Hebrew substantival participle, which often precedes the
clause and is resumed later by a suffix. The literal Greek rendering of this
would employ the corresponding form of αὐτός as a resumptive demonstrative pronoun. The LXX translates this, for example, in Gen. 9:6 ὁ ἐκχέων
αἷμα ἀνθρώπου ἀντὶ τοῦ αἵματος αὐτοῦ ἐκχυθήσεται. NT constructions in
this class are definitely under Hebrew influence, although the possibility of
Aramaic is not excluded, since the Greek participle could be a rendering of
an Aramaic relative clause. These occurrences are usually best translated
'when somebody', cf. Matt. 5:40 ὁ θέλων (D) σοι κριθῆναι καὶ τὸν χιτῶνα
σοῦ λαβεῖν, ἄφες αὐτῷ καὶ τὸ ἱμάτιον, '*when somebody would* sue you and
take your shirt, let him have your coat as well'.

From the Apc. Beyer cites examples in the following categories: (a) Participle as subject of main clause: Apc. 2:11*b* ὁ νικῶν οὐ μὴ ἀδικηθῇ ἐκ τοῦ
θανάτου τοῦ δευτέρου, '*The conqueror* shall not be hurt by the second
death' (i.e. 'he who conquers'); 3:5 ὁ νικῶν οὕτως περιβαλεῖται ἐν ἱματίοις
λευκοῖς, 'The conqueror shall be clad thus in white garments.' Here Charles
would add 11:10 οἱ κατοικοῦντες ἐπὶ τῆς γῆς and 19:9 Μακάριοι οἱ ...
κεκλημένοι; 22:17 καὶ ὁ ἀκούων εἰπάτω, Ἔρχου καὶ διψῶν ἐρχέσθω ὁ
θέλων λαβέτω ὕδωρ ζωῆς δωρεάν, 'and *the one hearing*, let (him) say,
come, and *the one thirsting*, come, and *the one desiring* (let him) take the
water of life freely'. (b) The participle as (indirect) object of the main
clause: Apc. 2:7*b* τῷ νικῶντι δώσω αὐτῷ φαγεῖν ἐκ τοῦ ξύλου τῆς ζωῆς,
'*to the overcomer* I will grant to eat of the tree of life'; 21:6 ἐγὼ τῷ
διψῶντι δώσω ἐκ τῆς πηγῆς τοῦ ὕδατος τῆς ζωῆς, '*to the thirsting one*
I will give water from the fountain of life'. (c) The participle which stands
before the main clause as *casus pendens* (a very Hebraic characteristic²⁸⁷):

Apc. 2:26 ὁ νικῶν καὶ τηρῶν ἄχρι τέλους τὰ ἔργα μου, δώσω αὐτῷ
ἐξουσίαν ἐπὶ τῶν ἐθνῶν, '*He who conquers* and *keeps* my works to the
end, to *him* will I give'; 3:12 τῷ νικῶν ποιήσω αὐτὸν στῦλον, '*He who
conquers*, I will make *him*'; 3:21 ὁ νικῶν δώσω αὐτῷ καθίσαι μετ' ἐμοῦ,
'*He who conquers*, I will grant *him* to sit with me'; 21:7 ὁ νικῶν (αὐτὸς
syr^ph) κληρονομήσει ταῦτα, '*He who conquers, he* shall inherit these
things.'[288]

Lancellotti, who also discusses the use of the participle in place of a
relative clause,[289] makes a very strong case for its Hebraic nature. His
point is strained because his desire to support his thesis of a Hebrew sub-
stratum for the Apc.[290] leads him to push the Hebrew evidence on this
point to the neglect of Aramaic and even Hellenistic Greek influence.
Instead of attempting to explain the many participles in the Apc. that
are used as relative clauses as due solely to Hebrew influence, it would be
safer to admit that while this explanation is likely, it is not conclusive nor
can it be proven in every case.

Even the fact that Aramaic usually preferred a relative clause where
Hebrew would have employed a participle does not exclude Aramaic
influence, contrary to Lancellotti,[291] since it is possible that Aramaic relative clauses, especially where they underlie Gospel passages, were translated by Greek participles. The fact that in the LXX a participle can be
used even when the Hebrew text does not employ a participle should be
fair indication that in Hellenistic Greek this usage existed in its own right.
Otherwise, remarks Beyer,[292] the 266 substantival participles used relatively in the NT, if understood as literal translations from a Semitic language, would have to be taken as representing exclusively Hebrew originals,
not Aramaic! This conclusion, obviously, is not convincing.

g. Atemporal participles

One notable distinction between Hebrew and Greek participles is seen in
their roles of expressing relative time. While Greek participles have their
own designation for time, which is indicated by the tense in which they
occur, there is no Semitic equivalent. S.R. Driver describes the Hebrew
participle, for example, in the following terms: 'In itself it expresses no
difference of time, the nature of the "tenses" not favouring, as in Greek,
the growth of a separate form corresponding to each; and the period to
which an action denoted by it is to be referred, is implied, not in the participle, but in the connection in which it occurs.'[293] We find Hebrew participles used of past, present and future time with no alteration of form, in
sharp contrast to their Greek counterparts.

(i) Atemporal substantival and adjectival participles

The mark which this distinction has left on biblical Greek is pointed out by Zerwick,[294] who calls attention to the use of the present tense participle ὁ βαπτίζων to describe John 'The Baptizer', even after his death. In the Pauline epistles also, such usage appears, e.g. in Phil. 3:6 Paul describes himself as διώκων τὴν ἐκκλησίαν and in 1 Thess. 1:10 Jesus is called ὁ ῥυόμενος ἡμᾶς ἐκ τῆς ὀργῆς, 'the one who delivered us', although the atemporal flavour of the participle may be intentional in this passage to stress the timelessness of deliverance.

In the Apc. Lancellotti finds this use (or misuse) in 3:12, where a present participle expresses a future sense: ὁ νικῶν ποιήσω αὐτὸν στῦλον, 'He who conquers (literally 'shall conquer') I shall make a pillar.'[295] Charles sees similar usage in 15:2 καὶ τοὺς νικῶντας ἐκ τοῦ θηρίου, 'and those who have overcome the beast'. Here he prefers to take the participle as expressing perfect tense.[296]

(ii) Atemporal circumstantial participles

Here again we refer to the fundamental distinction between Hebrew/Aramaic participles and their Greek counterparts. Thus, the relationship between a circumstantial participle and its main verb in Semitic languages is not temporal – that is, no sequence of events is expressed in which the action of the participle can be said to occur either before, simultaneously with, or after that of the main verb. The participle merely provides additional information about the action or state of the main verb. This is clearly seen in Canticles 2:8, where the participles *leaping* and *bounding* clarify the manner in which the young man approaches. Even a passage such as Nu. 16:27 'Dathan and Abiram came out, *standing*', which could be made to read paratactically 'came out and (then) *stood*', thus expressing a temporal relation, is best understood as purely circumstantial; to impose a sequence of chronological order is foreign to the nature of the Semitic construction. Classical Greek, however, employs the circumstantial participle to express precisely the temporal relationship. W.W. Goodwin notes that 'The tenses of the participle generally express time present, past or future relatively to the time of the verb with which they are connected.'[297] An aorist participle would then represent an action as past in reference to its main verb, a present participle would represent action occurring at the same time as its main verb, etc. While these categories of time are not totally inflexible, exceptions in classical Greek are so rare that when they do occur, they require special comment.

The aorist circumstantial participle in the NT is a striking exception in numerous places where it expresses not the customary past action, but action occurring at the same time as its main verb, or even following it in time.[298] The most disputed passage in the NT is Acts 25:13:[299] Ἀγρίππας ὁ βασιλεὺς καὶ Βερνίκη κατήντησαν εἰς Καισάρειαν ἀσπασάμενοι τὸν Φῆστον, 'Agrippa the king and Bernice arrived in Caesarea, *greeting* Festus.' The variant ἀσπασόμενοι is an obvious emendation to bring the passage into line with Greek syntax, the greeting thus following the arriving. These main positions have been held regarding this principle: (a) it indeed expresses an action which follows the main verb, contrary to Greek practice (so Burton and Howard); (b) it makes an additional assertion or modification of the act of the main verb, a usage foreign to classical Greek syntax, but found often in the NT (so Ballantine); (c) it expresses an act simultaneous with the main verb, which in classical Greek would be expressed by the present tense participle (so Moulton and Robertson); (d) the most candid admission, from no less an authority on Greek syntax than Blass, is that this use of the *aorist* participle 'is not Greek', meaning that the construction is not original.[300] But we prefer a different explanation, suggesting that the Semitic mode of employing a circumstantial participle, as discussed in this section, offers a plausible explanation for the timelessness of this and other circumstantial participles in the NT. As noted already, the Semitic construction was devoid of the idea of temporal relationship, ascribing rather additional circumstances to the main verb. Such an influence on ἀσπασάμενοι in the passage in Acts 25:13 would remove the difficulty of explaining how an aorist participle expresses an act which in fact should follow its main verb. The observation that these unusual aorist participles abound just in the NT[301] would also be more understandable if their existence were traceable to an underlying Semitic sense of the participle; likewise it would remove the objection that the temporal order of events is incorrect.

In the Apc.

In each case the tense of the participle does not coincide with that of the main verb, as would be expected in Greek: Apc. 7:1 εἶδον τέσσαρας ἀγγέλους ἑστῶτας . . . κρατοῦντας, 'I saw seven angels stand [taking the participle as an indicative, under Semitic influence] . . . *holding* (the four winds)'; 14:15 καὶ ἄλλος ἄγγελος ἐξῆλθεν . . . κράζων ἐν φωνῇ μεγάλῃ, 'and another angel came out . . . crying in a loud voice'; 18:15 οἱ ἔμποροι . . . στήσονται . . . κλαίοντες καὶ πενθοῦντες, 'the merchants . . . shall stand . . . weeping and mourning'; verse 18 καὶ ἔκραξον βλέποντες 'and they cried, seeing'.

h. The circumstantial accusative participle[302]

C.C. Torrey has drawn attention to what he designates as the 'adverbial' accusative use of the participle in the Apc., which is based on Semitic usage.[303] An illustration he cites is Apc. 7:9 ὄχλος . . . ἐστῶτες ἐνώπιον τοῦ θρόνου . . . περιβεβλημένους στολὰς λευκάς,[304] 'a multitude . . . standing before the throne . . . *clothed* in white garments'. Here a condition of the subject is expressed by an appended passive participle *in the accusative case*! Why? Hebrew grammarians recognise the adverbial accusative use of the participle to describe the manner in which an action or a state takes place.[305] These participles can be placed after the main verbs, as in the following cases: Nu. 16:27 *wĕdotān wĕ'ăbîrām yāṣ'û niṣṣebîm petaḥ 'ohā-lêkem*, 'Then Dathan and Abiram came out, *standing* at the opening of their tents'; Jer. 2:26f *kēn hōbîšû bēt yiśrā'ēl . . . 'ōmrîn lĕ'ēṣ 'abî 'attâ*, 'The house of Israel shall be ashamed . . . *saying* to a tree, "you are my father".' Cf. Ps. 7:3 'Lest like a lion they rend me, *dragging (pōrēq)* me away'; Job 24:5 'like a wild ass in the desert they go forth to their toil, *seeking (mĕšahărê)* prey'.

These passages, employing the *accusative* participle in subordination to the main verb, illustrate what is known as the looser subordination of the accusative to the verb.[306] They differ from the ordinary accusative of the direct object[307] by specifying not the object of the verb in question, but some more immediate circumstance affecting the action, such as place, time, measure, cause, or manner. The part of speech subordinated in this fashion may be a noun, an adjective, or, of special interest at this point, a participle.[308]

The circumstantial participle usually follows its main verb as in the Hebrew passages just cited. It can also precede the main verb: Gen. 44:11 *'Tying ('ōsĕrî)* his foal to the vine . . . he washes his garments in wine'; Ps. 56:2 'all day long *making war (lōḥēm)* they oppress me'.

The construction is found in biblical Aramaic: Dan. 2:22 *hû' gālē' 'ammîqātā' ûmĕsattĕrātā yāda' mâ baḥăšôkā'*, 'He reveals deep and mysterious things, *knowing* what is in the darkness'; Dan. 3:3 *bē'dayin mit-kanšîn . . . wĕqā'mîn lāqābēl ṣalmā'*, 'Then they were assembled . . . and *stood* (literally 'standing') before the image.' It should be noted that where the Targum of these Hebrew examples is available (i.e. Nu. 16:27, Jer. 2:26f, it also employs the circumstantial participle, a literal rendering of the Hebrew original.

While it is true that in Hebrew the case-endings have disappeared, it is generally agreed that Hebrew, like Assyrian and classical Arabic,[309] has three cases, with some remains of the case endings. Therefore the fact that the cases of the nouns, adjectives and participles loosely subordinated to the verb are accusative can be seen first from the fact that in some cases the *nota accusativi* ('*et*) is prefixed; secondly, that on certain occasions the old accusative termination (-*â*) is employed; thirdly, in classical Arabic these constructions are consistently set in the accusative.[310] On this basis Torrey argues that 'in an inflected Semitic language, as regularly in Arabic, such a participle would be shown as accusative; and where there is no inflection, as in Hebrew, this construction, the "adverbial" accusative, is recognized by grammarians'.[311] Other examples from the Apc. include 11:3: καὶ προφητεύσουσιν . . . περιβεβλημένους (ℵ*AP 046: -μενοι C); cf. 10:8: καὶ ἡ φωνὴ ἣν ἤκουσα . . . πάλιν λαλούσαν μετ᾽ ἐμοῦ καὶ λέγουσαν. Here Ozanne states that the force of ἤκουσα is carried over into the second part of the sentence,[312] and accordingly the two participles are adverbial/circumstantial in character. The Hebraism was here induced by attraction to ἤν.

Perhaps the simplest and strongest objection which has been raised against this alleged Semitism is that it is merely a solecism, a 'hanging accusative'[313] in the case of Apc. 7:9, which has been attracted to εἶδον. In fact, Turner has drawn attention to a similar (mis)use of the nominative and genitive circumstantial participles.[314] Nowhere in the Greek OT, however, have I found such a literal translation of a circumstantial accusative participle, so its use in Apc. cannot be justified by referring to a *conventional* translation equivalent. But even though unsupported by evidence from translation Greek, Torrey's explanation, that this un-Greek use of the accusative participle in the Apc. is due to Semitic influence, is not contradicted by the evidence assembled here. If accepted, it would defend the Seer against the accusation of committing a solecism at this point.

i. Participle for Hebrew infinitive absolute

Thoroughly Hebraic is the addition of an infinitive absolute to the finite verb to strengthen the verbal idea: *běkû bākô*, 'weep bitterly!'[315] Its influence on biblical Greek has been widely discussed because of the 'distortions' it produces when translated.[316] It has long been viewed as a feature of the classical period of Hebrew and is said to be absent from Mishnaic Hebrew,[317] and, with few exceptions, from Aramaic.[318] This means that wherever the NT reflects the infinitive absolute, it points to underlying Hebrew, not Aramaic, influence, and OT Hebrew at that! But is this construction more-or-less exclusively Hebraic? More precisely, is it absent from Palestinian Aramaic? Two recent challenges have arisen to the

accepted position. The first, admittedly tentative, is by Mussies,[319] who
suggested that since the infinitive absolute 'was absent from Mishnaic
Hebrew but frequent in Aramaic', its possible presence in several passages
in the Apc. points to Aramaic influence. But this suggestion cannot be
taken seriously, since it seems based on a misunderstanding both of a foot-
note in Segal's *Mishnaic Hebrew Grammar*,[320] and of the Aramaic language!
A more authoritative challenge is made by Fitzmyer, who implies the
occurrence of an infinitive absolute in the Aramaic of the *Genesis Apocryphon*, 20:10f. If so, then his discovery, in his own words, 'contrasts the
remarks of G. Dalman . . . and M. Black', about the exclusively Hebraic
influence behind the construction in the NT.[321]

But what Fitzmyer refers to is not, strictly speaking, an infinitive absolute at all. In the passage *wbkyt 'nh 'brm bky tqyp* (literally, 'But I Abram
wept a strong weeping') the main verb *bkyt* is strengthened *not* by a following infinitive absolute at all – there is none in the passage. Rather, it
concludes with the noun *bky/bk'* modified by the adjective *taqqîp*,
'strong'. The expression is the Aramaic equivalent to biblical Hebrew *bākâ
běkî gādôl*, found in Judg. 21:2, 2 Sam. 13:36, 2 Ki. 20:3, Isa. 38:3, and
called 'internal' or 'absolute object'. It serves the same purpose as the
infinitive absolute – intensifying the verb. But instead of attaching an
infinitive of the same stem to the verb, the absolute object consists of a
noun from the same stem as the verb to which it is subordinated.[322] In
some cases an adjective – such as *gādôl* – is added for intensity. This form
of the absolute object with *gādôl* is found about a dozen times in the
Hebrew OT, roughly one half of them occurring in the prophets and the
book of Daniel. Fitzmyer's discovery of this 'absolute object' simply confirms that it is Aramaic, as well as Hebraic; it in no way alters the fact
that the intensifying function of the infinitive absolute is a feature limited
to biblical Hebrew, and to Aramaic OT translations.

The discussion by Mussies[323] of the influence of the infinitive absolute
on the Apc. does not consider this 'absolute object' construction; thus his
comments on the five passages (not four, as he states) where he alleges this
occurs in the Apc., are inadequate. Apc. 16:9 καὶ ἐκαυματίσθησαν . . .
καῦμα μέγα and 17:6 καὶ ἐθαύμασα . . . θαῦμα μέγα are cognates accusative,
identical to LXX literal translations of the Hebrew absolute object (illustrated by LXX Gen. 12:17; Judg. 16:23; 1 Ki. 17:25; Zech. 1:2, 14, 15;
8:2; Dan. 11:2). This is a recognised NT Semitism, although it is found in
classical Greek as well.[324] The remaining three passages are true examples
of the OT Hebrew infinitive absolute, *viz.* Apc. 3:17, 6:2, 18:6. Apc. 6:2
ἐξῆλθεν νικῶν καὶ ἵνα νικήσῃ, as it stands, is neither Hebrew nor Greek. A
slight emendation, into ἐξῆλθεν ἵνα νικῶν καὶ νικήσῃ would yield 'he depar-

ted, in order that he might thoroughly conquer', bringing it into line with the most frequently-employed Greek form of the infinitive absolute in the LXX (where it is translated by a participle 171 times[325]). Apc. 18:6 διπλώσατε τὰ διπλᾶ, with the verb followed by an adjective from the same stem, is according to Charles, 'an extraordinary expression'.[326] This combination of verb plus adjective is also found in 3:17 πλούσιός εἰμι καὶ πεπλούτηκα. Both of these have been attributed to Hebrew infinitive absolute influence, but without supporting evidence. But the evidence is available in the form of one example in the LXX, where the infinitive absolute was also translated by an *adjective* plus verb:[327] Nu. 13:30(31) δυνατοὶ δυνασόμεθα (yākôl nûkal).

Even without resorting to the emendation suggested for 6:2 above, one can safely argue that the construction in all three passages owes its existence to the *biblical* Hebrew infinitive absolute. The construction does not appear in the portions of the LXX originating in Greek,[328] and elsewhere in the NT it occurs only in LXX translations.[329] Thus its appearance in the Apc. points unmistakably in the direction of OT Hebrew, not a later form of the language, as the pattern on which the Seer relied.

Summary of chapter 3, section 7

The resolution of a participle into a finite verb, along Hebraic lines, has been given considerable attention by a wide range of scholars as one of the best-attested Hebraisms in the Apc. When employed in biblical Greek as a finite verb, the participle reflects the well-established custom of Aramaic (and to some extent, Hebrew), but at the same time goes against the usage preferred in Hellenistic Greek. This speaks loudly, wherever it occurs in NT Greek, for quite direct Aramaic influence.

While the Hebraic nature of indeclinable λέγων has long been acknowledged, this study is apparently the first to distinguish the two meanings of the construction, *viz.* 'to say', versus λέγων plus a verb of saying, crying out, etc., meaning 'thus'. Both uses reflect Hebrew OT constructions, but should not, where they occur in the Apc. be used to argue for direct Hebrew influence since such usage would early have become stylised in biblical Greek.

Due to Hebrew influence the perfect passive participle, which in secular Greek is acceptable but infrequent in its use as an attributive, came to be used much more frequently. Explanation for this has been sought in Hebrew usage, where for attributive purposes a distinction of exegetical importance exists between an ordinary adjective, which represents a *fixed* state or quality, and a participle, which implies that the state or quality has been brought about in some way by action or activity. According to evidence from the LXX, the choice of *perfect* tense was influenced by one of two separate factors: the first was the suitability of the perfect tense for designating the same time period as the qal passive participle in the underlying Hebrew. The second and wholly independent factor is that of an underlying Hebrew participle in one of the derived conjugations, such as niphal, pual or hophal, where the meaning of the derived form of the verb differs considerably from its qal form. Here, the perfect tense would signal to the reader that the meaning of the 'derived' form of the participle was intended.

The addition to the subject of a circumstantial participle in the grammatically unacceptable accusative case in the Apc. reflects the Hebrew and Aramaic adverbial accusative use of the participle to describe the manner in which an action or state takes place. This over-literal Semitism, avoided in the LXX, seems to be employed deliberately in the Apc. in order to impress upon the reader the 'biblical' nature of the Seer's language.

The final point of Hebrew influence on biblical Greek participles to be examined here is the translation of infinitives absolute by Greek participles. The construction is frequent enough in the LXX, and occurs a few times in the Apc., though not always using participles. The construction is limited to OT Hebrew, thus pointing exclusively to influence from that direction. Recent attempts to establish it as an Aramaism have not succeeded.

4

SEMITIC INFLUENCE ON THE CLAUSE IN THE APOCALYPSE

Basic to the structure of the Hebrew and Aramaic languages and that of Semitic languages generally is the distinction between noun and verbal clauses or sentences. A noun clause, according to the standard grammarians,[1] has as both subject and predicate a *noun* or its equivalent (especially participles), e.g. Isa. 33:22 *Yahweh malkēnû*, 'Yahweh [is] our king'. A verbal clause on the other hand *always* contains a finite verb as predicate, and a noun or pronoun for its subject, e.g. Gen. 1:3 *wĕyyō'mer 'ēlōhîm*, 'and God *said*'.

This basic distinction between noun and verbal clauses is not of merely technical interest, but has an important role to play in expressing meaning, and according to Gesenius-Kautzsch,[2] 'is indispensable to the more delicate appreciation of Hebrew syntax . . . since it is by no means merely external or formal, but involves fundamental differences of meaning. Noun-clauses with a substantive as predicate represent something *fixed, a state* or in short, *a being* so and so; verbal clauses on the other hand, something *movable* and *in progress*, an *event* or *action*.'

After noting this important point of Semitic syntax, one is led to inquire whether a distinction of such basic significance in the OT left its mark on biblical Greek. In answering this query, the noun clause will be considered first, followed by the verbal clause.

1. Noun clauses

a. Noun clauses in the OT

As just noted, a noun clause contains no finite verb, but has as both its subject and predicate a noun or its equivalent. It stresses the subject's state of being, its existence, its attributes, always in the sense of a fixed state.[3]

All Hebrew noun clauses fall into one of seven categories, depending on the type of nominal construction which serves as predicate; e.g. (1)

with substantive for the predicate; (2) with adjective for predicate; (3) with participles for predicate; (4) with numerals for predicate; (5) with pronouns for predicate; (6) with adverbs for predicate; (7) with any other construction such as prepositional phrase, for predicate. Under each of these categories representative Hebrew/Aramaic examples will be cited, with the LXX translation following, where it shows a literal rendering into Greek of the Semitic nominal construction: (1) With substantive for predicate (this mode of expression is characterised by Gesenius–Kautzsch as 'especially Semitic'): Gen. 5:1 *zeh sēper tôldôt 'ādām*, 'This book [is] the generation of mankind'; LXX Αὕτη ἡ βίβλος γενέσεως ἀνθρώπων. Isa. 33:22 κριτὴς ἡμῶν κύριος = *Yahweh šōpēṭēnû*; ἄρχων ἡμῶν κύριος = *Yahweh mēhōqqēnû*; βασιλεὺς ἡμῶν κύριος = *Yahweh malkēnû*. (2) With adjective for predicate: Ezek. 41:22b *wĕqîrōtayû 'ēṣ*, 'its walls [were] of wood'; LXX καὶ οἱ τοῖχοι αὐτοῦ ξύλινοι (adjective). Gen. 2:12 *ûzăhab hā'areṣ hahî' ṭôb*, 'and the gold of that land [is] good'; LXX τὸ δὲ χρυσίον τῆς γῆς ἐκείνης καλόν. Gen. 13:13 *wĕ'anšê sĕdōm rā'îm wĕhaṭṭā'îm*, 'The men of Sodom [were] evil and sinners'; LXX οἱ δὲ ἄνθρωποι οἱ ἐν Σοδομοις πονηροὶ καὶ ἁμαρτωλοί. (3) With participle for predicate: Gen. 24:1 *wĕ'abraham ... bā' bayyāmîm*, 'And Abraham ... [was] advancing in days'; LXX καὶ Αβρααμ ... προβεβηκὼς ἡμέρων. Gen. 2:11 *hû' hassōbēb 'et kol-'eres*, 'it [is] the one flowing around the whole land'; LXX οὗτος ὁ κυκλῶν πᾶσαν τὴν γῆν. (4) With a numeral for predicate: Gen. 42:12a *šĕnêm 'āśār 'ăbadeykā*, 'the twelve (of us) [are] thy servants'; LXX δώδεκά ἐσμεν οἱ παῖδές σου. (5) With a pronoun for predicate: Gen. 2:4 *'ēlleh tôldôt*, 'these [are] the generations'; LXX Αὕτη ἡ βίβλος γενέσεως. (6) With an adverb for predicate: Ps. 136(135):1f *lĕ'ôlām ḥasdô*, 'His mercy [is] forever'; LXX εἰς τὸν αἰῶνα τὸ ἔλεος αὐτοῦ. (7) Another construction (usually a prepositional phrase) for predicate: Gen. 42:13b *haqqāṭōn 'et-'ābînû hayyôm*, 'The youngest [is] now with our father'; LXX ὁ νεώτερος μετὰ πατρὸς ἡμῶν σήμερον. Gen. 1:1 *wĕhōšek 'al-pĕnê tēhôm*, 'and darkness [was] upon the deep'; LXX καὶ σκότος ἐπάνω τῆς ἀβύσσου.

b. Noun clauses in the Apc.

The categories listed above are repeated here, with examples from the Apc. in each.[4] (1) With substantive for predicate (especially Semitic); Apc. 19:12 οἱ δὲ ὀφθαλμοὶ ... φλόξ (if ὡς is omitted); 20:5 αὕτη ἡ ἀνάστασις; 21:18a καὶ ἡ ἐνδώμησις ... ἴασπις; 21:18b καὶ ἡ πόλις χρυσίον; 21:21b καὶ ἡ πλατεῖα ... χρυσίον; 21:22b ὁ γὰρ κύριος ὁ Θεὸς ... ναὸς αὐτῆς (-εστιν 104* 459 al); 21:23b καὶ ὁ λύχνος αὐτῆς τὸ ἀρνίον; 22:13 ἐγώ τὸ ἄλφα καὶ τὸ ὦ, ὁ πρῶτος καὶ ὁ ἔσχατος. In addition, several examples could be listed which include the copula but, just as in the examples cited above from the LXX, are essentially noun clauses: Apc. 17:9 αἱ ἑπτὰ κεφαλαὶ ἑπτὰ ὄρη εἰσίν . . . καὶ βασιλεῖς ἑπτὰ εἰσιν. Cf. verse 12 καὶ τὰ δέκα κέρατα . . . δέκα βασιλεῖς εἰσιν; 17:15 τὰ ὕδατα . . . λαοὶ καὶ ὄχλοι εἰσὶν καὶ ἔθνη; 17:18 καὶ ἡ γυνή . . . ἔστιν ἡ πόλις ἡ μεγάλη. (2) With adjective for predicate: Apc. 1:3 ὁ γὰρ καιρὸς ἔγγυς; 14:13 μακάριοι οἱ νεκροί; 15:3 μεγάλα καὶ θαυμαστὰ τὰ ἔργα σου . . . δίκαιαι καὶ ἀληθιναὶ αἱ ὁδοί σου; 16:7b ἀληθιναὶ καὶ δίκαιαι αἱ κρίσεις σου; 18:8 ὅτι ἰσχυρὸς κύριος ὁ θεός; 19:2 identical to 16:7b above; 19:9a μακάριοι οἱ . . . κεκλημένοι. Add also 20:6; 21:16b, c, 19; 22:6. Cf. 19:11 ὁ καθήμενος ἐπ'αὐτὸν πιστὸς . . . καὶ ἀληθινός (‭א‬). (3) With participle for predicate: Apc. 1:16 ῥομφαία δίστομος ὀξεῖα ἐκπορευομένη; 2:17 ὄνομα καινὸν γεγραμμένον; 4.1 καὶ ἰδοὺ θύρα ἠνεῳγμένη; 4:5 καὶ ἑπτὰ λαμπάδες πυρὸς καιόμεναι; 12:1 γυνὴ περιβεβλημένη τὸν ἥλιον; 5:1 Βιβλίον γεγραμμένον . . . κατεσφαγισμένον; 14:4 οὗτοι οἱ ἀκολουθοῦντες τῷ ἀρνίῳ; 17:4 καὶ ἡ γυνὴ ἦν (ἡ Koine) περιβεβλημένη . . . καὶ κεχρυσωμένη . . . ἔχουσα; 21:19a οἱ θεμέλιοι . . . κεκοσμημένοι; 22:7b μακάριος ὁ τηρῶν; 22:8 Κἀγὼ Ἰωάννης ὁ ἀκούων καὶ βλέπων ταῦτα; 22:14 Μακάριοι οἱ πλύνοντες τὰς στολὰς; (4) A numeral for predicate: Apc. 13:18b καὶ ὁ ἀριθμὸς αὐτοῦ ἑξακόσιοι ἑξήκοντα ἕξ 'Six hundred sixty-six [is] his number.' (5) A pronoun for predicate: Apc. 1:6 αὐτῷ ἡ δόξα καὶ τὸ κράτος; 20:14 οὗτος ὁ θάνατος ὁ δεύτερος ἐστίν (-εστιν 104 680 1380), 'this is the second death'; 11:4 οὗτοι εἰσιν αἱ δύο ἐλαῖαι καὶ αἱ δύο λυχνίαι 'these [are] the two olive trees and the two lamps'. (6) An adverb for predicate: Apc. 14:12a ὧδε ἡ ὑπομονὴ τῶν ἁγίων ἐστιν (-εστιν 808 1893), 'here [is] the patience of the saints; 17:9 ὧδε ὁ νοῦς, 'here [is] the mind'. (7) Other constructions for predicate (usually prepositional phrases): Apc. 12:1 ἡ σελήνη ὑποκάτω τῶν ποδῶν αὐτῆς; 21:3b ἰδοὺ ἡ σκηνὴ τοῦ Θεοῦ μετὰ τῶν ἀνθρώπων; 21:3 καὶ αὐτὸς ὁ Θεὸς μετ' αὐτῶν ἔσται; 21:8 τὸ μέρος αὐτῶν ἐν τῇ λίμνῃ τῇ καιομένῃ πυρὶ καὶ θείῳ; 22:2b καὶ τοῦ ποταμοῦ ἐντεῦθεν καὶ ἐκεῖθεν ξύλον ζωῆς; 22:2c καὶ τὰ φύλλα τοῦ ξυλου εἰς θεραπείαν τῶν ἐθνῶν; 22:4b τὸ ὄνομα αὐτοῦ ἐπὶ τῶν μετώπων αὐτῶν; 22:12 ὁ μισθὸς μου μετ' ἐμοῦ; 22:15 ἔξω οἱ κύνες καὶ οἱ φαρμακοὶ καὶ οἱ πόρνοι.

While scattered references can be found in both Bl-D and Moulton–Turner to Semitic influence on specific, narrow aspects of certain types of nominal phrases in NT Greek,[5] neither they nor any other grammarians, so far as I am able to determine, have explained these as Semitic noun clauses in Greek dress. This correspondence appears to be close and widespread, and the fact that there is simply no phenomenon elsewhere in *Koine* Greek of quite the same order as the noun clause in the LXX and NT seems to exclude the possibility that the point under discussion simply underwent parallel but unconnected development in the two languages involved.

The recognition of the existence of these Semitic noun and verbal clauses in biblical Greek, with their basic distinction in sense and meaning, calls for a re-evaluation of many scriptural passages where such clauses occur, to determine what implications their presence might have for both translation and exegesis.

c. Noun clauses with copula in the OT

Note that in Hebrew a true noun clause may contain the copula *hāyâ* without surrendering its essential nominal quality. For example, in Gen. 1:2 we read 'and the earth *was* (*hāytā'*) waste and emptiness'; this cannot be regarded as a verbal clause, since *hāytā'* expresses past time, not a sense of action or progress. The clause would have identical meaning if the verb were omitted. The two conditions under which *hāyâ* can occur in a true noun clause are if: (1) *hāyâ* itself retains no verbal force of its own in the sense 'to become', 'to exist', but is weakened to become a mere copula; (2) the natural word order of subject–predicate is retained[6] (the natural word order for verbal clauses, on the other hand, is verb–subject).

This point of syntax is important for the Greek of the Apc., since it means that a clause containing the copula could still be regarded as a Semitic-type noun clause, provided it complies with the two general conditions just cited. This is in contrast to the Greek understanding of nominal phrases, which, of course, can exist *only* when the copula is absent. This fact requires illustration from the Hebrew OT and LXX, since it will be employed in the following section to explain a significant characteristic of the Greek of the Apc. The following Hebrew noun clauses are rendered in the LXX by use of the appropriate form of the verb εἶναι: Deut. 14:1 *bānîm 'attem layahweh*, 'You [are] children'; LXX Υἱοί ἐστε κυρίου. Gen. 42:13 *šēnêm 'āśār 'ăbādêkā*, 'The twelve (of us) [are] your servants'; LXX Δώδεκά ἐσμεν οἱ παῖδές σου. Gen. 42:21 *'ăbāl 'ăšēmîm 'anaḥnû*, 'Truly we [are] in the wrong'; LXX ἐν ἁμαρτίᾳ γὰρ ἐσμεν. Eccl. 1:7b *wehayyām 'ēnenû mālē'*, 'the sea [is] not filled'; LXX ἡ θάλασσα οὐκ ἔσται ἐμπιπλαμένη.

d. Noun clauses with participle in the OT

We have noted earlier (pp. 31ff) that a Hebrew participle was often translated in biblical Greek by the present indicative. This is the case even in some noun clauses – the Hebrew noun clause with a participle for predi-

cate can be translated into Greek by the use of a present indicative form
representing the participle. In each case where this occurs we would be
justified in understanding the indicative verb as expressing not the action
or motion of a verbal clause, although indeed a finite verb is employed,
but a state or quality, along the lines of the Semitic noun clause in which
it occurs. See, e.g., the following: Gen. 2:10 *wĕnāhār yōṣē'*, 'A river
flowing'; LXX ποταμὸς δὲ ἐκπορεύεται. Gen. 4:9 *hăšōmēr 'āḥî 'ānōkî*,
'Am I my brother's keeper?'; LXX μὴ φύλαξ τοῦ ἀδελφοῦ εἰμι ἐγώ;
Eccl. 1:7*a* 'All streams flowing (*hōlĕkîm*) to the sea'; LXX πάντες οἱ
χείμαρροι πορεύονται εἰς τὴν θάλασσαν.

e. Noun constructions in Greek.

The nominal clause is of course not unique to the Semitic languages. In
classical Attic the verb ἔστιν as a copula was often omitted,[7] producing
a nominal phrase which in appearance is identical to the Semitic noun
clause. Like Hebrew, the Attic noun clause could have as its predicate:
(1) an adjective; (2) adjectival participle (which was most frequent); (3)
an adverb (rare – limited to fixed formulae such as θαυμαστὸν ὅσον). The
copula was very often omitted in poetic expression.[8] Against these similari-
ties, however, we now cite some striking differences. For Attic, the copula
omitted was for the most part limited to the third-person singular present
indicative – ἔστιν.[9] Other forms of εἶναι, when omitted in Attic, call for
special mention in the grammars. Hebrew, however, could omit, with perfect ease and freedom, any person or tense of corresponding *hāyâ*. Furthermore, while Attic Greek makes a relatively wide use of the ellipsis of
the copula, the same is not the case for other epochs of the Greek tongue.
According to E. Schwyzer,[10] the predominant post-classical tendency was
to reserve noun clauses, which were viewed as ellipses, for use in archaic
poetic turns, fixed formulas and stylised expressions. The NT has in many
places gone even further than its contemporary literary *Koine* in employing the copula.[11] Hebrew and other Semitic languages, in contrast, make a
significantly wider use of the noun clause (without copula) than the Indo-
European family of languages.[12]

While both Semitic and Greek noun clauses frequently employ adjectives and participles as predicates, yet there is nothing corresponding in
Greek to the distinctive Semitic use of a *substantive* as predicate of a noun
clause, e.g. Ezek. 41:22 *hammizbēaḥ 'ēs*, 'The altar [was] wood.' This
category is especially characteristic of the Semitic mode of expression,
which emphasises the identity of the subject with its predicate.[13] Finally,
Semitic noun clauses stand in sharpest contrast to their Greek counterparts

on the question of expressing fixed states, attributes, etc. While this sense is basic to Semitic, there is no indication that Greek nominal phrases *per se* are to be taken to express states as opposed to actions. Such a use would be foreign to Greek nominal phrases.

2. Verbal Clauses

Verbal clauses, as noted above, always use a finite verb and thereby place primary emphasis on the *action* stated by that verb. Because of this emphasis, the natural position for the verb is preceding its subject.[14]

Since the verbal clause is the basic and commonest sentence structure of the Hebrew language, it seems unnecessary to cite here examples of it from the OT. It should be adequate simply to state that the LXX translators tended to render verbal clauses literally into Greek, retaining in most cases the original word order.

Verbal clauses in the Apc. cannot, of course, have any unique claim to Semitic influence such as was the case with Semitic type noun clauses, simply because such verbal constructions, using finite verbs, are basic and natural in Indo-European languages as well as those of the Semitic family. It is instructive for our purpose, however, to note the *word order* followed in certain cases by verbal clauses in the Apc.: (a) the natural Hebrew word order in a verbal clause is verb–subject (–object). (In secular Greek as a whole, this order is certainly possible, but is common only with verbs of saying.[15]) Cf. the following in the Apc., which reflect the Hebrew word order: Apc. 4:10 πεσοῦνται οἱ εἴκοσι τέσσαρες πρεσβύτεροι; 6:17 ἦλθεν ἡ ἡμέρα; 10:7 καὶ ἐτελέσθη τὸ μυστήριον; 11:18 ἦλθεν ἡ ὀργή σου; 12:16 καὶ ἤνοιξεν ἡ γῆ τὸ στόμα αὐτῆς. (b) The word order of object–verb–subject (also frequent in Hebrew[16]): Apc. 6:6 καὶ τὸ ἔλαιον καὶ τὸν οἶνον μὴ ἀδικήσῃς; 2:1 Τάδε λέγει ὁ κρατῶν; 2:3 καὶ ὑπομονὴν ἔχεις. (c) An order which is Hebraic, yet even more common in Aramaic,[17] is that of subject–object–verb: Apc. 1:7b καὶ οἵτινες αὐτὸν ἐξεκέντησαν. (d) Finally, it should be noted that in the arrangement very frequently found in the Apc. of subject–verb (–object), no Hebrew or Aramaic influence is present. It seems rather to be a favourite arrangement which belonged to the Seer's own style.

Summary of chapter 4, sections 1 and 2

No previous discussion of NT Greek syntax has considered the influence on Greek of the basic distinction of Aramaic and Hebrew into noun and verbal clauses. It was found that noun clauses in the Apc. can be sorted into the same categories as their Hebrew equivalents, depending on their mode of construction; their meaning is the same – that of a fixed state.

Verbal clauses, expressing action in contrast to a fixed state, are basic to both Greek and Hebrew, thus less can be said about Semitic influence upon them, except possibly regarding their word order.

The evidence cited here sheds important new light on biblical Greek syntax, and aids in better exegesis by underlining the distinction between a fixed state and an action; it is not of such a specific nature however, that it would serve to indicate direct translation of the Apc. from a Semitic source.

3. Syntax of the subordinate clauses

a. Relative clauses[18]

The great majority of relative constructions in the Apc. are expressed by use of the attributive participle, with or without the article:[19] Apc. 17:1 εἷς ἐκ τῶν ἑπτὰ ἀγγέλων τῶν ἐχόντων τὰς ἑπτὰ φιάλας, 'one of the seven angels *who had the seven bowls*'. This use of the participle is in full harmony with Greek syntax, but the frequency of occurrences in the Apc. is high. Quite frequently also the Apc. employs the relative clause proper, consisting of a relative pronoun followed by some form of the verb. Occurrences of this in the Apc. also follow normal Greek usage.

When these categories of the relative construction have been allowed for, there remain certain phrases which seem to demand a relative sense yet which are puzzling indeed when viewed only in the light of Greek syntax. In contrast to Greek, the Semitic languages frequently formulate a relative clause by using a noun clause, as follows: 2 Sam. 20:21 'a man of the hill country of Ephraim *whose name was Sheba*', šeba' šĕmô; an analogous instance from biblical Aramaic is Ezra 5:14 lĕšēšbaṣar šĕmēh 'to one *whose name was Sheshbazzar*'. Job 3:15 'with princes *that had gold*', zāhāb lāhem. This abbreviated form of relative clause omits the relative pronoun 'ăšer and is linked to its antecedent by simple co-ordination.[20] It has left its mark on the NT in four well-known passages which are identical to the example cited above, two of which are in the Apc.:[21] 6:8 καὶ ὁ καθήμενος ἐπάνω αὐτοῦ ὄνομα αὐτῷ ὁ θάνατος, 'and the one sitting on it, *whose name [was] death*'; 9:11 τὸν ἄγγελον τῆς ἀβύσσου ὄνομα αὐτῷ Ἑβραϊστὶ Ἀβαδδών, 'the angel of the abyss, *whose name is*'.[22]

The Hebrew relative clause is frequently introduced by 'ăšer, which is not a relative pronoun in the Greek sense, but an original *demonstrative* pronoun.[23] Since the demonstrative sense of 'ăšer is connected with its use in relative clauses, it is not surprising to discover that the Hebrew demonstrative pronoun proper (*zeh*, etc.), and sometimes the definite article, are used to introduce relative clauses, especially in poetic expression.[24] Under Hebrew influence the Apc. in several places uses the definite article to introduce a relative clause which consists of a preposition plus noun (or pronoun). First, a Hebrew example: Gen. 1:7 *hammayim 'ăšer mittaḥat lārāqîa'*, 'The waters *which were under the firmament*' (literally 'those under the firmament'), which in the LXX is rendered in such a way that *'ăšer* is represented by the genitive article τοῦ. This unusual syntax is found in the Apc. in the following passages: 5:13*b* τὰ ἐν αὐτοῖς πάντα, 'all [living things] *which are in them*'; Apc. 2:1, 2, 12, 18; 3:1, 7, 14 τῷ ἀγγέλῳ τῆς ἐν Ἐφέσῳ ἐκκλησίας, etc. The long-standing debate over whether τῷ should be read instead of τῆς is carried a step further by noting that in the LXX passage just cited the genitive article was used to translate *'ăšer*.[25] Apc. 8:3 τὸ χρυσοῦν τὸ ἐνώπιον τοῦ θρόνου, 'the golden [altar] *which is before the throne*'; 10:6 τὸν οὐρανὸν καὶ τὰ ἐν αὐτῷ καὶ τὴν γῆν καὶ τὰ ἐν αὐτῇ καὶ τὴν θάλασσαν καὶ τὰ ἐν αὐτῇ, 'the heaven and those things *which are in it*, and the earth and the things *which are in it*, and the sea and those things *which are in it*'; 20:13 τοὺς ἐν αὐτῇ, '*those which were in it*'; possibly also 1:4 ταῖς ἐν τῇ Ἀσίᾳ, 'to those *who are in Asia*'. To these examples without the relative pronoun we add the following, which are based on the same Hebrew construction but in which the pronoun occurs: Apc. 5:13 πᾶν κτίσμα ὃ ἐν τῷ οὐρανῷ, 'all creation *which is in heaven*' (from a construction employing *kol-'ăšer*); 1:4*b* ἃ ἐνώπιον τοῦ θρόνου αὐτοῦ, '*which are before his throne*'.

The common Hebrew practice, after employing a participle, to resolve the construction into a finite verb plus *Waw* is a familiar one, discussed elsewhere in this study.[26] It is cited here for the light it casts on certain relative constructions in biblical Greek which are introduced by an attributive participle which in the following portion of the relative clause is resolved into καί plus a finite verb. Some of the Hebrew examples cited by Driver illustrate the Hebraic nature of the phenomenon.[27] Gen. 27:33 *haṣṣād ṣayid wayyābē'*, 'who hunted game and brought it before me' (literally 'who hunted game, *and he brought*'). The LXX translates idiomatically with two participles: ὁ θηρεύσας θήραν καὶ εἰσενέγκας.

In several passages in the Apc. the same construction appears, which slavishly resolves the second participle (and any subsequent ones) into a finite verb: 7:14 Οὗτοί εἰσιν οἱ ἐρχόμενοι ἐκ τῆς θλίψεως τῆς μεγάλης καὶ ἔπλυναν τὰς στολὰς αὐτῶν καὶ ἐλεύκαναν, 'These are those who came through great tribulation, and *who washed* (literally 'and they washed') their robes and *who whitened them*' (literally 'and they whitened them');

possibly also 8:2 ἑπτὰ ἀγγέλους οἳ ἐνώπιον τοῦ Θεοῦ ἑστήκασιν καὶ
ἐδόθησαν αὐτοῖς ἑπτὰ σάλπιγγες, 'seven angels which stand before God,
to whom were given (literally 'and they were given') seven trumpets';
14:18 ἄγγελος . . . ἔχων ἐξουσίαν ἐπὶ τοῦ πυρὸς καὶ ἐφώνησεν, 'another
angel . . . who had control over the fire, and *who spoke*' (not 'and he
spoke'); perhaps also 20:12 καὶ εἶδον τοὺς νεκρούς . . . ἑστῶτας ἐνώπιον
τοῦ θρόνου καὶ βιβλία ἠνοίχθησαν, 'then I saw the dead . . . which stood
before the throne, and the books *which were opened*' (instead of 'and
the books were opened').

Lohmeyer,[28] followed by Ozanne,[29] has drawn attention to the relative
clause in the first verse of the Apc., which contains a Hebrew construction
practically identical to those cited above. The first clause, ἣν ἔδωκεν, is
continued by means of the resolved finite verb plus καὶ ἐσήμανεν, on the
analogy of the Hebrew construct following *ʾăšer*. Ozanne cites OT
examples exhibiting similar characteristics, such as Isa. 49:7: *lĕmaʿan
Yahweh ʾăšer neʾĕmān qĕdôš yiśrāʾel wayyibḥārekkā*, 'because of the Lord
who is faithful, the Holy One of Israel, *who chose you*' (literally 'and he
chose you').[30] On the basis of this verse, the similar syntax of Apc. 1:1
should lead us to translate 'the revelation of Jesus Christ which God gave
. . . and *which* He made known (not 'and he made it known').

Attention has been called by R.B.Y. Scott to a pair of verses in the
Apc., which have what he terms 'comparative relative clauses' expressed
with the finite verb instead of the participle.[31] He notes that the construction is well-known in Hebrew,[32] as relative sentences which are attached
to substantives which have the particle of comparison (usually *kĕ*): Job
7:2 *keʿeber yiš'ap-sēl*, 'as a servant *desiring* (literally 'he desires') the
shade'; Isa. 42:1*b* *wišûʿātāh kĕlappîd yibʿār*, 'and her salvation as a torch
burning' (literally 'as a torch burns'); LXX renders τὸ δὲ σωτήριόν μου ὡς
λαμπὰς καυθήσεται.

In these examples it is noted that the particle of comparison is attached
to the noun, and the following verb is finite, not participle. This construction occurs also in the Apc., in the following places: 1:16 ὡς ὁ ἥλιος φαίνει
(later corrected to φαινων by 1611 2067 *al*), 'as the sun *shining*' (not 'as
the sun shines'); 10:3 ὥσπερ λέων μυκᾶται (altered to μυκομενος 93), 'as
a lion *roaring*' (not 'as a lion roars'). As indicated by the presence of
variants, the corresponding Greek construction preferred a participle.

Beyer, in his detailed analysis of the Semitic element in NT conditional
relative clauses,[33] touches on a phenomenon which is found twice in the
Apc.[34] He notes that, while by nature the Semitic relative clause is singular,
referring for example, to 'when somebody', such clauses are often translated in the LXX in plural form since in Greek the plural indefinite relative

clause is very common. This is especially noted in the LXX when the finite verb of the main clause in Hebrew is plural. Thus the plural forms of the relative pronouns in the two Apc. passages may in fact reflect a Semitic type relative clause, as follows: Apc. 3:19 ἐγὼ ὅσους (ους 2019 syr[ph] vg) ἐὰν φιλῶ, 'those whom I love'; 13:15 ποιήσῃ ἵνα ὅσοι ἐὰν μὴ προσκυ- νήσωσιν, 'cause those who would not worship'. In supporting his point Beyer cites two striking OT parallels to the Apc. passages where the identical sense is expressed by the singular relative pronoun: Prov. 3:12 (cf. Apc. 3:19), and Dan. 3:6, 11 (cf. Apc. 13:15).

This examination has shown how the numerous relative clauses in the Apc. which do not follow the accepted Greek form actually preserve one of several types of relative constructions native to biblical Hebrew and Aramaic.

b. Circumstantial clauses[35]

Any words which relate a fact subordinate to the main flow of narrative, or which describe a circumstance connected with the action expressed by the main verb may form a circumstantial clause. Black gives the following apt definition:[36]

> 'One of the commonest of Semitic subordinate clauses, characteristic of both Hebrew and Aramaic, is the so-called Circumstantial Clause, by which circumstances are described which are attendant on or necessary to the understanding of the action of the main verb, but subordinate to it ... Its translation may vary with the requirements of the context, but it is usually best rendered by "now", "while", "when".'

This is illustrated by Gen. 19:1 'The two messengers came to Sodom in the evening, *while Lot was sitting in the gate of Sodom*'.

The inclusion of a circumstantial clause in a sentence in Hebrew or Aramaic is of course affected by the tendency of these languages towards simple co-ordination; in other words, the clause will appear to have been simply thrown into the sentence,[37] with a *Waw* providing the only syntactical link with what precedes.[38]

Word order in circumstantial clauses varies, but that encountered most frequently is: conjunction (*Waw*) plus noun (pronoun) plus verb (or participle or predicate noun, etc.). The primary position of the noun serves to arrest the attention of the reader, by altering the word order of the natural flow of clauses.

The Semitic circumstantial clause corresponds on the whole to the Greek circumstantial participle,[39] which denotes manner, accompaniment, etc. especially in its modal use; a good example is Demosthenes, *On the Crown* 217: λυπούμενος καὶ στένων καὶ δυσμεναίνων οἴκοι καθῆτο, 'he sat at home *grieving and groaning and fretting*'.

The striking difference between Semitic and Greek circumstantial clauses is of course a matter largely of syntax. The hallmark of the Semitic type clause is its introductory *Waw*, followed by a noun (pronoun), which is a construction not paralleled in Greek.[40] Note the following: 1 Ki. 19:19 'and he went thence and found Elisha, and *he was ploughing*', *wĕhû' ḥōrēš*; LXX translates literally: καὶ αὐτὸς ἠροτρία. Gen. 18:8 *'as he stood beside them* they ate', *wĕhû' 'ōmēd 'ălêhem*, LXX αὐτὸς δὲ παρειστήκει αὐτοῖς; 2 Chr. 10:2 'while he was in Egypt', *wĕhû' bĕmiṣrayîm*; LXX καὶ αὐτὸς ἐν Αἰγύπτῳ.

R.B.Y. Scott drew attention to the occurrence of this type of circumstantial clause in the Apc. in the following passages:[41] 2:18 καὶ οἱ πόδες αὐτοῦ ὅμοιοι χαλκολιβάνῳ, '*now his feet are like burnished bronze*';[42] 10:1 καὶ ἡ ἶρις ἐπὶ τῆς κεφαλῆς αὐτοῦ καὶ τὸ πρόσωπον αὐτοῦ ὡς ὁ ἥλιος, καὶ οἱ πόδες αὐτοῦ ὡς στῦλοι πυρός, 'now the rainbow was on his head, and his face was like the sun, *and his legs were like flaming pillars*'; 12:1 'a woman clothed with the sun, *with the moon under her feet*', καὶ ἡ σελήνη ὑποκάτω τῶν ποδῶν αὐτῆς; 17:11 'and the beast which was and is not, *now he is an eighth and is of the seven*', καὶ αὐτὸς ὄγδοός ἐστιν καὶ ἐκ τῶν ἑπτά ἐστιν.

Another type of circumstantial clause, which in Hebrew is introduced by *Waw* followed by the predicate with a preposition,[43] is also reflected in the Apc. A good Hebrew example is Isa. 3:7: 'I will not be a healer *while in my house is neither bread nor clothing*', *ûbĕbêtî 'ên leḥem*. Clauses of this sort have a somewhat more independent character than those discussed above but are still to be regarded as circumstantial clauses.[44] Note the following: Isa. 6:6 'and he sent one of the seraphim to me, *now in his hand was a glowing coal*', *ûbĕyādô riṣpâ*, LXX καὶ ἐν τῇ χειρὶ εἶχεν ἄνθρακα; Amos 7:7 'The Lord was standing beside a wall . . . *now in his hand was a plumb line*', *ûbĕyādô 'ănāk*, LXX καὶ ἐν τῇ χειρὶ αὐτοῦ ἀδάμας; 2 Sam. 13:18 *'now she was wearing a long robe*', *wĕ'ālêhā kĕtōnet*, LXX καὶ ἐπ' αὐτῆς ἦν χιτών.

Scott noted occurrences in the Apc. of clauses which fit this pattern, although he did not make any attempt to illustrate the Semitic nature of the construction or to distinguish between the two forms of the clause which are employed in Hebrew. Note the following: Apc. 2:17 'I shall give him a white stone *and upon the stone a new name written*', καὶ ἐπὶ τὴν ψῆφον ὄνομα καινὸν γεγραμμένον;[45] 12:3 'a dragon . . . having seven heads and ten horns, *now upon his heads were seven crowns*', καὶ ἐπὶ τὰς κεφαλὰς αὐτοῦ ἑπτὰ διαδήματα; 12:1 'a woman clothed with the sun . . . *now a crown of twelve stars was on her head'*, καὶ ἐπὶ τῆς κεφαλῆς αὐτῆς στέφανος ἀστέρων δώδεκα; 13:1 'then I saw a beast . . . *now ten crowns were on his horns'*, καὶ ἐπὶ τῶν κεράτων αὐτοῦ δέκα διαδήματα, 'and a name of blasphemy on his heads', καὶ ἐπὶ τὰς κεφαλὰς αὐτοῦ ὄνομα[τα] βλασφημίας; 14:1 'I saw and beheld the lamb standing upon mount Zion, *now a hundred forty-four thousand were with him'*, καὶ μετ' αὐτοῦ ἑκατὸν τεσσεράκοντα τέσσαρες χιλιάδες; 14:14 *'now upon the cloud was sitting'*, καὶ ἐπὶ τὴν νεφέλην καθήμενον; 17:5 *'now on her forehead a name was written'*, καὶ ἐπὶ τὸ μέτωπον αὐτῆς ὄνομα γεγραμμένον; 19:12 *'while many diadems were on his head'*, καὶ ἐπὶ τὴν κεφάλην; 21:12 *'now at the twelve gates were twelve angels'*, καὶ ἐπὶ τοῖς πυλῶσιν ἀγγέλους δώδεκα.

By comparing these passages with the LXX translations of Hebrew circumstantial clauses cited above it becomes clear that they are of the same character, both representing the purely Semitic mode of denoting circumstances attendant to the main action of the sentence in which they are found. The primary un-Greek feature is the introductory καί used in the Semitic type clauses.

c. Conditional Clauses[46]

A degree of uncertainty in the text of Apc. 6:1 indicates a measure of primitive dissatisfaction with the construction which according to the Received Text ends with two imperatives, ἔρχου καὶ βλέπε (ιδε ℵ 046 1828 2042 syr[ph] *al*). The phrase is repeated with similar textual support in verses 3, 5 and 7. A similar current dissatisfaction and uncertainty with the Received reading led some modern editors of the Greek NT (Nestle-Aland, United Bible Societies' Greek NT) to excise the καί plus second imperative, probably due in part to the repetitive sense which would result in three of the above-mentioned passages (verses 1, 5, 7) from the inclusion of the καὶ εἶδον which opens the following verse: cf. verse 5 Ἔρχου καὶ ἴδε, καὶ εἶδον, καὶ ἰδοὺ ἵππος μέγας (but there is in each case textual evidence for omitting καὶ εἶδον); cf. 16:1 Ὑπάγετε καὶ ἐκχέετε.

A glance elsewhere in the NT shows that this curious expression employing two imperatives coupled by καί is not limited to the Apc. but is found also in the reported sayings of Jesus. See for example John 1:46 where ἔρχου καὶ ἴδε occurs; cf. Mark 6:38 ὑπάγετε ἴδετε (και om).[47] Blass–Debrunner describe this construction as 'asyndeton instead of subordination with finite verbs',[48] and refer to the similar classical expression ἄγε, ἴθι. As used in the NT however, the two imperatives coupled by καί are distinguished from an ordinary imperatival construction such as 'rise, take up your pallet' (Mark 2:11) in one important sense. While the double imperative, known from classical Greek as well as in *Koine*, expresses a *command*, in the standard imperatival sense, the construction with which we are dealing can be best understood as a *conditional clause* of a decidedly un-Greek nature. Thus ἔρχου καὶ ἴδε should be translated in the Apc. by 'if you come, you shall see' – at once different from simple command.

Such construction is in harmony with a Hebrew construction scattered throughout the OT, described as an imperative in logical dependence on a preceding imperative.[49] The two are connected by *Waw* copulative, and while the first imperative as a rule contains a condition, the second states the consequences of that condition's fulfilment. The construction is used especially to express the consequence particularly desired by the speaker: Gen. 42:18 *zō't 'ăśû wiḥĕyû*, 'This do, and live' (i.e. 'if you do this, you shall continue to live'); note how the LXX translator altered the second imperative to future tense, bringing the construction more in line with ordinary Greek syntax: Τοῦτο ποιήσατε καὶ ζήσεσθε; Isa. 36:16 *'ăśû 'ittî bĕrākâ ûṣĕ'û 'ēlay wĕ'iklû*, 'make with me peace, and come out, and eat' ('if you make peace and come out, then you shall eat'); LXX εἰ βούλεσθε εὐλογηθῆναι ἐκπορεύεσθε. This Hebraic conditional clause is preserved in its most literal form in the Apc. passages cited above, where the two imperatives are preserved.

Beyer has drawn attention to the use of the conditional clause plus εἰ or ἐάν with the indefinite subject to express 'if anybody', etc.[50] This use of εἴ τις, ἐάν τις while acceptable Greek, is used frequently in the LXX to translate a Semitic conditional clause plus conjunction or, respectively, a conditional participle: Gen. 19:12 *wĕkōl 'ăšer-lĕkā*, 'and all whom you have' (i.e. 'if you have anyone with you'), LXX εἴ τις σοι. Note also the plural Hebrew protasis, rendered singular in the LXX.[51]

On the basis of this evidence Beyer reckons that frequently εἴ τις/ἐάν τις in the NT is based on a Semitic relative clause or conditional participle. From the Apc. he cites 13:9 εἴ τις ἔχει οὖς; cf. 2:7a ὁ ἔχων οὖς, where a substantival participle serves as protasis;[52] 14:11 εἴ τις λαμβάνει. In each passage the translation 'if somebody/anybody' is to be preferred, on the basis of the Hebrew pattern.

Semitic influence on individual conditional clauses in the Apc. is also treated by Beyer, who calls attention to occasions when, in Semitic languages, the customary sequence of protasis followed by apodosis is *reversed*, usually to express a strong wish, an oath, or a command.[53] This seems to have influenced the Apc. at three places: 14:11 καὶ οὐκ ἔχουσιν ἀνάπαυσιν ἡμέρας καὶ νύκτος . . . καὶ εἴ τις λαμβάνει τὸ χάραγμα, 'they have no rest day or night . . . whoever receives the mark' (i.e. 'whoever

receives the mark also has no rest'); 2:5 ἔρχομαί σοι καὶ κινήσω τὴν
λυχνίαν . . . ἐὰν μὴ μετανοήσῃς, 'I will come to you and remove your
lamp . . . if you do not repent' (i.e. 'if you do not repent, I will'); and
2:22 ἰδοὺ βάλλω αὐτὴν εἰς κλίνην . . . ἐὰν μὴ μετανοήσωσιν, 'Behold, I
will throw her on a sickbed . . . if they do not repent' (i.e. 'if they do not
repent, I will').

d. Temporal clauses

An oddity of biblical Hebrew is its custom of introducing a temporal clause
by imperfect consecutive *wayĕhî* (καὶ ἐγένετο), especially if the temporal
clause is slightly independent of the narrative in which it is embedded, or
if it opens a new section of that which has been narrated previously.[54] In
rare cases the perfect consecutive *wĕhāyâ* is used in similar fashion. In
translating, it is usually best to ignore the *wayĕhî*, which is redundant, and
begin with the temporal conjunction, as in Judg. 1:1: *wayĕhî 'aḥărê môt
yĕhôšu'*, which is translated by RSV rightly by 'After the death of Joshua'
(not 'It came to pass, after'). It is especially instructive for understanding
NT Greek to note that in this and other OT passages the LXX translates
literally: καὶ ἐγένετο μετὰ τὴν τελεύτην Ἰησοῦ. Cf. Gen. 22:1 *wayĕhî
'aḥar haddĕbarîm ha'ēlleh*, 'After these things' (not 'and it came to pass,
after'). The LXX καὶ ἐγένετο μετὰ τὰ ῥήματα ταῦτα. Ex. 17:11 *kĕ'ăšer
yārîm mōšeh yādô*, 'whenever Moses held up his hand'; LXX καὶ ἐγίνετο
ὅταν ἐπῆρεν Μωυσης τὰς χεῖρας.[55] Here note the less frequent use of the
perfect consecutive. The same construction appears in biblical Aramaic in
Dan. 3:7 *kĕdî šām'în kōl-'ammayyâ*, 'When all the people heard'; Theod.
καὶ ἐγένετο ὅταν ἤκουσαν οἱ λαοί. It is significant that in Theod. the redundant καὶ ἐγένετο introductory formula is employed, even though no
Aramaic counterpart to Hebrew *wayĕhî* appears.[56]

Along with the fully written introductory formulas, *wayĕhî/wĕhāyâ*,
biblical Hebrew employed an abbreviated introduction, retaining the *Waw*
and temporal conjunction, but omitting the *hāyâ/yĕhî*: Judg. 2:18 *wĕkî
hēqîm Yahweh*, 'whenever Yahweh raised up', which the LXX translates:
καὶ ὅτι (sic) ἐγείρεν κύριος; Judg. 3:31 (preposition) *wĕ'aḥărāyw hāyâ
šamgār*, 'after him there was Shamgar'; LXX καὶ μετ' αὐτὸν ἀνέστη
Σαμαγαρ.

In the first chapter of his *Semitische Syntax im Neuen Testament*[57]
Beyer surveys the temporal constructions under discussion here.[58] The
construction *wayĕhî* followed by temporal conjunction occurs about 400
times in the OT,[59] especially in the older portions of the Hebrew writings.[60]
He concludes from his study that, while this construction was an essential

syntactical medium for the original Hebrew narrators,[61] it was unnecessary for the LXX and other ancient versions of the OT. The oddity of this construction literally translated into Greek becomes apparent when the temporal clause in the LXX is compared with natural Greek idiom. Nowhere in secular Greek does there appear anything related to the construction under consideration. In the first place, temporal conjunctions do not often appear as the first element in classical and Hellenistic Greek temporal clauses. When they do however, they can stand alone: ὅταν ἀπολύωνται or, in most cases, they are followed by δέ or οὖν; ὅταν δ᾽ἁλίσκηται, ὅταν οὖν παραγίνομαι.

The majority of temporal clauses in the NT are written in good Greek style, employing δέ immediately following the temporal conjunction; cf. Matt. 6:16 Ὅταν δὲ νηστεύητε, 'When you fast'; Mark 13:14 Ὅταν δὲ ἴδητε τὸ βδέλυγμα, 'When you see the abomination'; Luke 12:11 Ὅταν δὲ εἰσφέρωσιν ὑμᾶς, 'When they bring you'. However there are scattered occurrences in the Gospels of temporal clauses which have a close similarity to the Semitic type noted in the LXX. Burney cites five cases in Matt. where the Hebraic καὶ ἐγένετο plus temporal conjunction is found, always at the conclusion of a narrative passage:[62] 7:28 καὶ ἐγένετο ὅτε ἐτέλεσεν Ἰησοῦς, 'when Jesus finished'; also 11:1, 13:53, 19:7, 26:1. This fully written form of the Hebraic temporal clause does not occur in the Apc.

An abbreviated form, based on examples from the OT noted above, is found in the NT, employing καί as the first element of the clause, followed immediately by the temporal conjunction (omitting ἐγένετο): Matt. 6:5 καὶ ὅταν προσεύχησθε 'when you pray'; the Lukan parallel 11:2 has eliminated the καί. Cf. Mark 11:25 καὶ ὅταν στήκετε; 12:11; 14:7, 25.

A search of Hoskier's apparatus yields several passages which preserve the Semitic καί preceding the temporal conjunction: Apc. 6:12 καὶ εἶδον καὶ ὅτε ἤνοιξεν τὴν σφραγῖδα, 'I looked when he opened the seal.' Here the second καί, supported by uncial P (Gregory 024) plus numerous minuscules, is totally unnecessary to the sense of the sentence from a Greek point of view, and is quite untranslatable. The only explanation for its existence seems to be that it represents a Hebrew Waw in wĕkî. Other occurrences are: 4:9; 6:3, 5, 7; 8:1; 10:4; 11:7; 12:4 καὶ (gig) ἵνα ὅταν τέκῃ, also verse 13; 17:10; 18:1; 19:1; 20:7; 22:8.

e. Final clauses

In Attic Greek, final clauses introduced by ἵνα or ὅπως employ either the subjunctive or, less frequently, the optative mood of the verb,[63] never the indicative.[64] In the NT the mood employed is generally subjunctive,[65] but especially significant is the occasional use, especially in Paul and the Apc., of the future indicative in place of aorist subjunctive,[66] as illustrated by Apc. 3:9 ἰδοὺ ποιήσω αὐτοὺς ἵνα ἥξουσιν (ηξωσι 046) καὶ προσκυνή- σουσιν (-σωσιν046) . . . καὶ γνῶσιν (γνωση ℵ), 'I will require of them that they come and prostrate themselves . . . and learn.'

The significant question, hitherto unsettled, may now be asked: is the intrusion of the future indicative in these NT final clauses to be attributed to a tendency in Hellenistic Greek to substitute indicative for subjunc- tive?[67] Turner, in his thorough treatment of NT final (purpose) clauses referred to in note 64 above states that the future indicative is used in final clauses in Hellenistic Greek. Examples can be found in Radermacher's Grammar:[68] note the following: ἀνάβαινε πρὸς με, ἵνα σοι ἀποτάξομαι,[69] 'come towards me that I may set you apart'. He cites nine others illustrat- ing this use of future indicative in Hellenistic literature, but one, Enoch 6:3, must be discounted because of its Semitic background. By his own admission, however, these are far from abundant,[70] so could hardly be called upon to explain the proliferation of ἵνα plus the future indicative in the NT, where Turner finds no fewer than thirty-seven examples.[71] It is safe to say that the substantial intrusion of these futures indicative in NT final clauses cannot be adequately explained as due to Hellenistic develop- ments. The NT as a whole exhibits neither carelessness nor indifference regarding the choice of mood.

On p. 28 of this study it was noted that, under specific conditions of Semitic influence, biblical Greek employed the future indicative where it would not be acceptable in Greek. This was often done in the LXX to represent an imperfect tense Hebrew verb.[72] A study of the final clause in biblical Hebrew demonstrates that when the clause is expressed by a final conjunction plus finite verb, that verb is always an imperfect.[73] It is natural for a translator sometimes to forsake idiomatic Greek, which would use ἵνα plus subjunctive, and to use instead the future indicative as the formal translation equivalent of the Hebrew imperfect tense. This is illus- trated by the following examples from the LXX: Deut. 19:28 ἵνα εὐλογήσει (Α)σε κύριος ὁ Θεὸς σου, 'so that the Lord your God might bless you' (MT verse 29), lĕma'an yĕbārekka Yahweh 'ĕlōhêkā; 3 Km. 2:3 ἵνα συνήσεις ἃ ποιήσεις, 'that whatever you do might prosper', MT lĕma'an taśkîl 'et kol- 'ăšer ta'ăśeh; cf. 2:4 ἵνα στήσει 'that the Lord may establish', MT lĕma'an yāqîm. The Hebrew passages are cited to illustrate how the imperfect verb always follows the final conjunction.

In the following passages from the Apc. the final clauses are identical in syntax to those from the LXX: in addition to 3:9 cited above, note Apc. 6:4 ἵνα σφράξουσιν, cf. verse 11 ἵνα ἀναπαύσονται (AP 046 1), 8:3 ἵνα δώσει, cf. verse 6 ἵνα σαλπίουσιν (2094 2321), 9:4 ἵνα μὴ ἀδικήσουσιν, verse 5 ἵνα βασανισθήσονται, verse 20 ἵνα μὴ προσκυνήσουσιν (ℵ CA) (13:12 is identical), cf. 8:13 ἵνα καὶ πῦρ ποιήσει (616 2084 2321), 14:13 ἵνα ἀναπαήσονται, 13:16 ἵνα δῶσιν, 18:4 ἵνα μὴ συνκοινωνήσετε (2044 2054 al), 19:18 ἵνα ᾠάγετε (051* 2056), 22:14 ἵνα ἔσται . . . καὶ εἰσελεύσονται (syr^ph).[74]

It is now necessary to examine final clauses of another type. Frequently in biblical Hebrew the final clause, like most other dependent clauses, may be joined to its main clause by simple *Waw* copulative without the final conjunction:[75] see for example Lamentations 1:19 'while they sought food (wĕyāšîbû 'et-nāpšām) that they might revive themselves'. Here the LXX translator felt obliged to indicate the final force of the clause by inserting ἵνα: ἵνα ἐπιστρέφουσιν (ℵ) ψυχὰς αὐτῶν; cf. 1 Ki. 11:21 'Send me away (wĕ'ēlēk 'et-'arṣî) that I may go to my land'; LXX in this instance renders literally, in very un-Greek manner: Ἐξαπόστειλόν με καὶ ἀποστρέψω εἰς τὴν γῆν μου.

Compare now the following final clauses from the Apc., which exhibit identical construction: Apc. 4:1b ἀνάβα ὧδε, καὶ δείξω σοι, 'come up here *so that I can show you*';[76] this is not Greek, but obviously represents the Hebraic mode of final clause. The tense used in both LXX and Apc. is future indicative. A passage which has caused considerable confusion to translators is Apc. 5:10 καὶ ἐποίησας αὐτοὺς . . . βασιλείαν καὶ ἱερεῖς καὶ βασιλεύσουσιν (ℵ P: not βασιλευουσιν of A 046 al) ἐπὶ τῆς γῆς, 'and you made them . . . kings and priests *that they might reign on the earth*' (not 'and they shall reign' of the RSV); 9:19 καὶ ἐν αὐτοῖς ἀδικήσουσιν (181), '*that with them they might injure*'.[77] Possibly also 11:7 'The beast shall make war with them (καὶ νικήσει αὐτοὺς καὶ ἀποκτενεῖ αὐτούς) *that he might conquer and kill them*'; 13:7f καὶ ἐδόθη αὐτῷ ἐξουσία ἐπὶ πᾶσαν φυλὴν καὶ λαὸν . . . καὶ προσκυνήσουσιν αὐτον, 'and authority was given him over all tribes and peoples . . . *so that they should worship him*'; 15:4 πάντα τὰ ἔθνη ἥξουσιν καὶ προσκυνήσουσιν ἐνώπιόν σου, 'all the nations shall come *that they might worship before thee*'; 20:7f λυθήσεται ὁ Σατανᾶς . . . καὶ ἐξελεύσεται πλανῆσαι τὰ ἔθνη, 'Satan shall be released . . . *that he might come forth to tempt the nations*'; 20:10 (possibly): καὶ ὁ διάβολος . . . ἐβλήθη εἰς τὴν λίμνην τοῦ πυρὸς καὶ θείου ὅπου καὶ τὸ θηρίον καὶ ὁ ψευδοπροφήτης, καὶ βασανισθήσονται, 'and the devil . . . is thrown into the lake of fire and brimstone, where the beast and false prophet are, *so that they might suffer*'.

f. Consecutive (result) clauses

This section on syntax will conclude with observations on the Semitic
nature of certain consecutive clauses in the Apc. The accepted Greek manner of expressing result is by use of ὥστε followed by an infinitive[78] or
indicative (rare in the NT): Romans 7:6 'we are set free *so that we might
serve*', ὥστε δουλεύειν.

In Hebrew however, the consecutive clause is most frequently added
by means of simple *Waw* copulative followed by the jussive.[79] This is
especially found after interrogative sentences, e.g. Hosea 14:10 *mî ḥākām
wĕyābēn 'ēlleh*, 'who is wise, *so that he understands these things*?' The
LXX translates literally: τίς σοφὸς καὶ συνήσει ταῦτα.

A clear occurrence of the same type of translation consecutive clause is
found in Apc. 21:3*a* 'Behold, God's presence is with men' καὶ σκηνώσει
μετ'αὐτῶν, '*so that He dwells with them*'.

Summary of chapter 4, section 3

The use of the attributive participle to express a relative clause is in line
with Greek syntax, but the high frequency of occurrences in biblical Greek
is difficult to account for, except as due to Semitic influence. The use of
the possessive pronoun in a relative clause is peculiar to the Semitic
languages, however, and is to be found influencing the phrase ὄνομα αὐτῷ
in the Apc. as well as in the Fourth Gospel. Introduction of the relative
clause by the use of an article, especially in the genitive case, can be
traced directly to Hebrew syntax, which sometimes uses a definite article
as a relative pronoun. This has influenced the Apc. in several places.

The translation of the Apc. is affected by the recognition that the attributive participle used to introduce a relative clause can, in Hebraic fashion,
be resolved into a finite verb yet still express the sense of the participle, as
in the Apc. 7:14 'these are those who came . . . and *who washed* . . . and
who whitened'. Such highly characteristic Semitic usage could be explained
as translation Greek, or as a deliberate attempt to reproduce Hebrew syntax in Greek. Scott's 'comparative relative clause', found twice in the Apc.,
is also best accounted for as due to the same phenomenon.

The occurrence in the Apc. of two distinctly Semitic circumstantial
clauses is difficult to explain apart from the hypothesis of direct Semitic
influence.

The conditional clause expressed by two imperatives linked by καί,
which Black cites where it occurs in the Gospels, is also found in the Apc.,

based here on OT Hebrew usage. Most significant in determining Semitic influence is the phenomenon noted by Beyer, where the customary sequence of the conditional clause is reversed, the apodosis followed by the protasis. This seems not to have any parallel in secular Greek, and can only be explained on the basis of such a reversal well-known in the Semitic languages. The three occurrences of this in the Apc., would seem to suggest Semitic influence.

The Semitic mode of introducing a temporal clause with *Waw* immediately followed by the temporal conjunction is found several times in the Apc. Its un-Greek nature is emphasised by the fact that in some places copyists excised the καί from their texts.

Final clauses in Hebrew are expressed by the imperfect tense of the verb, and this usage has influenced passages in the Apc. which employ the Greek future indicative instead of the customary subjunctive. Where this has occurred, Semitic influence is reponsible. Likewise, the joining of a final clause to its main clause by simple *Waw* has influenced the Greek of the Apc. in several passages. Such usage is foreign to the Greek language, and can be justified only by appealing to direct Semitic influence for each occurrence.

Finally, the Hebrew consecutive clause, expressed by *Waw* plus jussive verb, is seen as the explanation for the unusual syntax of Apc. 21:3.

5

CONCLUSION

The most significant observation that can be made regarding the Greek text of the Apc. is that there appears to be no manuscript or family of manuscripts which preserves a relatively higher number of more Semitised readings affecting verbs and clauses than any other manuscript. Research has failed here, as it has with previous studies, to turn up anything equivalent to the Western text of the Gospels and Acts with its greater number of Semitisms. Another fact, noted by previous researchers, has been observed again here as well, that the relative antiquity of the individual witnesses to the text of the Apc. has little to do with the number of Semitisms preserved by them. Of the Semitic constructions discussed in this study, which are preserved in fewer than five extant witnesses, the third-century p^{47} gives the more Semitised form in five places, but in four places the Semitism has been smoothed over. This hardly differs from a fifteenth-century minuscule, 2067, which alone, or with just a few others, has preserved in three places the more Semitised reading. From this it is evident that the reconstruction of the primitive text of the Apc. must proceed from a broad textual basis, not overlooking the testimony of any witness. It is interesting to note that codex Sinaiticus, while considered to be inferior to the other uncials in the text of the Apc., has preserved more of the Semitised readings cited in this study (a total of six) than has Alexandrinus, which is judged to be the best complete witness to the Apc. (it preserved only four Semitic readings in places where fewer than five witnesses support the variant, as compared to six for Sinaiticus). Thus while no single manuscript of the Apc. can be considered as superior in respect to its more Semitised nature, neither can any witness be *a priori* rejected on grounds of its age.

Regarding Hebrew meanings expressed by Greek verbs, a conjecture was made that passive occurrences of ϑαυμάζειν in the Apc. should be translated to express the sense 'be devastated', 'desolated'. Also the use of διδόναι for 'set', and causative 'require' is due to Hebrew usage, as is κληρονομεῖν when it expresses the taking of possession by force, a meaning foreign to Greek. The use of ἀδικεῖν for 'harm', and, in Apc. 6:6, 'fraudulently withold', plus ποιμαίνειν, 'to shepherd away', 'push aside', give further illustration to the importance of considering that in Semitised Greek the secondary meanings of Hebrew and Aramaic verbs may be imposed on Greek counterparts, even if in normal usage the Greek verbs did not express that secondary meaning.

The primary contribution of this study has been an increased understanding of the specific nature of Semitic influence in the important areas of verbal syntax and clauses in the Apc. The results may be applied to any Jewish Greek document. The findings may be summarised as follows.

Third-person impersonal plural: while recent scholarship has shown this construction to be more widespread in Hellenistic Greek than previously assumed, still it cannot account for the greatly expanded use of it in Greek documents under direct Aramaic influence. The use of this construction to avoid naming God when found in the Apc. is based on Aramaic usage. Concerning another problematic usage of the *voice* in the Apc., we argued that the two occurrences of intransitive εὐαγγελίζεσθαι express a causative sense, based on the Hebrew piel and hiphil stem verbs. The Semitic custom of employing an auxiliary verb has probably left its mark on the Apc. in those places where such constructions as 'go and pour out', 'take and pour out', occur. Regarding the long-standing puzzle of passive of θαυμάζειν in the Apc. we have cited new evidence showing it not to be merely a deponent preferring the aorist passive ending, but rather to reflect a Hebrew meaning. Finally, the passive μνησθῆναι was included as a member of that group of 'theological passives' used to avoid naming God, due to the influence of Hebrew niphal.

The use of the *mood* in the Apc. is subject to the following forms of Semitic influence: the deliberative question is cast in the present indicative instead of the customary subjunctive mood due to the influence of the Hebrew participle, which is used often for deliberative questions in the OT. Concerning the substitution of future indicative for aorist subjunctive, we noted how in the Apc. and elsewhere this can be explained as due to the tendency to translate Hebrew imperfect by Greek future indicative. Likewise the Greek future indicative with hortatory sense is due to a Hebrew cohortative.

Another important section of this study was that on the tenses of the finite verb, which developed more clearly than and differently from any previous study the formal translation equivalents employed in biblical and Jewish translation Greek. For the sake of clarity the relation between Greek and Semitic tenses has been presented in table form above (p. 53). At its most elementary level, the Greek present indicative represented a

Semitic participle, while Greek aorist was used to render Semitic perfect tense verbs. The Greek future was reserved for the Semitic imperfect, while the perfect can represent Hebrew derived conjugations. Such translation equivalents were of course not always adhered to, and exceptions can be found for any category cited here. On the other hand, the very simplicity of this pattern, when seen in light of the many illustrations cited in the relevant section above, argues for its general validity. One cannot escape the impression that the biblical Hebrew (and Aramaic) tense system, profoundly different from Greek, is to be seen nearly everywhere in the language of the Apc. The conventional Greek time sense of past–present–future is equally foreign to verb tenses in the Apc. and in OT; both must be interpreted to allow for the Hebrew/Aramaic feel for tense. In determining the time at which the action took place one must deal with biblical Greek tenses in the same manner as Hebrew or Aramaic verbs – rely on the context of the verb in question. The related problem of sudden shifts of tense in the Apc., which has puzzled generations of scholars, is likewise solved by appealing to the shift in tense made in biblical Hebrew/Aramaic.

Another Hebraic construction, the *Waw*-consecutive, has left its mark on the Apc. most clearly where it is used (represented in translation by *καί*) to introduce the apodosis of a conditional clause, thus creating a syntactical oddity unknown in secular Greek.

Regarding Semitic influence on the infinitive, we noted that long ago Charles laid the foundation for explaining the Semitic nature of *τοῦ* plus infinitive in certain passages in the Apc. as expressing necessity. Here for the first time evidence was cited demonstrating that the construction was even better known in Aramaic and Syriac than in biblical Hebrew. By availing ourselves of Hoskier's apparatus we have discovered occurrences of this construction in the Apc. which have escaped the notice of previous scholars. In the case of infinitives which are resolved into finite verbs, based upon a well-documented Hebrew practice, further examples in the Apc. have been added to those listed by Charles. Regarding the so-called 'nominal' use of the infinitive, ascribed by Lancellotti to Hebrew influence, it was noted in this section that the construction is found in Greek as well, although there is admittedly a Hebrew construction in the OT which is identical.

In the section on participles, it was shown that the resolution of a participle into a finite verb, on Hebraic lines, is well-attested in the Apc. New occurrences were added to those cited by previous scholars. The Seer's use of the perfect passive participle was seen to reflect Hebrew qal passive, or derived conjugations. On the widely-debated issue of whether participles used as relative clauses fall under some variety of Semitic influence, it is decided best to avoid the one-sided argument of exclusive influence of Hebrew, maintained by Lancellotti, and recognise that Hellenistic Greek made wide use of the same construction. In contrast to Greek participles, which usually denote time past, present, or future in relation to their main verb, Hebrew participles of themselves express no difference of time. This has been found to influence the tense of the participle in the Apc. Such usage appears most clearly in the circumstantial use of the participle. We noted also that when the tense of the participle did not coincide in proper chronological sequence with that of the main verb, along the lines of Greek syntax, it was due to this timeless nature of the Semitic participle. The very Hebraic and ungrammatical circumstantial accusative participle was seen to reflect in a literal way one particular feature of OT Hebrew syntax. Finally, the OT Hebrew infinitive absolute left its mark on the Apc. and elsewhere in biblical Greek, demonstrating that the influence originated in biblical Hebrew, not in a later variety.

Another aspect of Semitic influence on Greek presented here for the first time is that of Semitic noun and verbal clauses. It was seen that noun clauses which can be traced in the Apc. can be sorted into the same categories as their Semitic counterparts, depending on their mode of construction, and their meaning is the same – that of a fixed state. Verbal clauses, expressing action in contrast to a fixed state, are basic to both Greek and Semitic languages, thus no case can be made for Semitic influence upon them, except possibly regarding their word order, when it varies from usual Greek. While the evidence cited here sheds important new light on biblical Greek syntax, and aids in better exegesis by underlining the distinction between a fixed state and an action, it is not of such a specific nature that it would serve to indicate direct translation from Semitic sources.

The final chapter, dealing with Semitic-type subordinate clauses, showed that the use of the attributive participle to express a relative clause is in line with Greek syntax, but the high frequency of occurrences in biblical Greek is difficult to account for, except as due to Semitic influence. The use of the possessive pronoun in a relative clause is peculiar to the Semitic languages, however, and is to be found influencing the phrase ὄνομα αὐτῷ in the Apc. Introduction of the relative clause by the use of an article, especially in the genitive case, can be traced directly to Hebrew usage. This has influenced the Apc. in several places. The translation of the Apc. is affected by the recognition that the attributive participle used to introduce a relative clause can, in Hebrew fashion, be resolved into a finite verb yet still express the sense of the participle. R.B.Y. Scott's 'comparative relative clause', found twice in the Apc., is due to Hebrew influence also.

The occurrence in the Apc. of two distinctly Semitic circumstantial clauses is also difficult to explain apart from the hypothesis of direct Semitic influence. The conditional clause expressed by two imperatives linked by καί is found in the Apc., based on OT Hebrew usage. Most significant in determining Semitic influence is the phenomenon noted by Beyer where the customary sequence of the conditional clause is reversed, the apodosis followed by the protasis. This seems to have no parallel in secular Greek, and can only be explained on the basis of such a reversal well-known in biblical Hebrew and Aramaic. The Semitic mode of introducing a temporal clause with *Waw* immediately followed by the temporal conjunction is found several times in the Apc. Its un-Greek nature is emphasised by the fact that in some places copyists excised the καί from their texts. Final clauses in Hebrew are expressed by the imperfect tense of the verb, and this usage has influenced passages in the Apc. where the Greek future indicative occurs instead of the customary subjunctive. Likewise, the joining of a final clause to its main clause by simple *Waw* has influenced the Greek of the Apc. in several passages. Such usage is foreign to the Greek language, and can be justified only by appealing to Semitic influence for each occurrence. Finally, the Hebrew consecutive clause, expressed by *Waw* plus jussive verb, explains the unusual syntax of Apc. 21:3.

Of special interest to translators and exegetes are passages in the Apc. in which, on the basis of findings in this study, the translation should be altered. A few are listed here: Apc. 1:1 'which he made known' (p. 91); 11:10-13 extensive series of aorists (p. 40); 17:7 'Why are you appalled?' (p. 12); 17:8 'devastated'; cf. 13:3 (p. 13); 18:3 'cause to drink' – derived Semitic tense (p. 44); 20:12 'books which were opened' (cf. p. 91); 21:7 'gain possession of' (p. 14).

More important are the large number of new exegetical possibilities which emerge if the fundamental thesis of this study gains acceptance. It could lead to a new era in the exegesis of the Apc., with more attention being given to the contributions of OT Hebrew/Aramaic syntax, and fuller awareness of the Seer's indebtedness to the OT not only for symbols and metaphors but for his very language. What more appropriate style of language could there have been for communicating his conviction that the new age of the Spirit had dawned, and the gift of prophecy had returned?

It is too much to expect that on the basis of the new evidence presented in this study the vexing question of the original language of the Apc. could be finally and convincingly answered, but it would be disappointing if this research did not provide evidence toward the eventual solution of the problem. Briefly, there have been four replies to the question of original language: (a) the Apc. was originally written in post-biblical Hebrew and subsequently translated into Greek; (b) the Apc. was originally written in post-biblical Aramaic and subsequently translated into Greek; (c) the Apc. is in part a translation from Hebrew and/or Aramaic documents, with linking sections composed in Greek; (d) the Apc. is composed *de novo* in Greek, uninfluenced by direct translation from sources; its peculiar grammar and syntax is to be explained solely on grounds of the author's unusual style. The evidence here presented has, I believe, testified *against* (a) and (b), but *in favour of* very close links to *biblical* Hebrew/Aramaic, since the syntactical oddities examined were in some cases seen to be the same as those in the LXX, reflecting features exclusive to biblical Hebrew, such as the *Waw*-consecutive, and the infinitive absolute.

The related question of *which* Semitic language, Hebrew or Aramaic, underlies the relevant portions of the Apc. must also be reconsidered in the light of this study. R.B.Y. Scott, who maintained that the Apc. was wholly a translation from Hebrew, based his arguments partly on the obvious fact that the Apc. is very closely bound up with the Hebrew OT as far as citations and allusions are concerned. He and others adopting this view have been unable to account for a few syntactical constructions which are far more at home in Aramaic than in OT Hebrew, however.[1] Most noteworthy is the use of the participle in the sense of a finite verb, which is usual practice in Aramaic, but which occurs only occasionally in the Hebrew of the OT. Similarly, the use of the third-person impersonal plural verb is strongly Aramaic, rare in biblical Hebrew. Also, the use in biblical Greek of the genitive articular infinitive influenced by the use of *lĕ* plus the infinitive is much more widespread in Aramaic than in Hebrew. On the other hand, it is wise to avoid the opposite extreme of C.C. Torrey,[2] who insisted that *all* evidence pointed to an Aramaic source for the whole of the Apc. Most of the syntactical peculiarities cited in this study could in fact be ascribed to both Hebrew *and* Aramaic. Until we have evidence to the contrary, it is probably safest to assume that due to its strong links with the language of the OT prophets, the primary source of Semitic influence on the Apc. is biblical Hebrew, and biblical Aramaic.

Coming to a decision on (c) is not as simple as some would wish, due to two facts; first, the Semitisms affecting the verb and the clause are seen to be widely scattered throughout the Apc., thus preventing the formation of a hypothesis that Semitic sources lie behind only certain portions of our present text. But, secondly, there *are* portions of the Apc. which are nearly free from Semitisms – i.e. the epistles to the Seven Churches, and at the same time portions which contain a concentration of these constructions, such as chapters 11 and 12. This has been noted previously, especially by Bousset and Charles, and it effectively prevents the cursory decision that a Semitic source underlies the entire Greek text of the Apc. It is perhaps best to suspend judgment on the matter until the complete evidence of the Semitic influence on grammar and syntax of the Apc. has been presented.

One recalls Turner's statement about the Greek of the 'Testament of Abraham':[3] 'biblical Greek . . . is usually so drenched in Semitic idioms and forms of syntax that it is extremely difficult to decide whether a book has been translated from Hebrew into Greek or whether it was originally composed in that language'. For the 'Testament of Abraham' Turner believes that Hebraic influence is so strong that the book was either a direct translation, or it was composed in a form of Greek already influenced by Hebrew idiom and syntax. 'We may', he concludes, 'call this "Jewish Greek".' The Apc. can accurately be described in identical terms, and with no hesitancy be categorised as 'Jewish Greek', to the fullest extent of that term, in spite of recent protest.[4] Thus one might venture to suggest that, at least in the Apc., the Greek language was little more than a membrane, stretched tightly over a Semitic framework, showing many essential contours from beneath. Perhaps the necessity of expressing sacred themes in a gentile tongue was rendered less distasteful so long as it preserved the tenses and other essential syntactical features of the sacred language?

Appendix I: Ἔχων

Charles, followed by Ozanne, attributes ἔχων, which is seemingly employed as a finite verb in Apc. 1:16, to Semitic influence,[1] since it follows the pattern of participle equivalent to finite verb. But Beyer points out that ἔχειν has no verbal equivalent in Hebrew or Aramaic.[2] In illustrating this he cites statistics which show that the active participle of ἔχειν (except in expressions such as ἐν γάστρι ἔχειν, κακῶς ἔχειν, etc.) appears 115 times in the LXX, 60 of which are in 1–4 Maccabees.[3] He concludes from this fact that NT occurrences of the related substantival participle ὁ ἔχων reflect a Greek, not Semitic, mode of expression. While it is true that ἔχων is used in Greek with the sense 'to have', the manner in which it is found (with or without article) in some NT passages seems to reflect a Semitic construction which can be demonstrated.

In the description of the four beasts given in Dan. 7, the Aramaic lĕ- expresses the dative of possession: Dan. 7:4 wĕgappîn dî- nĕšar lah, 'and the wings of an eagle to it', cf. verse 6 wĕlāh gappîn 'arbá', 'and to it four wings'; note also its use in verses 7, 20. Now compare the description of the four living beings about the heavenly throne in Apc. 4:7f where the identical style of language is found: καὶ τὸ τρίτον ζῷον ἔχων τὸ πρόσωπον ὡς ἀνθρώπου, 'and the third being with the face of a man' (verse 8), καὶ τὰ τέσσαρα ζῷα . . . ἔχων ἀνὰ πτέρυγας ἔξ, 'and the four beings, each with six wings', καὶ ἀνάπαυσιν οὐκ ἔχοντες (2053: εχοντα 2023** 2321) ἡμέρας καὶ νύκτος, 'and no rest to them day nor night'. The Seer uses the participle of ἔχειν in this sense in the description of the New Jerusalem, Apc. 21:11, 12, 14 (καὶ ἔδειξεν μοι . . . Ἰερουσαλὴμ καταβαίνουσαν ἐκ τοῦ οὐρανοῦ) ἔχουσαν τὴν δόξαν του θεοῦ[4] . . . ἔχουσα τεῖχος μέγα . . . ἔχουσα πυλῶας δώδεκα ('and he showed me . . . Jerusalem descending from heaven') 'with the glory of God . . . with a great wall . . . with twelve gates . . . and the wall of the city with twelve foundations'.

Obviously ἔχων is no literal equivalent of Aramaic lāh expressing possession, nor of the Syriac 'iyt leh, which renders ἔχων every time it occurs in the Apc. The significance is to be found, however, in the fact that all the ἔχων clauses cited are the equivalents of Semitic noun clauses which in Aramaic/Syriac would be expressed by lāh/'iyt leh and in Hebrew lô, of possession.[5] The importance of the distinction between noun and verbal clauses in Semitic languages is universally recognised. The former always refer to a *fixed state*, the latter to *an act*. This basic difference of syntax plays an important role in OT exegesis,[6] and realisation that a similar mould was transferred by Jewish and Jewish Christian authors to biblical Greek opens the field for possible new insights into translation and exegesis of portions of the NT as well. The syntactical distinction in this case derives from the fact that in Hebrew and Aramaic the noun clause is often used in descriptions such as those just cited.[7]

It remains now to explain why the Seer would favour the participial form ἔχων to express possession in a (Greek translation) noun clause.[8] This is probably due to the fact that Semitic noun clauses contain only nouns or their equivalents, i.e. pronouns, adjectives, or *participles.*[9] A verbal clause, on the other hand, has as its predicate a finite verb. The Seer, in employing this descriptive quality of the Semitic noun clause, would choose the participle ἔχων; the finite ἔχω in such a context would signal a verbal clause instead of a descriptive noun clause, thus altering the sense. The growing tendency in Aramaic to employ participles as finite verbs[10] would of course blur somewhat the distinction between the two types of clauses in places where participles were used,[11] but this does not affect the construction under consideration because Aramaic possessive *lāh* and Syriac *'iyt leh* are of course not participial, and are firmly rooted in noun clause usage.

Appendix II: The resumptive pronoun

We now make an excursus to study another Semitic characteristic of relative clauses, the resumptive pronoun, and to survey the recent work of W.F. Bakker of the University of Amsterdam, who has made a significant contribution to our understanding of the resumptive pronoun in Greek relative clauses.[1] His study includes a rich selection of occurrences, arranged chronologically from Homer through the classical period, to Hellenistic Greek. Although tacitly confessing a lack of knowledge of Semitic languages,[2] the author does not hesitate to deal with Greek of the LXX (including the apocrypha) and the NT, and to contend with the closely-debated issue of Semitic influence on the frequently-occurring resumptive pronouns there.[3]

His primary contribution, stated in briefest form, is the distinction made for the first time between *non-essential* versus *essential* relative clauses. A non-essential (non-restrictive) relative clause is one which 'is not essential to the meaning of the sentence, but merely adds an idea. Such a clause does not determine the antecedent, but is almost independent.'[4] Into this category fall the resumptive pronouns in both ancient and *Koine* Greek, but it excludes most (not all) from biblical Greek. Thus the author can conclude that in ancient Greek the term *pronomen abundans* is a misnomer,[5] because where the pronoun is employed it is not redundant, but serves a definite purpose. The situation in *Koine* Greek differs, since in at least some cases the *pronomen abundans* serves to reinforce the relative pronoun, which had been reduced to a mere connective.

The function of the widely-employed resumptive pronoun in Semitic languages, according to Bakker, is altogether different. While truly Greek relative clauses which include a resumptive pronoun are non-essential, in Hebrew/Aramaic the relative pronouns $d\check{e}/'\check{a}\check{s}er$[6] have an inherent obscurity which is cleared up by addition of a personal or demonstrative pronoun. They become necessary to the full understanding of the sentence so are termed *essential*, in contrast to the non-essential Greek counterparts.

By applying this distinction to the resumptive pronouns in the LXX, the apocrypha, the NT and NT apocrypha, Bakker seeks to determine whether the resumptive pronoun in biblical Greek is due to Semitic influence. He finds eighteen occurrences of the resumptive pronoun in the NT (based on Nestle's text),[7] eight of which follow the Greek pattern (i.e. are non-essential). This number in a text the size of the NT corresponds favourably to the frequency of the construction in *Koine* Greek. Along with these are two examples termed 'uncertain'; then are listed eight cases where Greek would never have used a *pronomen abundans*, one in Mark (7:25), seven in the Apc. (3:8; 7:2, 9; 12:6; 13:8, 12; 17:9).[8]

Examination of Hoskier's critical apparatus of the Apc. shows the textual evidence to be surprisingly stable and consistent in transmitting the resumptive pronoun. The only possible instance not appearing in Nestle's text of the Apc. for which manuscript evidence exists is 2:18, τάδε λέγει ὁ υἱὸς τοῦ θεοῦ ὁ ἔχων τοὺ ὀφθαλμοὺς αὐτοῦ (ℵ C 025, 046) ὡς φλόγα πυρός, 'Thus says the Son of God, who has eyes like flames of fire' (literally 'who has *his* eyes').[9]

I accept the method so clearly developed and fully set out in Bakker's monograph, with but two criticisms. First, the crucial decision of whether or not the relative clause in question is essential allows for a measure of subjective opinion, and so cannot be relied upon as an absolute guide as to whether or not any given resumptive pronoun is essential. It would be safer to ask, after applying this rule, whether there is evidence for Semitic influence on the passage in question, before declaring that the resumptive pronoun is or is not Semitic. The author himself recognises this problem when he discusses the occurrences in the NT.[10] The second criticism concerns the accuracy of the statement made that the Hebrew *'ǎšer* used to introduce relative clauses is merely *nota relationis*.[11] There is a ground for arguing to the contrary, that it is *not* simply a loose connecting particle but is essentially a demonstrative pronoun, often belonging to the main clause.[12] This has support from the fact that the Hebrew demonstrative pronouns *zeh* and *zû* are sometimes used as relative pronouns.

Under this heading a conjecture will be put forward which, if accepted, would resolve a puzzling, if not particularly troublesome, verse. Apc. 1:1 is traditionally rendered 'The revelation of Jesus Christ, which God gave him, to show to his servants what must take place' (RSV). The versions, ancient and modern, do not stray from this, and indeed it is the only way to understand the present text. The relative clause 'which God gave him' is the heart of the puzzle, though. How could the Seer write of God giving a disclosure *of* Jesus Christ *to* Jesus Christ? Textual evidence hints at a bit of primitive uncertainty at this point as well: instead of ἣν ἔδωκεν αὐτῷ, 046 preserves the reading αὐτή, while 181 reads αὐτοῦ. It could be conjectured that αὐτή represents a corrupt form of an original resumptive pronoun αὐτήν; i.e. ἣν ἔδωκεν αὐτὴν ὁ θεός, 'which God gave *it*'. The verse would then be translated 'The revelation of Jesus Christ, which God gave to show his servants what must take place'. The traditional αὐτῷ would be a primitive corruption or alteration entering the text prior to the time when the ancient versions were translated.

NOTES

Introduction

1 R.H. Charles, *A Critical and Exegetical Commentary on the Revelation of St. John* (Edinburgh, 1920), I, 143 (hereinafter cited as Charles I (or II)).

2 'The Biblical Languages' in *The Cambridge History of the Bible* (Cambridge, 1970), I, 10f.

3 J.H. Moulton, *A Grammar of New Testament Greek*, IV, 'Style', by Nigel Turner (Edinburgh, 1976), 150.

4 See below, p. 79.

5 See M. Segal, *Grammar of Mishnaic Hebrew* (Oxford, 1927), p. 165.

6 *The Morphology of Koine Greek as Used in the Apocalypse of St. John. A Study in Bilingualism*, Supplement to *Novum Testamentum*, 27 (Leiden, 1971), p. 324.

7 See below, p. 53.

8 Below, p. 66.

9 Below, pp. 80ff.

10 Pp. 168–71.

11 Princeton, 1902. Thanks are due to Professor B.M. Metzger who provided a photocopy of this thesis.

12 Pp. 16f.

13 Pp. 19f.

14 I, clix.

15 Pp. cxxiii–cxxvii.

16 On p. cxxiii, note 1 he points out the relative confusion exhibited in chapter 11, ascribing it to the author's use of 'traditional material'.

17 *Ibid.*, p. cxxiv.

18 Charles here (p. cxxiv) and elsewhere notes usage of language which is more akin to Aramaic than to classical Hebrew; however, he does not seem seriously to consider the possibility of Aramaic sources behind portions of the Apc., nor does he say much about the influence of an Aramaic mother tongue on the author of the Apc.

19 I, 271–3.

20 I, cxliii.

21 *Ibid.*

22 Toronto University Press.
23 *Ibid.*
24 Cf. Gesenius–Kautzsch (Cowley), *Hebrew Grammar* (Oxford, 1910), §155 g (hereinafter cited as GK).
25 Scott, *The Original Language of the Apocalypse* (Toronto, 1928), p. 10.
26 *Saint Jean. L'Apocalypse,* 4th edn (Paris, 1933), pp. cliii–clv, where the verb is discussed.
27 *Apocalypse of John* (New Haven, 1958).
28 *Ibid.*, p. 57.
29 Collectio Assisiensis 1 (Assisi, 1964).
30 Cf. Lancellotti, *Sintassi Ebraica,* p. 116.
31 *The Morphology of Koine Greek.*
32 In J. Lambrecht, ed., *L'Apocalypse johannique et l'Apocalyptique dans le Nouveau Testament,* Bibliotheca Ephemeridum Theologicarum Lovaniensium 53 (Louvain, 1980), pp. 167–77.
33 *Ibid.*, pp. 171f.
34 3rd edn (Oxford, 1967).
35 I, 'Satzlehre' i (Göttingen, 1962).

1 Textual considerations

1 *Untersuchungen zur Geschichte der lateinischen Apokalypseübersetzung* (Düsseldorf, 1920).
2 *Concerning the Text of the Apocalypse* (2 volumes, London, 1929).
3 *Studien zur Geschichte des griechischen Apokalypse-Textes,* Part II, 'Die alten Stämme' (Munich, 1955). For a review of Schmid, see G.D. Kilpatrick, 'Professor J. Schmid', *Vigiliae Christianae* 13 (1959), 1–13.
4 Admirably summarised in an article by J.N. Birdsall, 'The Text of the Revelation of S. John', *Evangelical Quarterly* 33 (1961), 228–37.
5 Schmid, *Studien,* on pp. 12, note 2, and 150, note 1; cf. *ZNW* 59 (1968), 251, where this is repeated.
6 Published by F.G. Kenyon, *The Chester Beatty Biblical Papyri,* fascicle 3 (London, 1934). For evaluations see M.J. Lagrange, 'Les Papyrus Ch. Beatty', *Revue Biblique* 43 (1934), 488–93 and R.V.G. Tasker, 'The Chester Beatty Papyrus', *JTS* 50 (1949), 65ff.
7 *ZNW* 52 (1961), 82–8; *ZNW* 59 (1968), 250–8.
8 *ZNW* 59 (1968), 251.
9 *Novum Testamentum Graece* (Stuttgart, 1979), p. 53*.
10 'Le Texte de l'Apocalypse', in J. Lambrecht, ed., *L'Apocalypse johannique et l'Apocalyptique dans le Nouveau Testament,* Bibliotheca Ephemeridum Theologicarum Lovaniensium 53 (Louvain, 1980), p. 156.
11 *Ibid.*, pp. 156–61.

12   *Aramaic Approach*, 3rd edn, pp. 28f.
13   Chapter entitled 'Textual Criticism and Linguistics', p. 14.
14   'The Greek New Testament Text of Today and the Textus Receptus', in *The New Testament in Historical and Contemporary Perspectives: Essays in Honour of G.H.C. Macgregor*, edited by H. Anderson and W. Barclay (Oxford, 1965), pp. 205f.
15   'Professor J. Schmid', *Vigiliae Christianae* 13 (1959), 6.
16   *Ibid.*
17   *The Text of the New Testament*, 2nd edn, (Oxford, 1968), p. 233.
18   'Professor J. Schmid', *Vigiliae Christianae*, 13 (1959), 6.
19   Schmid, *Studien*, pp. 249–51.
20   'The Greek New Testament Text of Today', p. 126. See also his 'Atticism and the Text of the Greek New Testament', in J. Blinzler *et al.*, eds., *Neutestamentliche Aufsätze: Festschrift für Prof. Josef Schmid* (Regensburg, 1963).
21   See Delobel, 'Le Texte de l'Apocalypse', pp. 157f for a discussion of the use of eclectic method in this edition.

2 Greek verbs with Hebrew meanings

1   For a recent evaluation of words in the Apc. under real or supposed Hebrew influence, cf. Matthew Black, 'Some Greek Words with "Hebrew" Meanings in the Epistles and Apocalypse', in *Biblical Studies: Essays in Honour of William Barclay*, ed. J.R. McKay and J.F. Miller (London, 1976), pp. 135–46.
2   In later development the Hellenistic ϑαυμάζειν took the auxiliary definition of 'honour', 'admire'; cf. LS-J, *s.v.* ϑαυμάζω.
3   The term *šāmēm* has two definitions, with uncertain connection; 'desolated', and 'appalled'; cf. BDB.
4   On the passive form for possible active verbs, cf. Bl-D, §78, also section on voice, below, p. 24. Apc. 13:3 and 17:8 contain the only two occurrences of the passive form.
5   Cf. BAG, *s.v.* ϑαυμάζω 2, where 'wonder' is equated with 'worship'.
6   Here προσκυνέω without the sense of 'worship'.
7   See Black, 'Some Greek Words', pp. 145f; and Moulton–Turner, *Grammar*, IV, 154.
8   *Die Kasussyntax der Verba bei den Septuaginta* (Göttingen, 1928), pp. 52, 193.
9   Moulton–Turner, *Grammar*, IV, 154.
10   Black, 'Some Greek Words', pp. 135–46.
11   See LS-J, *s.v.* δίδωμι.
12   See BDB, *s.v.* *nātan*, 1, i.
13   Moulton–Turner, *Grammar*, IV, 154.
14   I, 230.
15   Cf. BDB, *s.v.* *yāraš*.
16   Cf. LS-J, *s.v.* κληρονομέω.

17 Cf. Bauer, *s.v.* κληρονομέω 2; this 'is Hellenistic Greek usage', he notes.
18 *Ibid.*, 1.
19 I, 59; II, 222.
20 As rendered by Black, 'Some Greek Words', p. 144.
21 I, 76.
22 Cf. the discussion under κληρονομέω above.
23 *Original Language*, p. 20; cf. Torrey, *The Apocalypse of John*, p. 107.
24 Moulton–Turner, *Grammar*, IV, 153f.
25 Cf. BDB, *s.v. mṣ'* niphal 2.
26 Moulton–Turner, *Grammar*, IV, 157.
27 Cf. Black, *Aramaic Approach*, pp. 138f.

3 Semitic influence on verbal syntax

1 Pp. 126f. Occurrences in the Gospels are cited. Cf. Beyer, *Semitische Syntax im Neuen Testament*, I, 226ff.
2 Charles I, 362; Dan. 4:13, 22, 23, 29; 5:20, 21; 7:12, 26. Ezra 6:5. Torrey, *The Apocalypse of John*, p. 42 cites this as evidence of an Aramaic origin of the Apc.
3 Bl-D, 130 (2); cf. Moulton–Howard, *Grammar*, II, 447, for a similar statement.
4 Moulton–Turner, *Grammar*, III, 292f. Cf. Moulton–Turner, *Grammar*, IV, 12, 32, 150.
5 See his book, *Fachprosa, Vermeintliche Volkssprache und Neues Testament*, Acta Universitatis Upsaliensis Studia Graeca Upsaliensia 5 (Uppsala, 1967). For a recent reaction to Rydbeck's position see Moulton–Turner, *Grammar*, IV, 159.
6 Rydbeck, *Fachprosa*, p. 27, note 1.
7 *Ibid.*, p. 28.
8 *Ibid.*, pp. 29f.
9 *Ibid.*, p. 34.
10 *Ibid.*, p. 35.
11 *Ibid.*, p. 36.
12 *Ibid.*, p. 37.
13 *Ibid.*, pp. 39–42.
14 Cf. Kautzsch, *Grammatik des biblisch-Aramäischen* (Leipzig, 1884), §96.
15 GK, §144 d–g.
16 Gen. 34:27; Job 7:3, 4:19, 6:2, 18:18, 19:26, 34:20; Ps. 43:11; Prov. 2:22, 9:11.
17 I, 269.
18 English translation (Edinburgh, 1902), pp. 224–6. More recent discussion is found in J. Jeremias, *New Testament Theology* (ET London, 1971) I, 9–14.
19 Conybeare and Stock, *Selections*, §84; cf. Bl-D, §309 (1).
20 *Philologische Wochenschrift* 49 (1929), 468.

21 In J. Ziegler, *Beiträge zur Ieremias-Septuaginta.* Nachrichten der Akad. d. Wiss. in Göttingen 2 (phil.-hist. Klasse, Jahrg. 1958).
22 Cf. Bl-D, §309 (1) for further examples.
23 Toronto, 1928, p. 10.
24 *ZAW* 85(1973), 197–219.
25 *Ibid.*, p. 200.
26 *Ibid.*
27 *Original Language*, p. 10; also Moulton–Turner, *Grammar*, IV, 157f, but cf. LS-J, *s.v.* ποιέω A.II.1*b*.
28 Mussies, *Morphology*, p. 321, notes that ἵνα plus subjunctive/fut. indic. could reflect the Semitic causative sense as could the infin. when following ποιεῖν.
29 Mussies, *loc cit.*, argues that the seemingly synonymous construction of δίδωμι plus infinitive, etc., really means 'permit', 'allow', rather than 'cause', thus not expressing a true causative sense (here also he should place 13:17 δύνηται ἀγοράσαι ἢ πωλῆσαι, which means 'no one able (permitted) to buy or to sell').
30 Cf. also Moulton–Turner, *Grammar*, IV, 155.
31 Bousset, *Die Offenbarung Johannis*, 6th edn (Göttingen, 1906), p. 162; Allo, *Saint Jean. L'Apocalypse*, 4th edn (Paris, 1933), p. 206; Charles I, 350f.
32 H.StJ. Thackeray, *A Grammar of the Old Testament in Greek* (Cambridge, 1909), I, 238f. Kühner-Blass, *Ausführliche Grammatik der griechischen Sprache*, I (Hanover, 1890), §324 contains a list of some fifty-five verbs which had already in classical Greek expressed deponents with aorist passive forms; cf. Bl-D, §78. Against Blass (followed by W. Bauer, *Wörterbuch*, *s.v.* θαυμάζω 2), who urges that θαυμάζειν was among that class of deponents preferring aorist passive forms, textual evidence indicates that the active ἐθαύμασα was preferred by later copyists.
33 *A Grammar*, p. 240, note 1.
34 The underlying Hebrew root, *ymr* or *'mr* (probably the latter, cf. BDB, *s.v.* *'mr*, p. 56 b) means 'act proudly'.
35 Cf. above, 'Greek verbs with Hebrew meanings', pp. 12f.
36 Cf. BDB, *s.v.* šāmēm.
37 Cf. Bl-D, §313; Moulton–Turner, *Grammar*, III, 58.
38 II, 52.
39 M. Zerwick, *Biblical Greek* (Rome, 1963), §236.
40 J. Jeremias, *New Testament Theology*, I, 11–14.
41 Cf. Moulton–Turner, *Grammar*, III, 58.
42 Schwyzer, *Griechische Grammatik*, II, 318; Bl-D, §366; Mandilaras, *The Verb*, §§397–9.
43 Jannaris, *An Historical Greek Grammar* (London, 1897), p. 466.
44 Bl-D, §366 cite Euripides, *Ion* 758 εἴπωμεν ἢ σιγῶμεν; ἢ τί δράσομεν; Cf. Moulton–Turner, *Grammar*, III, 98.
45 Deliberative subjunctives in the NT include among others Matt. 6:31, 16:26; Mark 12:14; Luke 14:34, 16:11f. Deliberative futures include Mark 6:37; Luke 11:5, 22:49; John 6:68; Romans 3:5.

46 *Selections*, §73.
47 This use of the deliberative present indicative was designated by
    Millar Burrows as 'one of the characteristic idioms of the LXX',
    in 'The Original Language of the Gospel of John', *JBL* 49 (1930),
    105. Of course the true Greek form of the deliberative appears
    often in the LXX as well; subjunctives in 2 Km. 23:3, 4 Km.
    6:15; Isa. 1:5. The future indic. in Gen. 27:37; Ps. 12:2, 3; 61:4.
48 GK, §116 p.
49 Charles I, 175 notes the occurrence of ἕως πότε plus deliberative
    in Matt. 17:17, ‖ Mk. 9:19 (future indicative), John 10:24 (present
    indicative), plus a number of places in the LXX Psalms. It seems
    that this construction is the Greek translation equivalent of
    Hebrew *'ad-mâ* and similar terms.
50 This mechanical translation of a Hebrew imperfect by a Greek
    future has been noted in other settings by Leslie Allen, *The Greek
    Chronicles*, supplements to *Vetus Testamentum* 25 (Leiden,
    1974), I, 42.
51 For an example of the deliberative question in the aorist tense,
    cf. Gen. 26:10 Τί τοῦτο ἐποίησας ἡμῖν; 'What is this you have
    done to us?' from a Hebrew perfect.
52 For a more comprehensive presentation of the Greek equivalents
    of Hebrew tenses, cf. 'Tenses of the finite verb', below, pp. 29–
    53.
53 Bl-D, §366.
54 Mayser, *Gramm.*, II, 2, 1; 236.
55 Conybeare and Stock, *Selections*, §106; Bl-D, §369 (2); Mandi-
    laras, *The Verb*, §413; Mussies, *Morphology*, p. 322.
56 Occurrences in the Apc. cited by Mussies are 2:22, 25; 3:9; 4:9f;
    6:4, 11; 8:3; 9:4, 5, 20; 13:12; 14:13; 15:4; 18:14. Since manu-
    script evidence can be cited for additional examples, Mussies
    rightly suggests that the number of futures indicative in the Apc.
    was originally higher, the aorists subjunctive lower. Scribal altera-
    tions account for the changed ratio.
57 Conybeare and Stock, *Selections*, §106.
58 Passages examined are: Gen. 16:2; Ex. 1:11; Deut. 14:28; 22:7
    (cf. verse 17); 3 Km. 2:3, 4; 2 Chr. 18:15; Prov. 6:30; Jer. 10:24;
    29:11; Lam. 1:19.
59 Mussies, *Morphology*, p. 322 explains this phenomenon in similar
    terms. He noted that since the Semitic verb system lacked a
    special subjunctive category, the imperfect tense came to bear,
    during later periods of the Hebrew language (i.e. first century
    A.D.) the value of a Greek subjunctive. Admittedly, this category
    was infrequent in the Hebrew/Aramaic of first-century Palestine.
    Had Mussies not insisted that the Seer was influenced only by
    late Hebrew, he would have seen the clear influence of earlier
    Hebrew at this point.
60 *Ibid.*, pp. 322f.
61 *Ibid.*, cf. Lancellotti, *Sintassi Ebraica*, pp. 69ff; Bl-D, §§362, 365.

62   καὶ ὅταν δώσουσιν ... πεσοῦνται ... καὶ προσκυνήσουσιν ... καὶ
     βαλοῦσιν. But this passage seems to fit the indicative instead of
     jussive sense, perhaps in a past tense, as suggested in Moulton–
     Turner, *Grammar*, III, 86.
63   Cf. Luke 2:15 Διέλθωμεν δὴ ... καὶ ἴδωμεν, which is the usual
     Greek hortatory construction.
64   GK, §48.
65   *An Idiom Book of New Testament Greek*, 2nd edn (Cambridge,
     1959), p. 181.
66   For discussion of this distinction, cf. Lancellotti, *Sintassi Ebraica*,
     chapter 1; Mussies, *Morphology*, chapter 12; Charles I, cxxiiiff,
     who devotes several paragraphs to the topic under consideration.
67   *Griechische Grammatik*, II, 273.
68   Moulton–Turner, *Grammar*, III, 63f.
69   Bl-D, §323; cf. E. De W. Burton, *Syntax of the Moods and Tenses
     in New Testament Greek*, 2nd edn (Edinburgh, 1894), pp. 9f,
     who cites examples in Mark 9:31 παραδίδοται; Matt. 26:18 ποιῶ,
     27:63 ἐγείρομαι; Luke 3:9 ἐκκόπτεται.
70   Cf. W.W. Goodwin, *A Greek Grammar*, 1st edn (London, 1879),
     §200, note 3.
71   *Neutestamentliche Grammatik*, 2nd edn (Tübingen, 1925), p.
     152.
72   A.N. Jannaris, *An Historical Greek Grammar* (London, 1897), p.
     434.
73   *Gramm.*, II, 1, 133f.
74   *The Verb*, §214ff.
75   S.R. Driver, *A Treatise on the Use of the Tenses in Hebrew*, 3rd
     edn (Oxford, 1892), p. 169. For a description of the use of the
     participle in biblical Aramaic cf. A.F. Johns, *A Short Grammar of
     Biblical Aramaic* (Berrien Springs, 1966), p. 25, and H. Bauer and
     P. Leander, *Gramm. des bibl.-Aramäischen* (Halle-Saale, 1927),
     pp. 291f, who note that, while the futuristic use of the partic. is
     not so common in biblical Aramaic, it comes to predominate by
     the time of Jewish–Palestinian Aramaic, where it tends to replace
     the futuristic imperfect. W.B. Stevenson, *Grammar of Palestinian
     Jewish Aramaic*, 2nd edn (Oxford, 1962), pp. 56f, can also be
     consulted for discussion of this use of the participle.
76   GK, §116 p.
77   Strictly speaking, *futurum instans* is employed only by grammarians
     in describing biblical Hebrew. However, since the corresponding
     Aramaic participle can express identical future sense, we follow
     C.F. Burney, *Aramaic Origin of the Fourth Gospel* (Oxford,
     1922), pp. 94f in extending the use of the term to include Aramaic
     as well.
78   *Gramm.*, 133f.
79   *Aramaic Origin*, pp. 94f.
80   Cf. *Aramaic Approach*, pp. 131f.
81   Knowing that the text of the NT often underwent scribal revising

and correction, and that this work was not carried out with consistency, even within the compass of single mss. (on this see *Aramaic Approach*, pp. 28–34), it is necessary to base a study of syntax on as wide a textual base as possible, to allow for the uneven revision of mss., and to aid in detecting more primitive readings. This comprehensive textual foundation has been provided for the Apc. by H.C. Hoskier's *Concerning the Text of the Apocalypse* (2 vols., London, 1929), which provides a collation of all Apc. Greek mss. known at the time, plus the testimony of the versions and patristic commentaries. To his *apparatus criticus* this study is indebted for practically all Greek ms. citations.

82   Charles I, 71.
83   Driver, *Hebrew Tenses*, p. 168.
84   Lancellotti, *Sintassi Ebraica*, p. 61, notes this corresponds to Hebr. *qôtēl* preceded by *hinnê*.
85   Cf. the expression common in Jeremiah: *hinnê . . . bā'îm*.
86   Charles I, cxlix, prefers to render this present as a future, ascribing it however, to influence of Hebrew imperfect rather than participle.
87   Cf. Simcox, *The Revelation of St. John the Divine* (Cambridge, 1893), p. 121, who notes that most of these presents are rendered as future in Latin.
88   This present is 'clearly jussive' according to G. Mussies, *Morphology*, p. 337; but we would prefer to see some precedent, from the LXX or other translation Greek, of Semitic jussives rendered by Greek presents indicative before accepting his explanation of this verb. In a brief examination of the LXX rendering of 18 Hebrew jussives, 8 were expressed by the Greek future (-ἔσται 3 times), 4 by subjunctives, 5 by imperatives, 1 by aorist indicative. In none was the present indicative employed; thus, we prefer to understand Apc. 13:10 as a futuristic present indicative.
89   Charles II, 131, compares here Isa. 11:3, where the sense is obviously future; thus the verbs in Apc. can well be taken as future also.
90   Charles II, 210, 'The future ἕξουσιν (A vg minusc.) is to be preferred to ἔχουσιν. All verbs in this description of the New Jerusalem are futures.' This might; however, be a case of shifting tenses, a characteristic of the Apc. based perhaps on the Hebrew tendency to alternate between participle and finite verb. The present tense is the more difficult reading.
91   *Ibid.*, I, cxxiii.
92   *Sintassi Ebraica*, pp. 67ff.
93   *Ibid.*, p. 68.
94   *Ibid.*, p. 67.
95   *Morphology*, pp. 312ff.
96   Princeton, New Jersey, 1902.
97   *Commentarius in Apocalypsin*, p. 39.
98   While this is a general rule, there are exceptions. Cf. Zech. 3:9 where present ὀρύσσω renders Hebrew perfect *nātatî*.

99   Moulton–Howard, *Grammar*, II, 456f; Moulton–Turner, *Grammar*, III, 60f; Bl-D, §321; Lancellotti, *Sintassi Ebraica*, pp. 62–6. For LXX examples cf. Thackeray, *The Septuagint and Jewish Worship*, 2nd edn (London, 1923), pp. 21f.

100   'The Influence of the Text and Language of the Old Testament on the Book of Revelation' (unpublished thesis, Manchester, 1964), p. 34.

101   Moulton–Turner, *Grammar*, III, 60.

102   *Aramaic Approach*, p. 130.

103   Cf. Driver, *Hebrew Tenses*, p. 166.

104   Cf. K. Beyer, *Semitische Syntax*, pp. 86ff.

105   Concerning the presence of the gnomic aorist in the NT Bl-D, §333 note that it appears infrequently, nearly always in comparisons. The same is true for classical Greek.

106   *Hebrew Tenses*, p. 18, note 2; p. 63. Cf. M. Black, 'The Christological Use of the OT in the NT', *NTS* 18 (1972), 10, note 4, for a NT occurrence.

107   The translation/revision by Theod. proves most suitable for this study for two reasons; first, since the LXX of Daniel is periphrastic in nature, and marked by the presence of textual expansions in some cases, it proves difficult to determine the Hebrew/Aramaic original behind it. Dan. 5:14a, for example, is missing in the LXX, though it appears in both the MT and Theod. Second, in the more literal version of Theod. there appears to be a text with less literary smoothing than the single tenth/eleventh-century A.D. ms. (codex Chisianus) which preserves the LXX text. A brief comparison of the two versions reveals that, where Theod. tacks phrases together in Semitised paratactic style, the LXX employs the smoother Greek hypotaxis. The fact that Theod. is dated second century A.D., thus making it much too late to have influenced the author of the Apc., does not reduce its value as biblical Greek. Evidence is strong for the existence of a 'proto-Theod.' text during the first century A.D., since characteristically Theod. readings from Dan. appear in works composed before this time. This makes it appear that Theod. revised a version which long pre-dated him. Cf. R.K. Harrison, *Introduction to the Old Testament* (Grand Rapids, Michigan, 1969), p. 1134; for the most recent discussion, with references, cf. E. Würthwein, *Der Text des alten Testaments*, 4th edn (Stuttgart, 1974), pp. 56f.

108   Bl-D, §333 (2).

109   *Biblical Greek*, 4th edn (Rome, 1963), §259 (incorrectly cited as §59 by R. Funk in Bl-D).

110   *An Idiom Book of NT Greek*, pp. 12f.

111   *Aramaic Approach*, pp. 129f.

112   Mussies, *Morphology*, pp. 337ff denies that the use of the aorist in the Apc. has anything peculiar about it, although he feels that it serves a number of times for the *futurum exactum*, as could the Hebrew/Aramaic qatal. He makes no mention, however, of

the Greek aorist indicative with a patently present sense which we have clearly illustrated.

113 Cf. Driver, *Hebrew Tenses*, pp. 13–26.
114 *L'Apocalypse*, p. 2.
115 Lancellotti, *Sintassi Ebraica*, p. 49, notes these aorists are used in the sense of Hebrew perfect.
116 Charles I, 265, explains this aorist as a Hebraism for *wĕnišlam*. Cf. Moulton–Turner, *Grammar*, IV, 152.
117 Mussies, *Morphology*, p. 338, considers this as aorist of proleptic past, based on the parallel passage in Isa. 21:9 (LXX πέπτωκεν). But the translation of this phrase by the present tense is acceptable – in any case, the Hebrew stative perfect *nāplāh nāplāh* has influenced the choice of the Greek aorist; cf. Charles II, 14.
118 Allo, *L'Apocalypse*, p. 306, suggests 19:20 ἐβλήθησαν should be future in meaning.
119 Charles II, 119f, found in Hebrew texts an idiom corresponding to this construction. See 2 Ki. 9:7 where perfect *wĕniqqāmtî* is employed.
120 Again, Charles II, 125 calls attention to the similar use of *mālak* in Ps. 97:1, where again we note that the Hebrew perfect is translated by aorist in the LXX.
121 For a discussion of Greek perfect participles for Semitic participles of the derived conjugations, cf. section on Participles, pp. 71–3. Black, *Aramaic Approach*, pp. 129f, drew attention to anomalous occurrences of the perfect in the Gospels.
122 *Grammar*, I, 142.
123 Bl-D, §343 is thus aptly titled 'Perfect for the aorist'.
124 E. de W. Burton, *Syntax of the Moods and Tenses in New Testament Greek*, p. 44.
125 §342 (4).
126 *Aramaic Approach*, p. 129f.
127 BDB, *s.v. kûn* hiphil, 2, a.
128 *Studien*, II, 'Die alten Stämme', p. 207.
129 Cf. Bl-D, §343.
130 Cf. Bauer, *Wörterbuch, s.v.* ἵστημι II, 2.
131 I, 212. I wonder, though, about his assertion that 'This aoristic use of the perfect is not found in the Fourth Gospel'. For examples cf. Moulton–Turner, *Grammar*, III, 70.
132 Cf. Charles I, cxxiv; Moulton–Turner, *Grammar*, III, 86; Zerwick, *Biblical Greek*, §281; Lancellotti, *Sintassi Ebraica*, pp. 65f; Mussies, *Morphology*, pp. 341ff.
133 As early as 1825 G.B. Winer argued against those who held that the future tense verbs in Apc. 4:9–10 referred to past time (*A Treatise on the Grammar of New Testament Greek*, trans. W.F. Moulton, 3rd edn (Edinburgh, 1882), p. 350.
134 *Commentarius in Apocalypsin*, pp. 38f.
135 *The Revelation of St. John*, p. 76.
136 Moulton–Turner, *Grammar*, III, 86; cf. his *Grammatical Insights*

Into the New Testament (Edinburgh, 1965), pp. 158ff, and Moulton–Turner, *Grammar*, IV, 152.

137 In this passage the Hebrew perfect plus *Waw*-consecutive *wenasa* with past meaning is curiously rendered several times in the LXX by future ἐξαροῦσιν. While at first this would seem to be contrary to the equation of Greek future = Semitic imperfect, yet we note that the Hebrew perfect plus *Waw*-consecutive, since it takes on the sense of whatever verb precedes it in a given context, can have the same meaning as imperfect.

138 *Morphology*, p. 335.

139 *Offenbarung*, p. 142.

140 But we prefer the explanation and translation given above, pp. 24f of this chapter, passive of θαυμάζειν.

141 Charles' term, 'thinking in Hebrew while writing in Greek', seems inadequate to account for the more peculiar usage noted in this section.

142 Lancellotti, *Sintassi Ebraica*, pp. 39–43.

143 The shift from aorist to present and even from present to future is not unknown in the NT, but a direct leap from aorist to future (or *vice versa*) is, so far as I can determine, limited to the Apc.

144 *Commentarius in Apocalypsin*, pp. 394.

145 *Ibid.*, pp. 168f.

146 *Ibid.*, p. 334.

147 I, cxxiiif.

148 *Sintassi Ebraica*, pp. 42f.

149 *L'Apocalypse*, p. 216.

150 Moulton–Turner, *Grammar*, III, 87–9; Bl-D, §§352–6.

151 Skrifter Utgivna av. den Kungliga Humanistiska Vetenskaps-samfundet i Uppsala 32, Part II (Uppsala, 1940).

152 In Paul Regard's *La Phrase Nominale dans la Langue du Noveau Testament* (Paris, 1919), pp. 111–85.

153 Björk, *Die Periphrastischen Konstruktionen*, pp. 59f, 67f, 123ff.

154 *Ibid.*, pp. 67f.

155 Cf. Bl-D, §353 (1); Mayser, *Gramm.*, II, 1, 223ff; Moulton–Turner, *Grammar*, III, 87.

156 *Die Periphrastischen Konstruktionen*, p. 96.

157 Conybeare and Stock, *Selections*, §72.

158 Cf. GK, §116 r.

159 Cf. Stevenson, *Grammar of Palestinian Jewish Aramaic*, p. 58, who also cites Dan. 2:31; 6:5, 11, 15.

160 Amsterdam, 1965 (cited by Mussies, *Morphology*, p. 304).

161 Moulton–Turner, *Grammar*, III, 87–9 cites many (perhaps all?) occurrences in the NT; cf. also discussions in Bl-D, §§352–6. Both allow for Semitic, especially Aramaic, influence. Black, *Aramaic Approach*, p. 130 is in agreement. For more recent discussion, cf. Mussies, *Morphology*, pp. 302–8.

162 Moulton–Turner, *Grammar*, III, 87–9.

163 Cf. GK, §116 r.

164 Cf. Bl-D, §352.
165 Further examples are cited by Aerts, *Periphrastica*, pp. 56ff.
166 *Morphology*, p. 331.
167 *Aramaic Approach*, p. 130.
168 According to Moulton–Turner, *Grammar*, III, 89.
169 Apc. 1:18 ἐγενόμην νεκρός is also cited by Turner, *Grammar*, III, 89, along with 3:2, 16:10.
170 The significant advance in understanding of the development and function of *Waw*-consecutive, from the earlier explanation given by S.R. Driver, through that put forward in 1948 by Henri Fleisch in his article *Sur le système verbal du sémitique commun et son évolution dans les langues sémitiques anciennes*, Mélanges de l'Université Saint Joseph 27 (Beirut, 1947–8), 39–60, which was adapted by Frank Blake of Johns Hopkins University, and is generally accepted today, serves as the position from which this section is written. For the standard presentation, see Blake's *A Resurvey of the Hebrew Tenses* (Rome, 1951), pp. 44–53.
171 GK, §§112ff.
172 Evidence has been presented for the influence of the *Waw*-consecutive on the redundant καί in the Apc. by the following: Allo, *L'Apocalypse*, p. 141; Beyer, *Semitische Syntax*, 66f; Black, *Aramaic Approach*, 3rd edn, p. 67, note 1; Bousset, *Offenbarung*, p. 160; Charles I, cxlviii; Bl-D, §442 (7); Moulton–Turner, *Grammar*, III, 334f, IV, 154; Scott, *Original Language*, p. 11.
173 Scott, *Original Language*, p. 11, considers 14:9f to be a causal clause
174 *L'Apocalypse*, p. 141. Cf. G.R. Driver, *JTS* n.s. 11 (1960), 386; Beyer, *Semitische Syntax*, p. 69.
175 Mussies, *Morphology*, p. 314.
176 *Ibid.*; cf. M.H. Segal, *A Grammar of Mishnaic Hebrew* (Oxford, 1927), pp. 72f.
177 M. Burrows, 'Orthography, Morphology and Syntax of the St. Mark's Isaiah Manuscript', *JBL* 68 (1949), 209f, lists only about twenty cases in which *Waw*-consecutive tenses are avoided. See Mussies, *Morphology*, p. 313, note 2 for further references to relevant literature.
178 Cf. Segal, *Mishnaic Hebrew*.
179 *Morphology*, p. 322.
180 Cf. GK, §§109, 110.
181 Cf. section 'Future indicative for semitic jussive', p. 27.
182 Schwyzer, *Griechische Grammatik*, II, 380.
183 Bl-D, §389.
184 Mayser, *Gramm.*, II, 1, 303–5; Moulton–Turner, *Grammar*, III, 78, and especially Mandilaras, *The Verb*, §316, who provides abundant examples of the imperatival infinitive from the papyri.
185 *Idiom Book*, p. 127.
186 I, 267.
187 See Mandilaras, *The Verb*, §318 for illustrative passages.
188 GK, §113, note 2.
189 *Ibid.*

190   I, 267.
191   Bl-D, §468 (2).
192   In 'Participle and Imperative in I Peter', appended note to E.G.
      Selwyn's *The First Epistle of Peter* (London, 1947), pp. 467–
      88 (summarised by W.D. Davies, *Paul and Rabbinic Judaism*, p.
      329).
193   Daube, in Selwyn, *First Epistle*, p. 471.
194   It is accepted by Moule, *Idiom Book*, p. 179, while Zerwick, *Biblical
      Greek*, also mentions it, §373. P. Joüon in his *Grammaire de
      l'hébreu biblique* (Rome, 1947), §121 e, note 2, cites the usage
      as a characteristic of Mishnaic Hebrew.
195   *The Verb*, §§922–4.
196   Dr A.J.M. Wedderburn's suggestion to me that στηρίζων be co-
      ordinated with γρηγορῶν and thus dependent on γίνου is pos-
      sible; it has, however, not been adopted by the leading English
      translations of this verse.
197   H.C. Hoskier, *Concerning the Text of the Apocalypse* (London,
      1929), I, 23, 122, 515.
198   *The Revelation of St. John*, p. 180.
199   Ozanne, 'The Influence of the Text', p. 36.
200   Occurrences of δεῦτε immediately followed by imperative in the
      LXX: Gen. 11:1; 4 Km. 1:6, 6:13, 22:13; Ps. 33:11, 65:16; Isa.
      66:9.
201   LS-J, *s.v.* δεῦτε.
202   §388.
203   Schwyzer, *Griechische Grammatik*, pp. 372f; Mandilaras, *The
      Verb*, §§815ff; Moulton, *Grammar*, I, 216f; Conybeare and
      Stock, *Selections*, §§59, 60; Jannaris, *Historical Grammar*, pp.
      482f, 578f.
204   Bl-D, §400 concentrate on these and other meanings of the con-
      struction.
205   *Ibid.*, cf. Conybeare and Stock, *Selections*, §59.
206   Mandilaras, *The Verb*, §§815ff.
207   *Ibid.*
208   GK, §114f; cf. Driver, *Hebrew Tenses*, pp. 275f.
209   Bauer and Leander, *Grammatik*, §85 a; cf. Stevenson, *Jewish
      Aramaic*, p. 53, who notes that in targumic Aramaic also 'an
      infinitive dependent on a governing verb is nearly always pre-
      ceded by *lĕ* even when there is no preposition in the Hebrew text'.
210   The use of *lĕ* plus infinitive in Syriac is obligatory in this type of
      construction, according to Nöldeke, *Kurzgefasste Syrische Gram-
      matik* (Leipzig, 1880), p. 197.
211   This orginally would have been written οὐ δεῖ τοῦ παραλλάξαι,
      with the τοῦ becoming misplaced during subsequent transmission
      of the text.
212   Cf. Ozanne, 'The Influence of the Text', pp. 36f, who rejects
      Aramaic influence.
213   The view that Semitisms in Luke-Acts were Septuagintisms sheds
      no light on this construction, since in the LXX it is not rendered

consistently. According to Charles, the LXX translators 'reproduced it in many ways', I, 356.

214 Bl-D, §400 (8).

215 The discovery of additional occurrences of this construction in the Apc. makes necessary the modification of an observation by A.T. Robertson that in the NT 'it is only in Luke (Gospel 23 times, Acts 21 times) and Paul (13 times) that τοῦ with the infinitive (without prepositions) is common' (cited by Moule in his *Idiom Book*, p. 129). According to Bl-D, §400 (3) this usage is also classical.

216 So Gunkel, *Schöpfung und Chaos* (Göttingen, 1895), p. 200, note 2; Charles I, 317; Lancellotti, *Sintassi Ebraica*, pp. 110f.

217 E.g. the nineteenth-century commentaries by Ewald and Züllich, who explained τοῦ πολεμῆσαι as due to the Hebrew infinitive absolute (cited by Lücke, *Versuch einer vollständigen Einleitung in die Offenbarung des Johannes* (Bonn, 1852, II, 453f).

218 Charles, I, 322; cf. GK, §114 k for an explanation of this use of the Hebrew infinitive construct.

219 Moulton–Howard, *Grammar*, II, 448f.

220 Moulton–Turner, *Grammar*, III, 141; cf. Turner, *Grammatical Insights*, 160f; also Moulton–Turner, *Grammar*, IV, 152.

221 Lancellotti, *Sintassi Ebraica*, p. 112.

222 Charles, I, 355f; cf. cxlvi.

223 Jannaris, *Historical Grammar*, p. 578, notes a total of 3 occurrences in Plato, 5 in Xenophon, and 12 in Thucydides.

224 Other occurrences in the Apc. include 1:12 τοῦ βλέπειν (598 2038); 2:14 τοῦ φαγεῖν (325 336 517 620); 16:9 τοῦ δοῦναι (628); 16:19 τοῦ δοῦναι (א 2014 2034).

225 Cf. GK, §114 g.

226 GK, §114 m, 116 m; Driver, *Hebrew Tenses*, pp. 136f; Charles, I, 146.

227 Driver, *Hebrew Tenses*, pp. 136f.

228 Cf. C. Rabin, *Zadokite Documents*, edited with a translation and notes (Oxford, 1954), p. 10, note 3.

229 See Driver, *Hebrew Tenses*, pp. 138f.

230 For the latter verb Hoskier wrongly cites Syriac evidence for an infinitive; in Gwynn's transcription the verb is peal imperfect.

231 I, cxlvi.

232 Cf. Charles I, cxlix (b).

234 *Sintassi Ebraica*, pp. 109f.

235 Lancellotti does not specify the nature of the influence, but refers to P. Joüon, *Grammaire de l'hébreu biblique*, §157 c, note 2.

236 LS-J, *s.v.* δίδωμι, list no fewer than eight secular examples where the verb followed by an infinitive means 'grant', 'concede', while for λέγω with the meaning 'command', ten cases are cited.

237 II, 52.

238 LS-J, *s.v.* μιμνήσκω for examples.

239 On the unusual construction in this passage of ἐμνήσθη ἐνώπιον

τοῦ ϑεοῦ as a modification of the Aramaic indefinite third-person plural, see above, p. 25.

240 I, cxlivf.

241 Cf. also GK, §116 x.

242 *Aramaic Origin*, pp. 96f. Lancellotti, *Sintassi Ebraica*, pp. 105f, declares that it is not found in Aramaic!

243 Burney, *Aramaic Origin*, pp. 96f, where he notes it also occurs in Pal. Syriac of John 1:32.

244 *Aramaic Approach*, p. 68.

245 *The Apocalypse of John*, pp. 43f.

246 'A Hebraic Construction in the Apocalypse', *JTS* 22 (1921), 371-6.

247 See discussion in Moulton–Turner, *Grammar*, IV, 155.

248 'Partizipium und Verbum finitum im Spätgriechischen', in *Kleine Schriften*, Studia Graeca et Latina Gothoburgensia 21 (Gothenburg, 1966), pp. 432-42.

249 Conybeare and Stock, *Selections*, §80; cf. Mandilaras, *The Verb*, §920, who points out that although this phenomenon is found in the papyri, yet the ten cases he cites occur mostly 'in letters or writings of less educated people', and that some cases represent nothing more than a stereoptyed mode of epistolary address. The obvious contrast between these and the literary nature of the Apc. makes it clear that the one can hardly be used to account for the other.

250 So Stevenson, *Jewish Aramaic*, p. 56; Bauer and Leander, *Grammatik*, §81; Nöldeke, *Syrische Grammatik*, §269.

251 Stevenson, *Jewish Aramaic*, p. 56.

252 Charles I, 316; Burney, *Aramaic Origin*, p. 88.

253 *Einleitung in die drei ersten Evangelien*, 2nd edn (Berlin, 1911), p. 14.

254 *Aramaic Approach*, pp. 68, 130.

255 *Grammar*, I, 222-4.

256 *Idiom Book*, p. 179. Relevant are Romans 5:11, 2 Cor. 5:12, 7:5, 8:4, 9:11.

257 *The Apocalypse of John*, pp. 43, 119f.

258 *Sintassi Ebraica*, p. 98.

259 Charles conjectures that λαλούσης μετ᾽ ἐμοῦ λέγων might be a Hebraism (*mĕdabbēr 'itî lē'mōr*) here and in 10:8.

260 Scott, *Original Language*, p. 9.

261 According to Lisowsky's *Konkordanz zum hebräischen Alten Testament*, p. 123; I found only eight such passages (he cites nine) where the infinitive absolute is thus employed.

262 My own count, based on Lisowsky's *Konkordanz*.

263 Cf. GK, §113 y.

264 Cf. GK, §113 r.

265 'The Influence of the Text', p. 19; but he seems to reverse his opinion on pp. 39f.

266 A. Cowley, *Aramaic Papyri of the 5th Century B.C.* (Oxford, 1923), 30:7, 16:8, 20:6.

267 *Lexicon Linguae Aramaicae Veteris Testamenti* (Rome, 1971), *s.v. 'āmar.*
268 Ozanne is mistaken when he says that parallels to the indeclinable form of the participle are extremely rare or non-existent in the LXX. Cf. 'The Influence of the Text', pp. 18f.
269 Bl-D, §368; Moulton–Howard, *Grammar*, II, 454.
270 Cf. Bl-D, §420 (3) where this use as a finite verb as in Hebrew is noted.
271 Charles I, cl; Bousset, *Offenbarung*, p. 243. Cf. Moulton–Turner, *Grammar*, III, 315. Some of the cases cited here could be explained as parataxis since two or more verbs (including λέγων) occur.
272 This occurs 67 times in codex Alexandrinus (so Mussies, *Morphology*, p. 348, 61 times in the text of the United Bible Societies, according to my count.
273 Moulton–Turner, *Grammar*, III, 152.
274 Mussies, *Morphology*, p. 347. Cf. Moule, *Idiom Book*, p. 103, who described Acts 4:12 οὐδὲ γὰρ ὄνομά ἐστιν ἕτερον ... τὸ δεδομένον as 'very odd usage' and acknowledged a Semitic background.
275 Mussies, *Morphology*, p. 348. Although noting that this type of participle occurs 67 times in the Apc., Mussies cites only 2 cases where, he alleges, it expresses the Hebrew qal passive participle: 13:8 ἐσφαγμένου and 18:2 μεμισημένου.
276 GK, §116 a.
277 *Ibid.*
278 *Ibid.*, §116 d, e.
279 Moulton–Turner, *Grammar*, III, 85. See also GK, §116 a–e, as referred to above, for an important discussion of the relationship of Hebrew attributive participle to time and to its subject.
280 GK, §116 a.
281 This usage is discussed by Mussies, *Morphology*, pp. 347f, who ascribes to the verbs a non-perfective meaning based not on Hebrew but on the new Hellenistic present stem στήκω.
282 Bl-D, §§412, 13; Moulton–Turner, *Grammar*, III, 150–3; Beyer, *Semitische Syntax*, pp. 196–216; Lancellotti, *Sintassi Ebraica*, pp. 75, 79f, 100–3; Schwyzer, *Griechische Grammatik*, pp 408f; Mandilaras, *The Verb*, §§882–9.
283 Note the similar phrase in LXX Isa. 28:16*b* καὶ ὁ πιστεύων ἐπ' αὐτῷ οὐ μὴ καταισχυνθῇ (here ὁ πιστεύων = participle *hamma'ămîn*).
284 The participle in Aramaic assumed the role of a finite verb, making it unsuitable for this use.
285 See Beyer, *Semitische Syntax*, p. 196.
286 But N. Turner (Moulton–Turner, *Grammar*, IV, 151f) notes the Hebrew idiomatic use of an anarthrous participle as the object of a sentence. This he cites as influencing the construction found in Apc. 2:14 ἔχεις ἐκεῖ κρατοῦντας τὴν διδαχὴν βαλαάμ.

287 So also Lancellotti, *Sintassi Ebraica*, p. 83; cf. Black, *Aramaic Approach*, pp. 51f for Aramaic examples.

288 This passage is listed by Beyer, *Semitische Syntax*, p. 196, under headings (a) as it stands in the text and under (c) if the Syriac variant is accepted.

289 See *Sintassi Ebraica*, pp. 75, 79, 83, 100f.

290 See *ibid.*, p. 83, note 3.

291 *Ibid.*, pp. 79, 83, note 3.

292 *Semitische Syntax*, pp. 205f.

293 *Hebrew Tenses*, p. 165.

294 *Biblical Greek*, §§371, 72.

295 *Sintassi Ebraica*, p. 82.

296 Charles II, 33.

297 *Syntax of the Moods and Tenses of the Greek Verb* (London, 1889), p. 47.

298 A few classical Greek examples of this usage are cited by Goodwin, *ibid.*, p. 52.

299 The literature on this aorist participle is extensive; the most important includes the following: W.G. Ballantine, 'Predicative Participles with Verbs in the Aorist', *Bibliotheca Sacra* 41 (Oberlin, Ohio, 1884), 789; Burton, *NT Moods and Tenses*, pp. 65f; C.D. Chambers, 'On A Use of the Aorist Participle in Some Hellenistic Writers', *JTS* 24 (1923), 183; W.F. Howard, 'On the Futuristic Use of the Participle in Hellenistic', *JTS* 24 (1923), 403–6; Zerwick, *Biblical Greek*, §264; Bl-D, §339 (1); Moule, *Idiom Book*, pp. 100, 206; Albert Wifstrand, 'Apostelsgeschichte 25, 13', *Eranos* 54 (Uppsala, 1956), 123ff. The latter article provides further bibliographical references, plus analyses, on this much-disputed participle.

300 *Grammar of New Testament Greek* (London, 1898), p. 197. Blass rejects the aorist participle adopting the poorly-attested future participle in its place.

301 Especially in Acts; cf. 3:26; 7:26; 10:29; 12:24, 25; 16:23; 21:24; 23:35; 24:23. The Gospels also contain several; cf. John 11:2, 3; Luke 2:16; Matt. 27:4; Mark 1:31, 14:39.

302 This differs from the circumstantial clause, for which see Black, *Aramaic Approach*, pp. 81f.

303 *The Apocalypse of John*, pp. 112f.

304 The accusative participle standing after a nominative is solecistic; cf. Moulton–Turner, *Grammar*, III, 314.

305 E.g. GK, §118 p.

306 GK, §118.

307 GK, §117.

308 GK, §118 n, o, p.

309 GK, §90.

310 GK, §118 b.

311 Torrey, *The Apocalypse of John*, pp. 112f.

312 'The Influence of the Text', p. 22.

313 Bl-D, §136 (2).
314 Moulton–Turner, *Grammar*, III, 314.
315 G. Dalman, *The Words of Jesus*, p. 34; *Jesus-Jeshua*, p. 126; Black, *Aramaic Approach*, p. 239 who explains the occurrence in Luke 22:15 as a Hebraism.
316 Moulton–Turner, *Grammar*, III, 156f; IV, 152; Bl-D, §198 (6); Conybeare and Stock, *Selections*, §81. For a variety of methods of translating the infinitive absolute in the LXX, cf. H. Kaupel, 'Beobachtungen zur Übersetzung des Infinitivus Absolutus in der LXX', *ZAW* n.s. 20 (1945–8 (1949)), 191ff.
317 'Never found in M[ishnaic] H[ebrew]', M.H. Segal, *A Grammar of Mishnaic Hebrew* (Oxford, 1927), p. 165.
318 So C.F. Burney, *Aramaic Origin*, p. 13; W.B. Stevenson, *Jewish Aramaic*, p. 53; G. Dalman, *Jesus-Jeshua*, p. 34, 'to Biblical Aramaic this style is foreign; in the Galilean dialect it is a rare exception; but in the Babylonian Jewish-Aramaic it is more frequent'.
319 *Morphology*, pp. 323f.
320 P. 165, note 3.
321 J.A. Fitzmyer, 'The Contribution of Qumran Aramaic to the Study of the New Testament', *NTS* 20 (1973–4), 401.
322 GK, §117 p.
323 *Morphology*, pp. 323f. Moulton–Turner, *Grammar*, IV, 152 also wrongly attributes Apc. 16:9 and 17:6 to Hebrew infinitive absolute influence.
324 Bl-D, §153; Moulton–Turner, *Grammar*, III, 245f.
325 According to Moulton–Turner, *Grammar*, III, 156f.
326 II, 99.
327 Noted by H. St John Thackeray, 'The Infinitive Absolute in the LXX', *JTS* 9 (1908), 600.
328 *Ibid.*
329 Moulton–Turner, *Grammar*, III, 157.

4 Semitic influence on the clause in the Apocalypse

1 E.g. GK, §141 a, b.
2 See §140 e.
3 Cf. C. Brockelmann, *Hebräische Syntax* (Neukirchen, 1956), p. 10.
4 Cf. Bl-D, §§127, 28; Moulton–Turner, *Grammar*, III, 294–310, gives a comprehensive analysis of the Greek nominal phrase, including tables of statistics for NT and *Koine* authors. It should be noted that the total of ninety-one occurrences of ellipse listed there for the Apc. is higher than that which is found in this study. This is due to the fact that here most cases of ellipse which occur in subordinate clauses are excluded, and will be treated separately under the various categories of clauses to be discussed below.
5 Bl-D, §128 (7); Moulton–Turner, *Grammar*, III, 295f.

6 GK, §§141 i, 142 c, f.
7 Kühner–Gerth, *Ausführliche Grammatik der griechischen Sprache*, II, I, 1, 40.
8 *Ibid.*
9 *Ibid.*, cf. Bl-D, §127, where it is termed the 'most frequent omission by far'.
10 Schwyzer, *Griechische Grammatik*, II, 623 (cited by N. Turner in Moulton–Turner, *Grammar*, III, 294).
11 Moulton–Turner, *Grammar*, III, 294.
12 Brockelmann, *Hebräische Syntax*, p. 10.
13 GK, §141 b.
14 GK, §142 a. This order can of course be reversed to subject–verb if special emphasis is to be put on the subject in question.
15 Bl-D, §472 (1).
16 GK, §142f.
17 E. Kautzsch, *Grammatik des biblische-Aramäischen*, §84, 1 b, who cites Dan 2:7, 10. For a Hebrew example, cf. Isa. 3:17.
18 Moulton–Turner, *Grammar*, III, 106–10; Bl-D, §§293–7.
19 Cf. Bl-D, §412 for general comments on the attributive participle.
20 GK, §155 e.
21 The other two are John 1:6, 3:7.
22 Cf. Burney, *Aramaic Origin*, pp. 30–2.
23 GK, §138 a.
24 GK, §138 g.
25 Cf. Charles I, clvif; J. Schmid, *Studien*, Part II, p. 198. G.D. Kilpatrick reviews both in *Vigiliae Christianae* 13 (1959), 7f.
26 See p. 66.
27 *Hebrew Tenses*, pp. 137f.
28 *Offenbarung*, p. 6; Burney, *Aramaic Origin*, pp. 95f, also discusses this construction.
29 In his Ph.D. thesis, 'The Influence of the Text'.
30 Also Gen. 24:14, Judg. 1:12, 1 Sam. 17:26.
31 *Original Language*, p. 9.
32 Cf. GK, §155 g.
33 *Semitische Syntax*, pp. 141–232.
34 *Ibid.*, p. 192.
35 Cf. Bl-D, §417.
36 *Aramaic Approach*, p. 81. Cf. Moulton–Turner, *Grammar*, IV, 152.
37 Driver, *Hebrew Tenses*, pp. 195f.
38 *Ibid.*
39 Designated as 'adverbial' in some grammars, cf. Bl-D, §411.
40 Cf. GK, §156.
41 *Original Language*, p. 11.
42 The following, cited by Scott, appear doubtful: Apc. 9:7, 8, 9, 17; 17:4. Turner (in Moulton–Turner, *Grammar*, IV, 152) rightly adds 3:20, 14:17, 17:11, 19:15 *bis* 21:7. But not 16:10 (the apodosis of a conditional clause), or 18:6.
43 Such a construction is found in Greek as well, but only with the

circumstantial participle. ἐπὶ τοῦ ἅρματος καϑήμενος τὴν πορείαν ἐποιεῖτο, 'he was making the journey *seated in his chariot*', Xenophon, *Anabasis* 1, 7, 20.

44   GK, §156 b.
45   Cf. Lancellotti, *Sintassi Ebraica*, pp. 98f.
46   See also chapter 3 above, 'Evidence of underlying *Waw*-consecutive constructions', pp. 53–6.
47   Cf. Bl-D, §461 (1) for further examples. Black, *Aramaic Approach*, has also discussed this idiom; cf. pp. 90f.
48   Bl-D, §461 (1); cf. Moulton–Turner, *Grammar*, III, 75.
49   GK, §110f.
50   *Semitische Syntax*, pp. 226ff.
51   Cf. *ibid.* for other examples.
52   For many similar passages in the Gospels cf. *ibid.*
53   *Ibid.*, pp. 75f.
54   GK, §111 f, g.
55   On the form ἐγίνετο in the LXX for iterative wĕhāyă, see M. Johannessohn, 'Das biblische καὶ ἐγένετο und seine Geschichte', *Zeitschrift für vergleichende Sprachforschung* 53 (1925), 163.
56   Burney, *Aramaic Origin*, pp. 12f. following Dalman, *Words of Jesus*, p. 32, declares that this construction belongs exclusively to biblical Hebrew, and that it has no Aramaic equivalent, in spite of the occurrence in Dan. 3:7 which Dalman himself cites. But, in light of the rendering of the passage by Theod. the question of direct Aramaic influence on the Greek temporal clause should remain open. While Dalman rightly states that Hebrew wayĕhî plus temporal conjunction is foreign to Aramaic, one must not overlook the fact that the temporal kĕdî was rendered by Theod. as καὶ ἐγένετο, seemingly as if the latter came to serve as a standard introductory formula for certain temporal clauses in Jewish translation Greek. Cf. Bauer and Leander, *Grammatik des biblisch-Aramäischen*, §109 g.
57   *Semitische Syntax*, 'Satzeinleitendes καὶ ἐγένετο mit Zeitbestimmung', pp. 29ff.
58   Cf. especially pp. 32–52.
59   For statistics in the OT see Johannessohn, 'Das biblische καὶ ἐγένετο, *Zeitschrift für vergleichende Sprachforschung* 53 (1925), p. 161.
60   *Semitische Syntax*, p. 30.
61   Cf. *ibid.*, p. 61, 'notwendige syntaktische Mittel'.
62   Burney, *Aramaic Origin*, p. 12. On pp. 11–13 are listed many instances of a closely related Hebrew idiom, that in which the introductory wayĕhî is followed by an infinitive with a preposition, usually bĕ or kĕ, rendered in the LXX by ἐν τῷ plus infinitive. Instances of this are to be found in the NT, especially in Luke–Acts. This type of temporal construction, however, is not found in the Apc.
63   Schwyzer, *Griechische Grammatik*, pp. 671ff; Kühner-Gerth, *Grammatik*, II, §553.

64   Cf. Moulton–Turner, *Grammar*, III, 100, 'Its mood was always subjunctive in classical Greek (or oblique optative).'
65   So Bl-D, §369.
66   Turner, in *Grammar*, III, 100 remarks that in Apc. and Paul the future indicative is used 'quite profusely' with aorist subjunctive as variant. See also Bl-D, §369 (2).
67   On the mixing of future indicative with aorist subjunctive, cf. Bl-D §§363, 369 (2), Radermacher, *Neutestamentliche Grammatik*, 2nd edn (Tübingen, 1925), p. 174.
68   Radermacher, *Neutestamentliche Grammatik*, p. 173.
69   BGU III, 884, ii, 14.
70   Radermacher, *Neutestamentliche Grammatik*, p. 173, 'doch sind die Beispiele nicht häufig'.
71   Turner, *Grammar*, III, 100. Radermacher, *Neutestamentliche Grammatik*, p. 216, gives further examples outside the NT.
72   Cf. also Bl-D, §363.
73   Cf. GK, §165 a, c; 107 g.
74   Turner, *Grammar*, III, p. 100, cites examples elsewhere in the NT which employ future indicative in final clauses, indicating that this Semitism was widespread in biblical Greek.
75   GK, §165 a.
76   *Not* jussive as was suggested by Lancellotti, *Sintassi Ebraica*, p. 71.
77   Lancelotti, *ibid.*, pp 62f would make Apc. 9:19*b* a circumstantial clause; I would prefer, on the basis of the syntax described here to understand it as a final clause.
78   Moule, *Idiom Book*, p. 141.
79   GK §166 a.

Conclusion

1   Cf. J.A. Montgomery, 'The Education of the Seer of the Apocalypse', *JBL* 45 (1926), 79, note 5, argues that the Apc. 'betrays no traces of Aramaic'. More recently Beyer, *Semitische Syntax*, p. 17, maintained that the Apc. stands exclusively under Hebrew influence ('wie ausschliesslich die Apc.').
2   *The Apocalypse of John.* Apparently followed now by Frank Zimmerman in an appendix on the Apc. in his *The Aramaic Origin of the Four Gospels* (New York, 1979).
3   *NTS* 1 (1955), 222f.
4   Note in particular L. Rydbeck's 'What Happened to New Testament Grammar after Albert Debrunner?', *NTS* 21 (1975), 425: 'peculiar language of a peculiar people is too much of a polemical slogan'.

Appendix I

1   Charles I, 29, 316; Ozanne, 'The Influence of the Text', pp. 18f, who cites Apc. 5:6, 10:2, 14:14, 17:3, 21:24.
2   *Semitische Syntax*, pp. 208f.

3   *Ibid.* Cf. H. Hanse, *TDNT* II, 817.

4   ῎Εχων here seems to express 'with', 'accompanied by', rather than simple possession, thus paralleling what Bl-D, §419, term 'pleonastic' meaning 'with', which occurs in Luke 2:42: 'and when he was twelve years of age, his parents went up to Jerusalem *with* him', ἀνέβησαν οἱ γονεῖς αὐτοῦ ἔχοντες (D) αὐτόν. Cf. Mussies, *Morphology*, pp. 325f.

5   Lancellotti, *Sintassi Ebraica*, p. 88, reaches similar conclusions along Hebrew lines.

6   GK, §140 e: the distinction 'is indispensable to the more delicate appreciation of Hebrew syntax . . . involves fundamental differences of meaning'.

7   Cf. Bauer and Leander, *Grammatik des biblische-Aramäischen*, p. 326: 'drucken einen Zustand aus und dienen der Beschreibung und Schilderung'. The distinction between noun clauses and verb clauses in Syriac is less distinct (cf. Nöldeke, *Syrische Grammatik*, p. 215).

8   Of course not every occurrence of ἔχων in the Apc. should not be assigned a Semitic sense: ἐν γαστρὶ ἔχουσα is good Greek, likewise ἔχων ἐν τῇ χειρί has close parallels in other Greek literature.

9   GK, §140 a, §141 b.

10   Bauer and Leander, *Grammatik des biblisch-Aramäischen*, p. 326.

11   *Ibid.*

Appendix II

1   *Pronomen Abundans and Pronomen Coniunctum.* Verhandelingen der Koninklijke Nederlandse Akademie van Wetenschappen, Afd. Letterkunde, n.s. 82 (Amsterdam and London, 1974).

2   *Ibid.*, on p. 34, note 103 credit is given to P.W. van der Horst 'for his assistance in interpreting the Hebrew texts' of the OT.

3   See especially *ibid.*, pp. 34–42.

4   *Ibid.*, pp. 13, 36; cf. p. 29 'not only in Ancient Greek, but also in the *Koine*, the *pronomen abundans* is used for clearness' sake and in order to emphasise a certain word'.

5   Cf. *ibid.*, p. 32.

6   Described by the author as merely *nota relationis*, therefore by nature weaker and more ambivalent than a true relative pronoun.

7   See *ibid.*, p. 42.

8   Bakker also cites four Semitic type resumptive pronouns occurring in codex D (Luke 8:12, 12:43; Matt. 10:11, 18:20), but failed to include them in the statistics. Cf. Black, *Aramaic Approach*, p. 101, who notes 'The construction [resumptive pronoun] again predominates in the text of D.'

9   Cited by Lancellotti, *Sintassi Ebraica*, pp. 101f.

10   Bakker, *Pronomen Abundans*, pp. 39f.

11   Cf. *ibid.*, pp. 33, 36.

12   GK, §138 a, e.

BIBLIOGRAPHY

Abel, F.-M. *Grammaire du Grec Biblique*, 2nd edn, Paris, 1927.
Aerts, W.J. *Periphrastica*, Amsterdam, 1965.
Aland, K. *et al.*, eds. *Novum Testamentum Graece*, 26th edn, Munster, 1979.
Allen, Leslie. *The Greek Chronicles*, supplements to *Vetus Testamentum* 25 and 27, Leiden, 1974.
Allo, E.-B. *Saint Jean. L'Apocalypse*, 4th edn, Paris, 1933.
Bakker, W.F. *Pronomen Abundans and Pronomen Coniunctum*, Verhandelingen der Koninklijke Nederlands Akademie van Wetenschappen, Afd. Letterkunde, n.s. 82, Amsterdam and London, 1974.
Ballantine, W.G. 'Predicative Participles with Verbs in the Aorist', *Bibliotheca Sacra* 41 (Oberlin, Ohio, 1884), 787–99.
Bauer, H. and P. Leander. *Grammatik des biblisch-Aramäischen*, Halle-Saale, 1927.
Bauer, W., W.F. Arndt and F.W. Gingrich. *A Greek–English Lexicon of the New Testament and other Early Christian Literature*, 2nd edn, revised and augmented by F.W. Gingrich and F.W. Danker, Chicago, 1979.
Beyer, Klaus. *Semitische Syntax im Neuen Testament*, I, 'Satzlehre', Göttingen, 1962.
Birdsall, J.N. 'The Text of the Revelation of Saint John', *Evangelical Quarterly* 33 (1961), 228–37.
Björk, G. HN ΔΙΔΑΣΚΩΝ *Die Periphrastischen Konstruktionen im Griechischen*, Skrifter Utgivna av den Kungliga Humanistiska Vetenskapssamfundet i Uppsala, 32, Part II, Uppsala, 1940.
Black, Matthew. *An Aramaic Approach to the Gospels and Acts*, 3rd edn, Oxford, 1967.
'The Biblical Languages', *The Cambridge History of the Bible*, I, ed. P.R. Ackroyd and C.F. Evans, Cambridge, 1970.
'Some Greek Words with "Hebrew" Meanings in the Epistles and Apocalypse', in J.R. McKay and J.F. Miller, eds., *Biblical Studies: Essays in Honour of William Barclay*, London, 1976.
'The Christological Use of the Old Testament in the New Testament', *NTS* 18 (1972), 1–10.
Blake, F.R. *A Resurvey of the Hebrew Tenses*, Rome, 1951.
Blass, F. *Grammar of New Testament Greek*, translated by H.St J. Thackeray, London, 1898.
and A. Debrunner. *A Greek Grammar of the New Testament and Other*

Early Christian Literature, trans. and rev. by Robert Funk, Chicago, 1961.

Bousset, W. *Die Offenbarung Johannis*, 6th edn, Meyer's Kommentar, Göttingen, 1906.

Brockelmann, C. *Hebräische Syntax*, Neukirchen, 1956.

Brown, F., S. Driver, C. Briggs. *A Hebrew and English Lexicon of the Old Testament*, Oxford, 1907 (reprinted with corrections, 1972).

Burney, C.F. 'A Hebraic Construction in the Apocalypse', *JTS* 22 (1921), 371-9.

The Aramaic Origin of the Fourth Gospel, Oxford, 1922.

Burrows, Millar. 'Orthography, Morphology and Syntax of the St. Mark's Isaiah Manuscript', *JBL* 68 (1949), 209-17.

'The Original Language of the Gospel of John', *JBL* 49 (1930), 95-139.

Burton, E.De W. *Syntax of the Moods and Tenses in New Testament Greek*, 3rd edn, Edinburgh, 1898 (reprinted 1955).

Chambers, C.D. 'On a Use of the Aorist Participle in Some Hellenistic Writers', *JTS* 24 (1923), 183-7.

Charles, R.H. *A Critical and Exegetical Commentary on the Revelation of St. John*, The International Critical Commentary, 2 vols., Edinburgh, 1920.

Conybeare, F.C. and George Stock. *Selections from the Septuagint*, Boston, 1905.

Cowley, A. *Aramaic Papyri of the 5th Century B.C.*, Oxford, 1923.

Dalman, G. *Jesus-Jeshua*, Studies in the Gospels, ET London, 1929.

Words of Jesus, Edinburgh, 1902.

Daube, David. 'Participle and Imperative in I Peter', in E.G. Selwyn, ed., *The First Epistle of Peter*, London, 1947.

Davies, W.D. *Paul and Rabbinic Judaism*, 2nd edn, London, 1962.

Delobel, J. 'Le Texte de l'Apocalypse', in J. Lambrecht, ed., *L'Apocalypse johannique et l'Apocalyptique dans le Nouveau Testament*, Bibliotheca Ephemeridum Theologicarum Lovaniensium 53, Louvain, 1980.

Driver, G.R. Review of C.C. Torrey, *The Apocalypse of John* in *JTS* n.s. 11 (1960), 383-9.

Driver, S.R. *A Treatise on the Use of the Tenses in Hebrew*, 3rd edn, Oxford, 1892.

Ewald, George H. *Commentarius in Apocalypsin Johannis Exegeticus et criticus*, Leipzig, 1828.

Fitzmyer, J.A. 'The Contribution of Qumran Aramaic to the Study of the New Testament', *NTS* 20 (1973-4), 382-407.

Fleisch, H. *Sur le système verbal du sémitique commun et son évolution dans les langues sémitiques anciennes*, Mélanges de l'Université Saint Joseph 27, Beirut, 1947-8.

Frisk, Hjalmar. 'Partizipium und Verbum finitum im Spätgriechischen', *Kleine Schriften*, Studia Graeca et Latina Gothoburgensia 21, Gothenburg, 1966, pp. 432-42.

Gesenius-Kautzsch (Cowley). *Hebrew Grammar*, 2nd edn, Oxford, 1910.

Goodwin, William W. *A Greek Grammar*, London, 1891.

Bibliography 137

Goodwin, W.W. *Syntax of the Moods and Tenses of the Greek Verb*, London, 1889.
Gunkel, H. *Schöpfung und Chaos in Urzeit und Endzeit*, Göttingen, 1895.
Gwynn, John, ed. *The Apocalypse of St. John in a Syriac Version Hitherto Unknown*, Dublin, 1897.
Hanse, H. Ἔχω, in G. Kittel, ed., *Theological Dictionary of the New Testament*, II, ET Grand Rapids, 1964.
Harrison, R.K. *Introduction to the Old Testament*, Grand Rapids, Michigan, 1969.
Helbing, R. *Die Kasussyntax der Verba bei den Septuaginta*, Göttingen, 1928.
Hoskier, H.C. *Concerning the Text of the Apocalypse*, 2 vols., London, 1929.
Howard, W.F. 'On the Futuristic Use of the Participle in Hellenistic', *JTS* 24 (1923), 403–6.
Jannaris, A.N. *An Historical Greek Grammar*, London, 1897.
Jeremias, J. *Die Abendmahlsworte Jesu*, 3rd edn, Göttingen, 1960.
   New Testament Theology, I, 'The Proclamation of Jesus', ET London, 1971.
Johannessohn, M. 'Das biblische καὶ ἐγένετο und seine Geschichte', *Zeitschrift für vergleichende Sprachforschung* 53 (1925), 161–213.
Johns, A.F. *A Short Grammar of Biblical Aramaic*, Berrien Springs, 1966.
Joüon, P. *Grammaire de l'hébreu biblique*, 2nd edn, ed. R.P.L. Semkovski, Rome, 1947.
Katz, P. in J. Ziegler, *Beiträge zur Ieremias-Septuaginta*. Nachrichten der Akademie der wissenschaften in Göttingen 2 (phil.-hist. Klasse), Göttingen, 1958.
Kaupel, H. 'Beobachtungen zur Übersetzung des Infinitivus Absolutus in der LXX', *ZAW* n.s. 20 (1945–8 (1949)), 191–2.
Kautzsch, E. *Grammatik des biblisch-Aramäischen, Mit einer kritischen Erörterung der aramäischen Worte im Neuen Testament*, Leipzig, 1884.
Keder-Kopfstein. 'Die Wiedergabe des hebräischen Kausative in der Vulgata', *ZAW* 85 (1973), 197–219.
Kenyon, F.G. *The Chester Beatty Biblical Papyri*, Fascicle 3, London, 1934.
Kilpatrick, G.D. 'Atticism and the Text of the Greek New Testament', in J. Blinzler *et al.*, eds., *Neutestamentliche Aufsätze: Festschrift für Prof. Josef Schmid*, Regensburg, 1963, pp. 125–37.
   'The Greek New Testament Text of Today and the Textus Receptus', H. Anderson and W. Barclay, eds., *The New Testament in Historical and Contemporary Perspectives: Essays in Honour of G.H.C. Macgregor*, Oxford, 1965.
   'Professor J. Schmid on the Greek Text of the Apocalypse', *Vigiliae Christianae* 13 (1959), 1–13.
Kühner, R. *Ausführliche Grammatik der griechischen Sprache*, I, 'Elementar- und Formenlehre'; 3rd edn by F. Blass, 2 vols., Hanover, 1890–2.
   Ausführliche Grammatik der griechischen Sprache, II, 'Satzlehre'; 3rd

edn by B. Gerth, 2 vols., Hanover and Leipzig, 1898–1904 (reprinted 1955).

Lagrange, M.J. 'Les Papyrus Ch. Beatty', *Revue Biblique* 43 (1934), 488–93.

Lancellotti, A. *Sintassi Ebraica nel Greco dell'Apocalisse*, I, 'Uso delle forme verbali', Collectio Assisiensis 1, Assisi, 1964.

Laughlin, T. C. *The Solecisms of the Apocalypse*, Princeton, 1902.

Liddell and Scott-Jones. *Greek-English Lexicon*, 9th edn, with a supplement edited by E.A. Barber, Oxford, 1968.

Lisowsky, A. *Konkordanz zum hebräischen Alten Testament*, Stuttgart, 1958.

Lohmeyer, E. *Die Offenbarung des Johannes*, 2nd edn, Handbuch zum Neuen Testament, Tübingen, 1953.

Lücke, F. *Versuch einer vollständigen Einleitung in die Offenbarung des Johannes und in die gesamte apokalyptische literatur*, 2 vols., Bonn, 1852.

Mandilaras, Basil G. *The Verb in the Greek Non-literary Papyri*, Athens, 1973.

Mayser, E. *Grammatik der Griechischen Papyri aus der Ptolemäerzeit*, I, 'Laut- und Wortlehre' Leipzig, 1906; II, 'Satzlehre', Berlin, 1926–34.

Metzger, B.M. *The Text of the New Testament*, 2nd edn, Oxford, 1968.

Montgomery, J. A. 'The Education of the Seer of the Apocalypse', *JBL* 45 (1926), 70–80.

Moule, C.F.D. *An Idiom Book of New Testament Greek*, 2nd edn, Cambridge, 1959.

Moulton, J.H. *A Grammar of New Testament Greek*, I, 'Prolegomena', 3rd edn, Edinburgh, 1908.

and W.F. Howard. *A Grammar of New Testament Greek*, II, 'Accidence', Edinburgh, 1929.

and Nigel Turner. *A Grammar of New Testament Greek*, III, 'Syntax', Edinburgh, 1963.

and Nigel Turner. *A Grammar of New Testament Greek*, IV, 'Style', Edinburgh, 1976.

Mussies, G. 'The Greek of the Book of Revelation' in J. Lambrecht, ed., *L'Apocalypse johannique et l'Apocalyptique dans le Nouveau Testament*, Bibliotheca Ephemeridum Theologicarum Lovaniensium, 53, Louvain, 1980.

The Morphology of Koine Greek as used in the Apocalypse of St. John, supplement to *Novum Testamentum* 27, Leiden, 1971.

Nöldeke, T. *Kurzgefasste Syrische Grammatik*, Leipzig, 1880.

Ozanne, C.G. 'The Influence of the Text and Language of the Old Testament on the Book of Revelation', unpublished Ph.D. thesis, Manchester University, Manchester, 1964.

'The Language of the Apocalypse', *The Tyndale House Bulletin* 16 (April, 1965), 3–9.

Rabin, C. *Zadokite Documents*, edited with a translation and notes, Oxford, 1954.

Radermacher, Ludwig. *Neutestamentliche Grammatik*, 2nd edn, Handbuch zum Neuen Testament, Tübingen, 1925.
Regard, P. *La Phrase Nominale dans la Langue du Nouveau Testament*, Paris, 1919.
Rydbeck, Lars. *Fachprosa, Vermeintliche Volkssprache und Neues Testament*, Acta Universitatis Upsaliensis Studia Graeca Upsaliensia 5, Uppsala, 1967.
  'What Happened to New Testament Greek Grammar after Albert Debrunner?', *NTS* 21 (1975), 424–7.
Schmid, Josef. 'Neue Griechische Apokalypsehandschriften', *ZNW* 59 (1968), 250–8.
  Studien zur Geschichte des griechischen Apokalypse-Textes, Part II, 'Die alten Stämme', Munich, 1955.
  'Unbeachtete und unbekannte griechische Apokalypse-handschriften', *ZNW* 52 (1961), 82–8.
Schmid, Wilhelm. Review of R. Helbing, *Kasussyntax, Philologische Wochenschrift* 49 (1929), 468.
Schwyzer, E. *Griechische Grammatik*, I, Munich, 1939; II 'Syntax und syntaktische Stilistik', completed and edited by A. Debrunner, Munich, 1950.
Scott, R.B.Y. *The Original Language of the Apocalypse*, Toronto, 1928.
Segal, M.H. *A Grammar of Mishnaic Hebrew*, Oxford, 1927.
Selwyn, E.G. *The First Epistle of Peter*, London, 1947.
Simcox, W.H. *The Revelation of St. John the Divine*, Cambridge Greek Testament, Cambridge, 1893.
Stevenson, W.B. *Grammar of Palestinian Jewish Aramaic*, 2nd edn, Oxford, 1962.
Tasker, R.V.G. 'The Chester Beatty Papyrus of the Apocalypse of John', *JTS* 50 (1949), 60–8.
Thackeray, H.StJ. *A Grammar of the Old Testament in Greek*, Part I, Cambridge, 1909.
  'The Infinitive Absolute in the LXX', *JTS* 9 (1908), 600–2.
  The Septuagint and Jewish Worship, 2nd edn, London, 1923.
Thayer, J.H. *Greek–English Lexicon of the New Testament* (translation and augmentation of C.L.W. Grimm, *Lexicon Graeco-Latinum in libros NT auctore*, Leipzig, 1868), New York and Edinburgh, 1886.
Torrey, C.C. *The Apocalypse of John*, New Haven, 1958.
Turner, Nigel. *Grammatical Insights into the New Testament*, Edinburgh, 1965.
  'The Testament of Abraham: Problems in Biblical Greek', *NTS* 1 (1955), 222–3.
Vogels, H.J. *Untersuchungen zur Geschichte der lateinischen Apokalypse-übersetzung*, Dusseldorf, 1920.
Vogt, E., ed. *Lexicon Linguae Aramaicae Veteris Testamenti*, Rome, 1971.
Wellhausen, J. *Einleitung in die drei ersten Evangelien*, 2nd edn, Berlin, 1911.
Wifstrand, Albert. 'Apostelsgeschichte 25, 13', *Eranos* 54 (Uppsala, 1956), 123–37.

Wilcox, Max. *Semitisms of Acts*, Oxford, 1964.

Winer, G.B. *Grammatik des neutestamentlichen Sprachidioms*, Leipzig, 1822 (ET W.F. Moulton, *A Treatise of the Grammar of New Testament Greek*, 3rd edn, Edinburgh, 1882).

Würthwein, E. *Der Text des Alten Testaments*, 4th edn, Stuttgart, 1974.

Zerwick, M. *Biblical Greek*, 4th edn, ET Joseph Smith, Rome, 1963.

Zimmerman, Frank. *The Aramaic Origin of the Four Gospels*, New York, 1979.

INDEX OF REFERENCES

Euripides, *Ion*
758   117

Eusebius, *Ecclesiastical History*
7, 25, 7ff   1

Genesis Apocryphon
20:10f   80

1–4 Maccabees   109

Oxyrhynchus papyrus
1477   30

Testament of
    Abraham   108

GENERAL INDEX

absence semitism, 6
absolute object, 2, 80
absolute use of participle, 2
accusative, 22, 78
accusative participle, 78, 129
active voice, 12, 29, 117
adjective, 81, 84, 87
adverb, 84, 87
adverbial accusative, 78, 82
adverbial participle, 6
Aerts, W.J., 51, 124
Aland, K., 11
Allen, Leslie, 118
Alexandrinus, codex, 10, 102
Allo, E-B., 4, 8, 41, 47, 49, 56, 117,
    122, 124
analytic causative, 23
Anderson, H., 115
animated speech, 30
antecedent, 111
antonym, 43
apocrypha, 3, 111
apodosis, 38, 54, 56, 101, 104, 106, 131
Arabic, 78
Aramaic, 1, 3, 17, 18, 20, 21, 31, 51,
    53, 61, 65, 68, 70, 74, 75, 79, 81,
    83, 92, 103, 104, 107, 109, 113,
    123, 127, 128, 132, 133
Aramaic, Palestinian, 79
Aramaism, 25, 69, 82
Aristotle, 20
articular genitive infinitive, 60–3, 107
Assyrian, 78
asyndeton, 94
atticism, 11, 44
Attic literature, 57, 87, 97
Attic prose, 30
attributive participle, 5, 90, 105
auxiliary verb, 23, 26, 51, 103

Babylonian Jewish Aramaic, 130

Bakker, W.F., 6, 111, 112, 134
Ballantine, W.G., 77, 129
Barclay, W., 115
Bauer, H. and P. Leander, 61, 119, 125,
    127, 132, 134
Bauer, W., 15, 116, 117, 122
Beyer, Klaus, 7, 74, 91, 92, 95, 96, 101,
    106, 109, 116, 121, 124, 128,
    129, 133
biblical Aramaic, 1, 51, 61, 64, 68, 96,
    104, 106, 107, 119, 130
biblical Greek, 20, 26, 29, 30, 31, 33,
    38, 56, 61, 67, 71, 73, 76, 79, 81,
    83, 86, 90, 98, 100, 105, 110,
    111, 121, 133
biblical Hebrew, 1, 2, 51, 55, 58, 64, 65,
    80, 96, 104, 105, 106, 107, 113,
    119, 132
Birdsall, J.N., 114
Björck, G., 50, 123
Black, Matthew, 1, 6, 7, 9, 11, 14, 15,
    16, 18, 24, 32, 35, 39, 43, 44, 52,
    66, 69, 80, 92, 100, 115, 116,
    121, 122, 123, 124, 129, 130,
    132, 134
Blake, Frank, 124
Blass, F., 77, 117, 129
Blass, F. and A. Debrunner, 18, 22, 23,
    26, 27, 29, 39, 43, 60, 61, 62, 63,
    70, 85, 94, 115, 116, 117, 118,
    119, 121, 122, 123, 124, 125,
    126, 128, 129, 130, 131, 132,
    133, 134
Blinzler, J., 115
Bousset, Wilhelm, 2, 8, 47, 70, 107, 117,
    124, 128
Brockelmann, C., 130, 131
Burney, C.F., 32, 66, 67, 68, 97, 119,
    127, 130, 131, 132
Burrows, Millar, 118, 124
Burton, E. de W., 43, 77, 119, 122, 129

case, 78
casus pendens, 74
causal clause, 55, 60
causative verb, 3, 22–4, 26, 102, 117,
Chambers, C.D., 129
Charles, R.H., 1, 2, 3, 8, 14, 16, 18, 21,
    23, 25, 32, 33, 36, 40, 41, 45, 46,
    47, 58, 61, 62, 63, 64, 65, 66, 67,
    68, 70, 74, 76, 81, 104, 107, 109,
    113, 116, 117, 118, 119, 120,
    122, 124, 126, 127, 128, 129,
    131, 133
circumstantial clause, 92–4, 100, 106,
    129, 133
circumstantial participle, 5, 105, 131
classical Greek, 15, 18, 19, 20, 22, 25,
    27, 29, 35, 37, 38, 44, 52, 70, 73,
    76, 80, 87, 95, 97, 111, 117, 121,
    126, 129, 133
clause, 7, 83–101
cohortative, 5, 28
comparative relative clause, 91, 105
conditional clause, 3, 54, 94–6, 101,
    104, 106, 131
conditional participle, 95
conditional relative clause, 91
conjunction, 55, 92
connecting particle, 112
consecutive clause, 100, 106
context, 32, 42, 53
Conybeare, F.C. and George Stock, 22,
    23, 26, 116, 118, 123, 125, 127,
    130
co-ordination of clauses/parataxis, 89,
    92
co-ordination of present and future
    tenses, 34
copula, 86
Cowley, A., 127
crasis, 55
critical apparatus, 8, 112, 120

Dalman, Gustaf, 20, 21, 22, 80, 130,
    132
Daube, David, 58, 59, 125
Davies, W.D., 125
definite article, 89
deliberative question, 26, 28, 103, 117,
    118
Delobel, J., 9, 115
demonstrative pronoun, 73, 89, 112
Demosthenes, 93
deponent, 12, 24, 26, 103, 117

derived conjugation verb, 42, 53, 73,
    103
Dionysius, 1
Dioscurides, 19
dittography, 62
Driver, G.R., 124
Driver, S.R., 32, 37, 38, 63, 66, 75, 90,
    119, 120, 121, 122, 124, 125,
    126, 131
'durative' sense, 33, 36

eclectic textual method, 9
Elephantine papyri, 70
Elliger, K. and W. Rudolph, 11
ellipsis, 87, 130
emendation, 14, 77, 80
epistolary address, 127
epistolary aorist, 40
Eusebius, 1
Ewald, G., 34, 45, 46, 47, 126
exegesis, 106

final clause, 97–9, 101, 106, 133
final conjunction, 99
finite verb, 81, 83, 88, 91, 110, 120,
    128
Fitzmyer, J.A., 80, 130
Fleisch, Henri, 124
fourth Gospel, 32
frequentative future tense, 45
Frisk, Hjalmar, 67
Funk, R., 121
futurum exactum, 121
furuturm instans, see prophetic future
    tense
futuristic present tense, 29–34

genitive absolute, 6
genitive articular infinitive, 60–3, 107
Gesenius–Kautzsch, 21, 53, 73, 83, 84,
    114, 116, 118, 119, 123, 124,
    125, 126, 127, 128, 129, 130,
    131, 132, 133, 134
gnomic aorist, 37, 39, 40, 41, 121
Goodwin, W.W., 76, 119, 129
Greek, 18, 21, 23, 24, 74, 123, 134
Greek accusative plus infinitive, 6
Greek O.T. versions, 3
Grimm-Thayer, 24
Gunkel, H., 24, 126
Gwynn, John, 126

'hanging' accusative, 79
Hanse, H., 134

Wikgren, A., 11
Wilcox, Max, 18
Winer, G.B., 45, 46, 122
word order, 88, 92
Würthwein, E., 121

Xenophon, 19, 126, 132

'Zadokite' document, 64
Zerwick, M., 25, 39, 46, 76, 117, 122,
    125, 129
Ziegler, J., 117
Zimmerman, Frank, 133
Züllich, C.F.J., 126